LIST OF ILLUSTRATIONS

STUDYING ALTERITY: BACKGROUNDS AND PERSPECTIVES

Raymond Corbey & Joep Leerssen

All human cultures articulate, situate themselves by categorizing the world. Such a predicative act necessarily involves a distinction between that which is allowed into the sphere of culture, and that which is excluded; the circumscription of cultural identity proceeds by silhouetting it against a contrastive background of Otherness. It is this Otherness, both created by, and providing the cognitive background to, articulations of cultural identity (in ethnic, sexual or other terms), which was the topic of an interdisciplinary conference held at Amsterdam in the autumn of 1988 under the joint auspices of the Dutch Sociological and Anthropological Association (NSAV) and the University of Amsterdam's Department of European Studies. This book presents, in reworked versions, the papers discussed on that occasion.

The articulation of culture can be traced in all societies and periods. Various ethnic groups apply to themselves a name which is cognate or even synonymous with the word for *human* or *a user of language*, implicitly arrogating for the social in-group this fundamental human *proprium* and relegating outsiders and aliens to the status of inferior semi-humans. The name for *stranger* can often be synonymous with that for *enemy*, *slave* or *one who blabs gibberish*. What is more, leadership structures within most societies stipulate certain requirements (age, sex, descent) to which a given individual must conform before being given a position of authority; so that here, too, human dignity is distributed unequally between an elite and its Others.

That tendency can be traced in Indo-European vocabulary and institutions as elucidated by Émile Benveniste;[1] in the classical European tradition it is compounded by the specifically civic virtues current in Greece and Rome. Greek society saw its cultural identity and superiority manifested mainly in the institution of the *polis*, and classical Rome developed that human ideal of civic virtue which Cicero so resoundingly formulated into perhaps the central aspect of Rome's bequest to subsequent European civilization. 'Civic', that is, as in the socially regulated life of cities (so far superior to the nomadic or irregular life of rustics); and 'virtue' in the classical sense of Roman *virtus*, which sees in the self-control, courage and 'manliness' of the adult/mature male the ideal type of human values.

This formulation of cultural values already marginalizes a number of human types: strangers, children, women, rustics, brutes and those who cannot control their passions. The inferiorization of this type of excluded Others, who fall short of the canonized set of cultural values, remains a constant throughout the development of European thought, up to and including Freud (cf. Corbey's contribution).

To be sure, the articulation of cultural identity in these terms does not *by definition* imply a denigration of the Other. As Cieraad traces in her contribution, and as Lovejoy and Boas have shown in their classic study on *Primitivism and Related Ideas in Antiquity*, there has from the earliest times onwards been an appreciative mode of viewing Otherness: the appreciation of artlessness, of innocence, of freedom from social constraints. The encounter with strangers can result, not only in hostile mistrust and denigration, but also in admiration for the (universally positive) virtue of hospitality. The Odyssey, for instance, is one long testimony to the idea that hospitality towards strangers is a central marker of true positive humanity, regardless of cultural or social background.

But in a world fraught with dangers and uncontrollable incident, the more current mode of encountering the Other is a defensive one. The

---

[1]   *Le vocabulaire des institutions indo-européennes* (Paris, 1969) traces, in the examples of Indo-European tribal appellations such as *arya* and *slav*, a fundamental ethnocentrism and sense of in-group superiority vis-à-vis aliens. 'Dans le nom qu'un peuple se donne il y a, manifeste ou non, l'intention de se distinguer des peuples voisins, d'affirmer cette supériorité qu'est la possession d'une langue commune et intelligible' (p. 368).

unknown is by definition a threat to one's cognitive grip on the world; it is the locus for fantasies about uncouth monsters and dangerous adventures: that uncomfortable fantasmagoria runs from, again, the Odyssey to the speculative geography of Pliny and Solinus. Strange lands are strange in a double sense: unfamiliar and weird.

The expansion of European control over the geographic environment, which took place at a time when the Ciceronian notions of civic virtue and progressive superiority were revived, thus goes hand in hand with an attempt to subdue the strangeness of the Other in cognitive terms. Civility is articulated in a double sense: brought into being by having it discursively formulated, and given a discriminatory distribution by having it assigned in varying degrees to different parts of the world or different spheres of society.

The exclusion and subjection of Otherness thus forms a red thread throughout European intellectual and political history. The treatment of medieval rustics, of nineteenth-century proletarians, of Jews, of natives in distant colonies, of homosexuals, of blacks, of women, of madmen: in all these multifarious instances the history of social (inter)action can be seen in its underlying structures if we see it in terms of the accompanying discourse, that of the articulation of civility and the exclusion of Otherness.

Recently, the notion of Otherness as a fundamental category of experience and reflection, and as an important perspective in the study of human thought, intercourse and culture, has been advanced in the human and social sciences. The question immediately poses itself whether this development occurred coincidentally in separate fields of study, or whether it spread from one field of inquiry to others. The Other has been placed on the agenda by pursuits as diverse as women's studies, literary image studies, psychology, philosophy and, most importantly perhaps, in the social sciences. The contributions to the present book intend to offer a survey of the issue as it is conceptualized in various fields

A majority of the following contributions are connected with the social sciences: those sciences which analyse the interaction between various subjects or cultures. Reflection on the nature of identity and alterity was made an especially pressing concern in anthropology, which has begun to study its own antecedents and ideological preassumptions in a critical self-analytical *Wissenschaftsgeschichte* and which is now grappling with the fact that it has traditionally defined its scientific *raison d'être* on the embarrassing criterion: its object's non-European, non-elite's exotic Otherness — an Otherness which is now recognized as a byproduct of colonialism, exoticism and Eurocentrism. With the growth and recent revival of cultural relativism in anthropology, and with the rationality debate of the 1960s (which concerned the translatablity and commensurability of cultures[2]), anthropologists have come to query many tenets (which were once central to their scholarly tradition) as a problematic construct based on the marginalization and denigration of their Others — those who were external enough to Western elite culture to become the object of anthropological inquiry. The influential study *Time and the Other* by Johannes Fabian[3] has demonstrated the discursive and ideological presuppositions behind supposed scientific, neutral ethnography and came to challenge the entire epistemological basis of the anthropological endeavour. Such self-reflexive reassessments of presuppositions and methods paved the way towards a constructivist rather than positivist view of ethnography (as in the subtitle to Fabian's book), and brought anthropological practice to an increasing awareness of the problematic character of *ethnography*, in the sense of 'writing the Other's culture'.[4] This emphasis on writing as construction rather than representation helped to place such critical self-reflexion in a general interest, prevalent in a number of disciplines, in the poetics of the writing act and its implications for the communication and formation of theories and ideas. Thus Lemaire, in her contribution, can read an anthropological text with the help of critical tools developed in literary studies.

Indeed the insight is not restricted to anthropologists: that the differentiation between Self and Other is not a neutral category of

---

[2]   Cf. M. Hollis & S. Lukes (eds.), *Rationality and Relativism* (Oxford 1985); S.J. Tambiah, *Magic, Science, Religion and the Scope of Rationality* (Cambridge U.P., 1990).

[3]   *Time and the Other. How Anthropology Makes its Object* (Columbia U.P., 1983).

[4]   The trend is exemplified also by the impact of Clifford Geertz. Cf. generally Geertz, *The Anthropologist as Author* (Stanford 1988); J. Clifford & G.E. Marcus, *Writing Culture. The Poetics and Politics of Ethnography* (Berkeley 1986); iid., *Anthropology as Cultural Critique. An Experimental Moment in the Human Sciences* (Chicago/London 1986); J. Clifford, *The Predicament of Culture. Twentieth-Century Ethnography. Literature and Art* (Harvard U.P., 1988).

cognition open to all sentient individuals in like manner; that its distribution is fraught with ideological implications: this has been advanced by
feminist scholars of different methodological persuasions (cf. Van der Kley
and Lemaire), and by literary or social historians working on national or
ethnic identity formations in cultural praxis (cf. Van Alphen, Leerssen,
Nederveen Pieterse). Indeed there are signs that this awareness may be part
of a general, paradigmatic shift of emphasis in scholarship generally — the
early signs were noticeable, for example, in linguistics, when Saussure and
Troubetzkoy began to locate the meaning of verbal or phonetic language
elements in terms, not of a 'meaning' inherent in the individual sign's
relation to its reference, but rather in a pattern of semantic differentiation,
where the meaning of a word or sound was seen to lie, not in its *identification* with its real-world reference, but rather in its being distinct from
all other words or sounds in the linguistic referential system. In like
manner, some historians have developed a historiographical theory which
is based on the notion of the past as *changes* and *discontinuities* rather than
individual situations or events. [5] In a parallel development, the idea of the
Other has been given a prominent position of the historiographical
agenda. [6] Again, imagology, in comparative literary studies, resulted from
a growing awareness that the cultural units between which 'international'
literary traffic took place, were not so much pre-given eternal categories,
self-sufficient and discrete national 'identities', but rather literary constructs
in themselves, results of confrontation, projection and the articulation of
cultural differentiation and discontinuity (cf. Leerssen's contribution).
Similar patterns in the vexed relation between biological sexual difference
and social gender construct have occupied feminist scholars; and in gay
studies the very notions of identity and alterity (or homo- and hetero-ness)
can be seen to interact in a curious combination of blatant social prejudice

---

[5]   Thus Paul Veyne defines an historical event as an *événement différentiel*,
i.e. an event which allows obne to see a difference between two subsequent
situations. Veyne shows himself to be deeply indebted to Foucault (cf. *Comment
on écrit l'histoire, suivi de Foucault révolutionne l'histoire*, Paris, 1979). Again,
the work of Michel de Certeau addresses similar patterns of 'making differences';
cf. his *Heterologies: Discourse of the Other* (Manchester U.P., 1986).

[6]   Witness the topic for the 16th Congrès International des Sciences
Historiques (Stuttgart 1985), which was on *L'image de l'Autre. Étrangers, Mino-
ritaires, Marginaux*.

and intimate personal self-experience (cf. Hekma, below). Whether homosexuality is a mode of being or a mode of behaving; whether it is a fundamental category of sexual identity or an ideological construct resulting from specific historical needs and circumstances; such questions, paradigmatic perhaps for the study of alterity between essentialism and constructivism, pose themselves with special urgency in this field.

The central thinker, whose influence has become manifest in all the disciplines represented in this book, is Michel Foucault. His influence in the social sciences, again, is overwhelming; however, it may be of use to place his thought in its context and to trace it as part of a reaction against Hegel as the culmination of modern thought.

Most philosophers who within the present century have addressed the problematics of alterity and difference were grappling, in one way or another, with Hegel. Hegel's thought is still constructed along the lines of identity and of unifying, harmonizing identification: in a reflexive process, *Geist* gradually apprehends itself and reality as it gains insight into itself and the world. The resulting system is one of increasing expansion and incorporation, assimilating or at least harmonizing all otherness in terms of an expanding identity. Contrast, plurality and difference, in Hegelian thought, are moments in a movement towards reconciliation, unity and harmony.

Hegel's notion of a dialectical *Vermittlung* between Self and Other was abandoned by a number of later thinkers. They take to a philosophy of division, which may be more or less pessimistic: Bataille's distinction between profane homogeneity and sacred heterogeneity; or Sartre's social ontology in *L'être et le néant*; or René Girard's notion of the I's mimetic desire for an Other which is both a role model and an obstacle;[7] or Lyotard's notion of dissenting parties. Within the chorus of post-Hegelian reflection of Otherness, an important position is taken up by the great figure of Emmanuel Lévinas, whose thought is more hermeneutically inspired. For Levinas, the Other's autonomous presence is irreducible to, indeed prior to subjective identity; on that hermeneutically-inspired basis Lévinas comes to query the very idea of an identity-based ontology which

---

[7]   For the process by which the Other may be made to serve as scapegoat so as to restore social order by being expulsed, see Girard's *Le bouc émissaire* (Paris, 1982).

is operative even in Heidegger, and which is ethically questionable in its
intolerant ego-centrism, its reluctance to acknowledge the fundamental
irreductibility of the Other to the self. [8]

It is in this anti-Hegelian differential thought (which might be
traced through Nietzsche and the impact of thinkers like Kojève and
Bataille) that we should see Foucault's work. He replaces the Hegelian
dialectic of *Aufhebung* by a sociohistorical mechanism of exclusion (as
Karskens analyses in greater detail); he argues that the forceful exclusion
and exorcism of what is Other is an act of identity formation, and
elaborates on the historical case of the exclusion of unreason and madness
as part of the self-definition of the rational humanistic ideal, which thereby
suppresses and denies a part of the human personality. History, for
Foucault, is still one of human self-constitution; but unlike the Hegelian
process of recuperation and finding-towards-oneself, and the growth of an
articulated identity, it is now described in terms of exclusion and estrangement, of the subordination of otherness by the hegemony of self. Thus
madness is no longer negated in the Hegelian sense but socially segregated,
outcast and obliterated. [9]

---

[8]   *Totalité et infini* (The Hague, 1961); *Autrement qu'être ou au-delà de
l'essence* (The Hague, 1974). The importance of the Other in hermeneutical
thought is manifest in Gadamer's critique (in *Wahrheit und Methode*) of what he
considers Dilthey's naive *verstehen* of the other. Gadamer has had an important
impact on the hermeneutical school in literary scholarship (Jauss, Iser) thematizing
the relationship text-reader.

[9]   The name of Foucault, in literary studies and cultural criticism, is often
seen as part of 'Post-structuralism' and bracketed with those of Barthes, Derrida
and Lacan. Indeed Derrida's view are comparable to those of Foucault, though
more radical: In Derrida's view, thought as such stands indited for being based on
the principle of exclusion. As soon as the *logos* articulates itself it excludes nonsense and madness (cf. 'Cogito et histoire de la folie', in *L'écriture et la
différence*, Paris 1967, 51-97). For Derrida, thought itself is a form of hegemony,
and totalitarian in its claims to understand, to comprehend, to force Otherness and
Absence in terms of presence and understanding. Thus the Derridean notion of
différance is not only the well-known version of semantic deferral, but also a
radical recognition of the constant refusal, in logocentric thought, to acknowledge
difference. *Différance*, in Derrida's thought, is a fundamental category, un-
thinkable, differentiation-generating, and irreducible to a fundamental or ultimate
identity.

However, unlike Foucault, the work of Derrida is more directly related to

Foucault's influence has been very important in all those spheres where the interaction between 'culture' and 'society' has been studied, and the results of discursive identity-articulations or attitudes can be measured in their social repercussions. Edward Said's pioneering, influential and controversial analysis of the Orient as the product of a Western, hegemonic exoticism is an obvious example, which in turn has led to a whole new genre in critical Orientalism and post-colonial studies: witness the work of Rana Kabbani and Homi Bhabha; [10] a similar project has been started in the work of V.Y. Mudimbe, which studies the construction of Africa as a

---

the insights of his precursor Saussure. The impact of Derrida's thought on literary studies (exemplified here in Schrover's contribution) should, furthermore, be seen as an attempt to counteract that part of Structuralist poetics which continued the aesthetic programme of the Russian Formalists. Formalist thought (Shklovski, Ejchenbaum, Propp) had spread to French academic circles partly through the mediation of East-European emigrés like Todorov, Kristeva and Greimas, and had been incorporated into the structuralist study of literature around the review *Tel Quel* and the work of men like Gérard Genette and Philippe Hamon. The Formalist programme was fundamentally, however, to establish the *identity* of literature, to formulate a theory of *literariness* and to pinpoint the differences between literary and 'normal' texts. As a result, Formalist-inspired analyses often tried to assess the individual achievement of the literary text, 'what made it tick', its artistic integrity. It was this tendency which was counteracted by Derrida's impact: 'deconstructionist' analyses began to look, not for the harmony and integrity in which the text manifested its artistry, but for the way in which a text showed its underlying tensions, its negated contradictions, the traces of its inescapable self-referentiality which it purported to transcend or else obliquely thematized.

Whereas Formalist-influenced mainstream Structuralism looked for the signature of the individual text, post-structuralism began to query this textual individuality. More important perhaps than Derrida's apodictic *il n'y a pas de hors-texte* was Julia Kristeva's elaboration of the notion of an *intertext*, which she defined as the textual-semantic equivalent of what the social sciences called *intersubjectivity*. In Kristeva's case, then, it was the notion of an individual subjectivity behind the text which came to be queried. Kristeva's problematization of subjectivity was partly adopted from Lacan (who did to Freud what Derrida did to Saussure), partly a result of her reflection on feminine identity, with which she exercised enormous influence in the field of women's studies (cf. Van der Kley, below); it eventually led to her more general reflections on human identity and the Other which she laid down in her *Étrangers à nous-mêmes*.

[10]   Said, *Orientalism* (London, 1978); Kabbani, *Europe's Myths of Orient: Devise and Rule* (London, 1986); Bhabha, *Nation and Narration* (London, 1991).

non-European Otherness and object of exoticist projections. [11] The entire field of racial studies has been affected, though it generally remains oriented along neo-Marxist lines — that is to say, in a perspective which affords primacy to actual (material, economic) power relations and explains the hegemonic cultural *Überbau* from socioecomic basis rather than *vice versa*. In this respect, such postcolonial studies into the configuration of race and class follow the lines set out by men like Frantz Fanon and Antonio Gramsci; thus in the London Institute for Race Relations' review *Race and Class*, or in the work of Jan Nederveen Pieterse (cf. his contribution to the present volume). Others have also adopted Immanuel Wallerstein's view of world-ecomic developments in terms of a 'world system' (Etienne Balibar, André Gunder Frank).

Within Europe, Said's model has been applied to Ireland; [12] and Europe's relations with the New World have likewise been studied as an instance of the confrontation with Otherness. Peter Hulme and Tzvetan Todorov [13] are two cases in point; a more Derridean way of reading this confrontation is performed by Peter Mason, who brings anthropological *Wissenschaftsgeschichte* and Derrida-inspired literary analysis together in a deconstructive interpretation of ethnographical representations of the New World. [14] A similar encounter in a key work of modern fiction is analysed here in Els Schrover's contribution.

The impact has spread beyond this culture-geographical inventory of Eurocentrism. Anthropology has also begun to query its traditional way

---

[11]   Mudimbe, *The Invention of Africa. Gnosis, Philosophy and the Order of Knowledge* (Indiana U.P., 1988).

[12]   W.J. McCormack, 'The Question of Celticism' in his *Ascendancy and Tradition in Anglo-Irish Literature* (Clarendon Press, 1985), pp. 219-238; David Cairns & Shaun Richards, *Writing Ireland* (Manchester U.P., 1988); and the new international research project on 'Celticism' sponsored by the Royal Irish Academy and the European Science Foundation.

[13]   Peter Hulme, *Colonial Encounters. Europe and the Native Caribbean, 1492-1979* (London, 1986). Tzvetan Todorov, *La conquête de l'Amérique: La question de l'Autre* (Paris 1988); Id., *Nous et les Autres* (Paris 1988).

[14]   E.g. his contribution in this book, and his *The Deconstruction of America: Representations of the Other* (London, 1990), which refuses to measure the European monologue on the New World in terms of its (imponderable) distortion of an extratextual extra-European reality.

of viewing the relation of humanity to its non-human natural environment. The circumscription of a civilized, ordered space from the wildness of nature has been charted by British symbolic anthropologists (following more general reflection by, for instance, Mircea Eliade and Gaston Bachelard), and their approach has been followed up by historians like Keith Thomas. [15] The further implication of this relationship has been addressed by Donna Haraway's analysis of ideological constructs in our study of primates and apes, and even in our perception of the natural world in general. [16] Recently, initiatives such as the 'African Apes Project' have been a significant illustration of the ongoing intensification of this trend: a 'Declaration on African Apes' is being prepared which challenges the automatism of traditional exclusion mechanisms by arguing to include African apes within the community of man's moral equals. [17]

The study of the Europan confrontation with Otherness on this global scale has been able to draw also on another important scholarly tradition in this field: that of feminism. Many publications register a continuum in the exclusion of 'naturals' be they in the guise of animals or of women (who are thus conflated in terms of their marginality vis-à-vis phallocentric values); a similar path is pursued by Barbara Noske. [18] Within the Western world, the exclusion of women from the formulation of cultural values has of course been a central topic in women's studies. Indeed the very personality of the female subject as an Other has become a central concern, frequently tackled with reference to Freudian or to Lacanian thought; as Van der Kley shows in her contribution to the present volume, the status of Freud [19] and of Lacan on either side of the Atlantic matches a certain divergence in the respective agenda's of women's

---

[15]   *Man and the Natural World. Changing Attitudes in England 1500-1800* (London, 1983).

[16]   Haraway, *Primate Visions. Gender, Race and Nature in the World of Modern Science* (New York/London, 1989).

[17]   By the Italian Paola Cavalieri and the Australian Peter Singer, who are editing a collection of essays around this topic, due to appear soon.

[18]   Noske, *Humans and Other Animals. Beyond the Boundaries of Anthropology* (London, 1989).

[19]   The value of psychoanalysis as an analytical tool in the study of otherness is queried in Corbey's contribution, which argues that Freud's thought instantiates, rather than reflects on, traditional alterity constructs.

movements and feminist scholars in America and Europe. Within Europe
(and especially in France, under the influence of Derrida, Lacan and
Kristeva there, cf. note 9 above), ideas have been developed on *écriture
féminine* and on the playful 'micrologies' with which women authors try
to circumscribe an alternative, Other, specifically feminine sphere of
experience.

So many manifestations of alterity — clearly Otherness has become a very
prominent concern in contemporary thought. The traditional Western articulation of cultural identity has excluded so many Others who are now, each
individually, posing a moral and epistemological problem to modern
scholarship. Alongside anthropology, and in close conjunction with a
revolutionized literary criticism, a branch of Cultural Studies has sprung up
which addresses the most diverse manifestations of alterity. A scholar like
Sander Gilman has addressed a whole series of stigmatized and scape-
goated Others: blacks, the insane, the sick, women, homosexuals, Jews, and
has demonstrated structural constants in the stereotypical imagination of all
these disparate and heterogeneous groups, linked only in their common
marginalization. [20] Peter Stallybrass and Allon White have published a
seminal study on how various domains (the slum, fairgrounds, the
carnivalesque, certain bodily practices) were constructed as 'low' and
'disgusting': an alterity against which post-Renaissance bourgeois identity
could silhouette itself. [21] The literary-cum-historical analysis of travel
descriptions has burgeoned, and exoticism has become a leading focus of
interest in the history of ideas. [22] The topical (indeed, almost trendy)
nature of the subject transpires from the fact that many publications in this
area consist of conference proceedings (indeed, the present volume is a

---

[20]   Cf. *On Blackness without Blacks: Essays of the Image of the Black in
Germany* (Boston, 1982); and *Difference and Pathology. Stereotypes of Sexuality,
Race and Madness* (Cornell U.P., 1985).

[21]   *The Politics and Poetics of Transgression* (London, 1986). The study of
'popular culture' generally has gained mauch interest, and frequently invokes the
antecedents of Peter Burke, or M.M. Bakhtin's notions of the carnivalesque.
Witness the work of historians like Nathalie Zemon Davis, Emmanuel Le Roy
Ladurie and Arthur Mitzman.

[22]   Witness *Exoticism in the Enlightenment*, ed. G.S. Rousseau & R. Porter
(Manchester 1990).

case in point) or accompany expositions. Among the former we should mention the collections *'Race', Writing and Difference* and *Europe and its Others*[23], among the latter there is Jan Nederveen Pieterse's *Wit over Zwart* or the exhibition catalogues of *Europa und der Orient, 'Primitivism' in Twentieth-Century Art, Exotische Welten - Europäische Phantasien* and *Der geraubte Schatten.*[24]

Perhaps the profusion of 'other'-related themes is bewildering; what is more, the topic tends to cut across existing divisions between various disciplines in the human and social sciences and offers a *fil conducteur* in which, for example, ethnographical texts are read with the expertise of the literary critic, or literary texts are read with the expertise of the anthropologist. Psychology, sociology, iconography, Image Studies, Women's Studies, Gay Studies, disciplines old and new, defined along different criteria of competence or terrain, all meet in their common interest in the subject of Alterity. They bring different perspectives, different priorities and methodological presuppositions; at times their respective views on one and the same issue in human culture can be irreconcilable. It is uncalled for, at this point, and given the nature of the shared topic, to bring all these endeavours under a single heading. The following collection merely aims to present, in a wholly artificial (alphabetical) order, the scala of approaches in all its variety; the meeting which is thereby documented was, if nothing else, exciting, inspiring, and continues to give cause for further reflection.

The construction of Otherness can be detected at the root of much injustice and suffering; it is a topic which cannot be studied without eliciting a certain amount of ethical discomfort. However, it would be all too easy to see in this ethical discomfort an escape hatch, a point where the modern scholar can feel comfortably different from the objectionable discourse s/he studies. The temptation exists: to define one's methodological justification in terms of an ethical quality, to denounce and to expose.

However it seems that to do so makes for poor scholarship. The

---

[23]   Ed. H.L. Gates (Chicago, 1986); originally special issues of *Critical Inquiry* (12 #1, 1985; 13 #1, 1986). and ed. F. Barker et. al.: Proceedings of the Essex Conference on the Sociology of Literature, July 1984 (Colchester, 1984).

[24]   Amsterdam, 1990; Berlin, 1989; New York, 1984; Stuttgart, 1987; and München, 1989, respectively.

editors believe that ethical values may guide one in one's choice of topic
— to study alterity bespeaks another set of concerns than to study the
development of the sonnet in European symbolism — but that ethical
considerations are doubtful guarantors of the methodic soundness of one's
research. The aim of alterity studies cannot be merely to point the accusing
finger. Our purpose is not to quixotically denounce the makings of
intolerance, merely to expose them.

Indeed it would be questionable to see the very topic of alterity in
primarily ethical terms, as something which contains an inherent moral
danger-signal. Otherness, whatever the social implications it may have
elicited, is a categorical fact of life, and as such ethically neutral. Otherness
will not go away: we know the world by subdividing it in spheres that we
do or do not identify with. We have values and express them in endorsing
or rejecting parts of our experience — or in selecting the type of topic we
feel is worth studying. We are all ineluctably implicated in the world of
human experience and cannot transcend its patterns either to pass
judgement on them or to define their limitations.

Similarly, the categorical pre-given fact that our subjective identity
exists in a constant confrontation with a sphere outside its cognitive
purview (as Voestermans also traces) seems to offer little reason why we
should militate against that state of affairs. To do so would lead to
solipsism (and the inability to define the status of our disbelief in the
objective existence of the world) or to that epistemological nihilism which,
in the wake of Derrida, sees the very notion of Self as a hegemonistic
intrustion on the virgin shores of Otherness. Such a decentering of
subjectivity often invokes an ethical rather than an epistemological cause;
but the question 'whose ethics if not those of the subject, and how
communicated?' must in this case remain unanswerable.

The unknowability of that otherness which yet, by lying contiguous
to our cognitive purview, invites acquaintance; which cannot become
known in its own terms and which, in the process of becoming known,
changes the subject to which it becomes known: that relationship is
fundamentally hermeneutic. It ceases to be an epistemological mousetrap
or an invitation to guilt if we can deal with that relationship on the basis
of respect for the separateness between the Other and oneself, and a
willingness to let the Other change one.

THE OTHER WITHIN [1]

Ernst van Alphen

> Si je suis étranger, il n'y a pas d'étrangers.
> Julia Kristeva, *Étrangers à nous-mêmes*

'Identity' and 'alterity' are concepts with a past. They have had different meanings throughout history, and they have created history by their application to different objects. When applied to imperialistic expansion, identity and alterity are primarily defined in terms of race or ethnicity. When applied to threatened boundaries and changing governmental systems, they are defined in terms of nationality. When applied to changing gender roles they are defined in terms of sexuality. In other words, 'identity' and 'alterity' pertain to concrete historical situations and to the preoccupations relevant to each of those historical situations.

The very fact that these concepts have a past indicates that identity and alterity are constructs rather than preconditions or ontological categories. The questions, then, are: How do these constructions come

---

[1]   Research for this paper was sponsored by NWO (Dutch Foundation for Scientific Research) which awarded me a post-doctoral fellowship in the 'Word and Image Studies' Programme at the Free University of Amsterdam.

about and what motivates them? What do they ultimately mean? I propose
to take a closer look at the concepts themselves by confronting three
different approaches to them which turn out to be related and to lead to
similar conclusions, although they are fruitful to different degrees. Those
three approaches are the hermeneutical, the epistemological and the
psychological ones.

A *hermeneutical approach* will raise the following question: how can
'identity' or 'alterity' be understood? Does an identity have intrinsic
characteristics which can be described and re-produced, or can we
understand an identity only by opposing it to what it is not (by differentiating it from its 'other')? In his *Nous et les autres* (1989), Tzvetan
Todorov has argued that we-other relations such as nationalism and
exoticism are both *relativisms*. No fixed, concrete content is valorized or
defended. Our own or the other culture only gains content in relation to the
values of the observer. In the case of exoticism, the other culture is seen
as superior to the culture of the observer. In the case of nationalism, the
observer's country is seen as superior to the other country or countries. In
both cases, the contents of 'other' as well as 'self' are fundamentally
relative, and as such they can only be defined in relation to their other, to
what they are not.

    This principle of relativism seems at first sight comparable to what
in semiotics is called *differentiation* as the principle of meaning production.
A sign does not *have* meaning, but *receives* meaning in its contradistinctive
relation with other signs. A meaning is not a thing which exists, but the
product of the process of differentiation. The relative relationship between
identity and alterity would, then, be an example of how meaning is
produced in the process called *semiosis*. This comparison suggests that the
terms are the result of a proper meaning-making procedure rather than of
suspect self-centered reasoning and appropriation.

    Yet this resemblance is misleading. Todorov shows convincingly
that alterity in exoticism and nationalism is not at all a concrete object
which is understood by differentiating it from the observer's (national,
cultural...) identity. In semiosis, the sign has objective existence and is
given meaning (i.e., turned into a sign) by the volition of the interpreter.
One can choose to take or not to take, say, the colour of the sky as a sign
of the weather the day will bring, but the colour of the sky is there all the
same. In contrast, descriptions of alterity are never based on a 'real' other,

but on a denial of the self, of the observer's identity. The preference for the other in the case of exoticism is not produced by an interest *in* and subsequently by knowledge *of* the other, but by a negative view of the observer's own identity or culture. The other is not the description, not even an interpretation of a reality, but the formulation of an ideal, desired identity. In the case of nationalism, descriptions of the other are phantasms of the potential enemy, not interpretations of a real one in any sense. Because of the fact that the other has no objective existence outside the interpreter's perception, not even as a virtual sign, the comparison between alterity and semiosis falls through. Hence, the very attempt to approach self and other hermeneutically is bound to fail.

Indeed, the hermeneutical approach leads finally to the conclusion that the other cannot be understood — that the concepts fail to be hermeneutically disentangled and substantiated. An attempt at reading the other remains caught in evocations of utopian self-images or feared self-images. This implies that the concept of alterity does not have the same status as that of identity. While 'alterity' is a screen for the imagination, 'identity' is the content of that imagination. In terms of the comparison with semiosis, alterity and identity are not, cannot be, two signs, mutually differentiating in order to reach meaning; rather, alterity is a code which helps identity to become meaningful, i.e. to gain content. Alterity, then, *is* nothing, has no meaning; it is mere a device of meaning-production, and since it is unacknowledged as such, and would be disowned if this proper function of the term were brought to awareness, it cannot be innocently used.

An epistemological approach seeks to examine the conditions of knowledge and insight; as we will see, these also have their ramifications in the production of meaning. The epistemological approach involves the following questions: How can we recognize identity, and its derived counterpart, alterity, as objects of knowledge? What kind of objects are they? What are their constituent parts?

The individualistic preoccupations of modern Western society have made the notion of identity more and more encompassing. Michel Foucault has argued that from the Middle Ages onwards the identity of self becomes the legitimizing point of reference for the individual. Where somebody in earlier epochs could refer to the relationships s/he had with others (family, the guild, patronage), to legitimize herself, the Renaissance introduced a 'truth discourse' about the inner self as a mode of legitimation. In the wake of that development, confession became a fundamental device of legitimation. The subject must confess the truth about her inner self, her identity. The notion of identity has developed from the relationships one has with others in a community, in the idea of an inner self, or inner truth.

The confessional mode becomes the predominant instrument by which people can come to know themselves, and by which the existence of identity is confirmed. The power of confession lies in its self-realization and the confirmation it affords the individual. Confession as a mode of revealing the inner self, presupposes, then, that there *is* or should be something — identity — which can be the object of confessing. This identity is seen as an origin which generates behaviour, the acts and artifacts produced by the owner of that identity. Acts, behaviour and artifacts can be read, then, in terms of their originator's identity. The producer's identity is mirrored in her/his products. This implies that identity does not cover the inner self only, but also the outer self, one's actions in the outer world.

In *Histoire de la Sexualité*, Foucault traces how in the nineteenth century sexual acts become incorporated into the realm of the identity concept. In earlier centuries homosexuals or heterosexuals did not exist as such: one's identity was not defined by one's sexual acts. In the Middle Ages homosexuality was seen as a crime, a criminal act, which had to be discouraged by the deterrent of capital punishment. Later on, homosexuality was no longer conceptualized as an *act*, but as a *state*: it was a certain state, an illness, which defined the identity of an individual as sick, depraved, and deviant.

The changing realm of the concept of identity makes it obviously impossible to decide which 'entities' constitute an identity. We are currently inclined to see identity as a centre or focus of meaning behind an individual or culture. Such a notion of identity, and subsequently of its corollary, alterity, is a typical instance of what Derrida has called Western logocentrism. Logocentrism, the metaphysics of presence, is the Western tendency to refer all questions of meaning to a singular founding presence which is imagined to be 'behind' the objects which ask for signification. That founding presence can be the author's or artist's identity and intention, historical reality, or cultural identity, or God. In spite of the self-evident importance of intention in our culture, I will argue that to see identity/alterity as an enabling presence of meaning or truth inevitably leads to reductive significations. Therefore, identity or alterity should not be defined in terms of how they underpin the meaning of a given cultural act or artefact; rather, it is more fruitful and more realistic to see identity/alterity as the effect produced by a given cultural (artef)act.

This is where the epistemological approach complements the hermeneutic one. For the effect we are dealing with is an effect of meaning. In terms of Austin's speech-act theory, it is not so much the *constative* aspect of a cultural (artef)act which defines its identity (that what it has to say or what can be said about it) but its *performative* aspect (what is done in the act of speaking it). This view would imply that discussions on the problematics of identity and alterity should not focus on the intrinsic characteristics of a cultural artefact, but on the interlocutionary situation in which such an object receives its meaning. [2]

Let me illustrate this by examining the consequences of this view in light of the controversial paintings of the German painter Anselm Kiefer. The case has particular relevance to our subject of discussion, because his paintings have given rise to discussions about what Kiefer does with the image of German cultural identity. At stake in the discussion is whether or not Kiefer subscribes to Germany's Nazi past, which he evokes in his paintings. German critics feel very uncomfortable with Kiefer's paintings, because they read them as promoting a resurrection of the Nazi past; in fact, Kiefer does undeniably and explicitly insert allusions to this past into his paintings, which often convey a gloomy atmosphere of threat and destruction. In much criticism Kiefer's treatment of the major icons of German Nazism is seen as an evocation of German national identity and thus as an attempt to relegitimize the Third Reich (Huyssen 1989: 29). Especially Kiefer's early work, his series of self-photographs entitled *Besetzungen* (1969) (ill. 1) in which he gives the fascist salute in various locations, sometimes accompanied by images of Nazi sculpture, has given

---

[2]   In later work Austin has proposed to analyse speech acts according to three dimensions: the *locutionary* dimension, which is the sound, sense and reference of an utterance; the *illocutionary* dimension, which is the intentional and conventional force of an utterance; the *perlocutionary* dimension, which is the actual effect of an utterance. For the approach of identity and alterity this differentiation implies that we should not so much look for the locutionary or illocutionary dimension of a cultural (artef)act, but for its perlocutionary dimension.

ill. 1

rise to indignation in the German press. The retrospective exhibition of his work at the German Pavilion at the Venice Biennale in 1980 provoked fellow-Germans to heated critical attacks. He was seen as 'flaunting his Germanness' and flirting with the 'ghosts of the Fatherland'.[3] The Kiefer exhibition in Jerusalem in 1984 was almost cancelled because press reviews of a previous showing in Düsseldorf, earlier that same year, had said that it contained various implications of 'neo-fascism'.

In contrast, American critics, who do not share Kiefer's nationality, generally praise Kiefer for his Germanness, for the authenticity with which his paintings deal with the ghosts of the fatherland and especially with the terror of recent German history (cf. Rosenthal 1987). According to Schjeldahl (1985) Kiefer did not resurrect or relegitimize the past in those pictures where he gives the Nazi salute; rather, 'Kiefer posed to himself some tactless questions then gnawing at many young Germans: "What happened?", "How could it have happened?" and "What would *I* have done?"' (p. 7) This typically German problematic has, however, been transcended by Kiefer into an issue of general concern, according to Schjeldahl:

> Kiefer's essential project, it seems to me, is to test the ability of consciousness to confront and assimilate — to master — history's overpowering paradigms, its terrorizing patterns of objectification: 'German', 'Jew', etc. Kiefer has imaginatively entered, and dissolved into his own maturing mind, one pattern after another. All have been specific to his national, generational, and personal identity, but the nature of his effort is compelling in the most general way. It adds up to a new proposition of what 'the artist' is and does in a culture that might somehow, someday, be termed 'ours'. (p. 11; cf also Schjeldahl 1988)

Kiefer is said to use typically German motifs, while at the same time reworking and transcending the negative past to which German identity has led, into a universally human identity. Rosenthal, to quote yet another sample of this response, says that 'Kiefer's investigation is traditionally religious, for implicit in it is an inquiry into the existence and nature of the Supreme Being, and by extension, the possibility of redemption' (1987:

---

[3]   For a discussion of German reactions to Kiefer's work, see Schwartz 1983.

18). When Kiefer in the early eighties began to use German architecture as the primary stage set of his paintings, this is read as an appropriation of Nazi architectural designs to create memorials to various personages, especially the artists. Thus in the painting *Interior* (1981), which is in the Amsterdam Stedelijk Museum (ill. 2), we recognize the mosaic room in the Reich Chancellery, a design by Albert Speer. The light-filled space of the original room has, however, been crudely intruded upon. The interior is blackened, stained and a kind of ceremonial, even ritual fire is depicted in the foreground. Rosenthal summarizes this kind of use of Nazi architecture by Kiefer unproblemat   urning Nazi buildings to more worthwhile uses' (p. 121).

A more ambiguous response to Kiefer's work, and specifically to *Interior*, is voiced by Andreas Huyssen, a German who works and lives in the United States. His lack of a clear national identity enables him to read Kiefer's work in a more complex way. He finds the paintings of the early 1980s problematic because they are devoid of satire or irony, in contrast to Kiefer's treatment of fascist icons in the 1970s. They seem, rather, to exude melancholy. Although Huyssen first saw in *Interior* the ruins of fascism represented in the mode of an allegory that seemed to hold the promise of transcendence, the second stage of his response gave him the feeling of 'having been lured into fascinating fascism, having fallen for an aestheticization of fascism which today complements fascism's own strategies' (p. 38). He eventually formulates his dilemma as follows:

> [I do not know] whether to read these paintings as a melancholy fixation on the dreamlike ruins of fascism that locks the viewer into complicity, or, instead, as a critique of the spectator, who is caught up in a complex web of melancholy, fascination, and repression. (p. 39)

It is clear that identity and alterity are the central issues in the response to Kiefer's paintings. At stake in the discussion is his alleged identification with, or aloofness from, a German national identity, while the positions within the discussions are in fact in both cases determined by the same factor, namely the national identities of the critics. Yet both German and American critics share the presupposition that Kiefer's painting should be read as having a fixed meaning or position about or attitude towards German national identity. German critics are horrified by it, because they

ill. 2

are convinced that Kiefer represents German fascism as part of, or even as a metaphor for, Germanness, while foreign critics applaud the work because German fascism is represented as something important that still weighs on contemporary identity; as something which has to be remembered.

These evaluations (with the exception of Huyssen's) show a conflation: the visual evocation of a national past is seen as a metaphorical mirror image of national identity. This conflation emerges thanks to the logocentric presupposition which entails that the manifestations of a culture, such as of its past, are a metaphorical entry into the identity of that culture. Kiefer's visual representations of a black page of German history are read as a constative definition of German identity.

The fact that Kiefer uses such controversial icons in his paintings suggests that he intends to challenge his audience. As Huyssen has argued, Kiefer's intention cannot be to open the wounds or to evoke uncomfortable truths in front of his countrymen who want to forget the fascist past.

> The issue is not whether to forget or to remember, but rather how to remember and how to handle representations of the remembered past at a time when most of us, over forty years after the war, only know that past through images, films, photographs, representations. (p. 30)

This implies that Kiefer's paintings should not be read as metaphors for German identity, representing the founding presence behind German fascism. They should be read in relation to Kiefer's contemporary audience. He challenges the ways they remember German history. The meaning of Kiefer's works, then, consists primarily of the actual effects they bring about: rather than the constative, one must mobilize the perlocutionary dimension of the works. And that this is so, is evidenced precisely by the very responses which remain enclosed within their constative horizon. The responses which these paintings evoke are instances of the performative meaning, which consists of an erroneous illusion of constative meaning. The constative meaning is an imputed one, and a painful one; the responses show that what matters is this illusion *plus* its assault on the respondent: its effect.

In Kiefer, one might argue, German fascism is not read as a metaphor, as a figure which replaces one thing (icons of Nazism) with another (German identity), but as a metonymy, as a figure which is *in touch* with its meaning; a figure which refers to something else with which it has a relation of proximity, of juxtaposition, of contiguity. Read metonymically, the references to Nazism are figures of an identity which is determined by *the way in which it relates to* the past of German fascism. In such a reading, identity is not 'the underlying presence', but the result of an ongoing process of reworking the self: an affect.

The psychological approach addresses the question of meaning also in terms of effect, or rather, examines the relation between meaning, effect and affect. Within such a perspective, Freud's psychoanalytical theory has radically changed the concepts of identity and alterity. Self and other are no longer counterparts; from now on, the other is part of the self. We are our own others. The other is always the other within. While the ethics and politics implied by the traditional concepts of identity and alterity consist of the will to understand and to integrate the other, the ethics and politics of psychoanalysis pursue, not the integration of the other, but the disintegration of the self. This assault on the self is often misunderstood, remains unacknowledged or often (I suggest) denied by critics who reject psychoanalysis as a whole.

Freud's analysis of the German words *heimlich* and *unheimlich* in his famous essay on 'the Uncanny' is of exemplary value for the role of the other in psychoanalytic theory. Freud points out that the word *heimlich* has two meanings: 1) familiar, intimate, pleasant and 2) secret, dangerous. Paradoxically, this second meaning is also the meaning of the opposite of *Heimlich*, namely *Unheimlich*. According to Freud this strange semantic structure occurs because sometimes things which are known are repressed, hence, are both known, familiar, and disavowed, becoming strange and spooky.

> [...] we can understand why linguistic usage has extended *das Heimliche* into its opposite, *das Unheimliche*; for this uncanniness is in reality nothing new or alien, but something which is familiar and old, established in the mind and which becomes alienated from it only through the process of repression (p. 364)

Something uncanny is, in short, something which is known and familiar, but repressed, made strange and thereby displaced onto an alien other.

Problematic, terrifying feelings experienced, or experiences undergone by a subject threaten the unity of a self that feels no longer in control. From this perspective, the uncanny other is a creation, the result of repression. This repression is motivated by the 'need' to defend the coherence of the self and to conserve its fragile unity and integrity. The other who arouses uncanny feelings is then in fact a return of that which has been repressed and was once part of the self; this other is not so other after all.

This return of the repressed has the effect of depersonalization. Julia Kristeva in her book *Étrangers à nous-mêmes* (1989) insightfully describes the effect of depersonalization which the uncanny meeting with the other can have:

> Étrange, en effet, la rencontre avec l'autre — que nous percevons par la vue, l'ouïe, l'odorat, mais n''encadrons' pas par la conscience. L'autre nous laisse séparés, incohérents; plus encore, il ne peut que nous donner le sentiment de manquer de contact avec nos propres sensations, de les refuser ou, au contraire, de refuser notre jugement sur elles — sentiment d'être 'stupides', 'floués'. [...] Face à l'étranger que je refuse et auquel je m'identifie à la fois, je perds mes limites, je n'ai plus de contenant, les souvenirs des expériences où l'on m'avait laissée tomber me submergent, je perds contenance. (p. 276)

The phenomena of uncanniness and depersonalization also enable us to reach a better understanding of the responses to Kiefer's paintings. This is not surprising: Shoshana Felman has demonstrated the close alliance between psychoanalysis and speech act theory in her astute study *Le scandale du corps parlant*. The confrontation with Kiefer's paintings is for many Germans a return of that which had been repressed. After the Second World War the most easy way to regain a respectable self-image was to forget this black page of German history. But this is easier said than done; the overt and silent complicities with, and contaminations by, Nazism cannot but burden Germans in many troubled ways, and instead of forgetting what will not be pushed out, the more likely effect of this desire will have been repression, in the specifically Freudian sense: repression from consciousness into the unconscious where it remains lurking. Kiefer's evocation of this past threatens this fragile, precariously regained self-image, which is too broadly based on repression to be sturdy and resistant against this kind of assault. The War is turned into the other, which does not belong to 'their' past. Instead of analysing the symptom of the uncanny feelings which Kiefer's paintings have provoked — instead of using these works as a catalyst to their repressed but re-emergent feelings, they repress their 'other within' a second time by accusing Kiefer of the complicity with that fascism they fear they might not keep at bay.

But the positive responses of the American audience can also be analysed in terms of uncanniness. Americans relate differently to the represented icons because their position is historically and geographically different from that of the German critics. But their self-image is different as well. Americans often evince a sense of inferiority. On the one hand this is so because they interpret (again metaphorically) their short history as a *lack* of identity (not unrelated, by the way, to another genocide, the extermination of native American peoples). On the other hand, American national identity is impaired because of the multi-ethnic composition of American society. Americans not only lack national identity, they are also burdened with a *double* allegiance, where Americanness is complemented by origin in another land. [4] This doubleness does nothing to increase the sense of national identity; by blurring identity, it increases the lack of it. Post-war Germans, in contrast, suffer from an *excess* of identity. The world of their national image (myths, literature, music) has been perverted by the Nazis into ornaments of superiority and power. Post-war Germany felt the need to purge contaminated parts of its national identity. The German crisis of identity is in that sense exactly the symmetrical counter-part of the American one.

When they praise Kiefer for the way he uses the power of art to transcend German identity into the universally human, American critics do something more specific than just endorsing the universalist fallacy (although that is also what they do). More particularly, they exorcize the alterity of Kiefer's representations. His paintings are said to evoke the opposite of uncanniness. These laudatory critics do not recognize something familiar which has been repressed, but rather something alien which is desired. Paradoxically, this is yet another form of exoticism. The desired otherness is an excess of identity, which is called to fill their own lack. This is not unproblematic in this case, for it is not just any identity,

---

[4] The problematics of national identity are complicated even further in the case of Kiefer criticism, when we consider that many of these American critics are of Jewish origin.

but *German* identity that is at stake. But that problem is solved not by repressing its Germanness, but by sublimating German history into the universally human — which, as usual, cancels the otherness out in the very move of appropriating it.

This gesture of appropriation implied in universalism is demonstrated most convincingly by Rosenthal's assessment of Kiefer's 'maturity', where he expresses his satisfaction to see the artist integrate German and American features into a unity that excludes all others:

> When Kiefer searched for models of the largely abandoned tradition of painting, he looked at the American Abstract Expressionist [Jackson Pollock] for muscular, large-scale work. Having grappled with Pollock's vision of art, Kiefer has brought forth his summation of how a new art might be formed, producing canvases that have considerable pictural complexity owing to the visual tension between the two-dimensional plane and three-dimensional space. These tensions are representative of one of the largest issues in his art, the attempt to unite the scale and visual richness of Abstract Expressionism with meaningful subject-matter. In other words, to unite the poles of form and content, the concrete and the ideal, and art and life (1987: 155).

I will not stop to discuss the criteria for the praise here ('muscular' inevitably evokes masculinity, while 'complexity' endorses cliché notions of 'high' art). [5] But more importantly, the final set of pairs could as well include 'American and German', for that pair constitutes the background of this assessment. That the ideal is to unite, and that the unification of nationalities happens to coincide with a harmony between form and content, seems hardly a coincidence. The universalization of this art not only reduces the troubling Germanness to the content that Americanness lacked; it also elides all other possible national identities, for 'form and content' allow of no other inside the sign.

Huyssen, in contrast to both German and American critics, and probably because of his double identity, seems to have enough distance from this issue to be able to stay out of this troublesome identification

---

[5]   Nor do I go into the self-other distinction inherent in the very notion of artistic 'maturity' — ageism is part and parcel of the problematics at stake in this discussion.

problem. His response demonstrates that national identity is not a prison in which one is fatally caught up, but a factor which can be faced, and by facing it, dismissed, relativized, or bracketed.

Conclusion

The hermeneutical, epistemological and psychological perspectives on identity and alterity all contribute to one conclusion. Identity and alterity are not 'givens', they are not presences behind the self or the other, but changeable products of the ongoing process of constituting a self-image. Speaking about the self is not the equivalent of speaking about the other. The other is other because s/he is focalized by the self of the observer. While the self is in the position of subject of focalization, the other is by definition the object. The only way to know the other is by letting the other speak about me, by giving the other the position of 'I'. When 'I' speak about the other, I remain in fact caught in the process of defining or demarcating my self-image. The other is used as screen on which ideals or terrors can be projected, or as location to which problematic feelings about the self can be displaced.

These conclusions should not be read as pessimistic. What they imply finally is that 'we' cannot analyse alterity without at the same time analysing 'our' identity. Or the other way around. Because of the very fact that identity is constituted by the creation of alterities, our object of knowledge can never be just 'identity' or 'alterity', but only the observer's identity (re)creating a self-image and the image of the other. In other words, and in convergence with the conclusions drawn by critical anthropologists (e.g. Fabian 1981), the study of identity and alterity only makes sense if we do it self-reflexively.

Bibliography

J. DERRIDA, 1980. *Of Grammatology*. Transl. and intr. by Gayatri G. Spivak (Johns Hopkins University Press).
J. FABIAN, 1981. *Time and the Other: How Anthropology Makes its Object* (Yale University Press).
SH. FELMAN, 1980. *Le scandale du corps parlant* (Paris: Seuil).
M. FOUCAULT, 1976. *La volonté de savoir* (vol.1 of *Histoire de la Sexualité*)

(Paris: Gallimard).

S. FREUD, 1985 (1919). 'The Uncanny', *The Pelican Freud Library* vol. 14: 335-76 (London: Penguin Books).

R. FUCHS, 1984. '[...]', *Anselm Kiefer*, catalogue Städtische Kunsthalle Düsseldorf, Musée d'art Moderne de la Ville de Paris, The Israel Museum, Jerusalem, pp. 6-17.

A. HUYSSEN, 1989. 'Anselm Kiefer: The Terror of History, The Temptation of Myth', *October* 48: 25-46.

J. KRISTEVA, 1988. *Étrangers à nous-mêmes* (Paris: Fayard).

M. ROSENTHAL, 1987. *Anselm Kiefer* (Chicago/Philadelphia: Art Institute of Chicago/Philadelphia Museum of Art).

P. SCHJELDAHL, 1985. 'Anselm Kiefer and The Exodus of the Jews', *Art and Text* 19 (October-December): 5-15, 1988 'Our Kiefer', *Art in America* 3 (March).

S. SCHWARTZ, 1983. 'Anselm Kiefer, Joseph Beuys, and the Gosts of the Fatherland', *The New Criterion* 1 #7 (March): 1-9.

T. TODOROV, 1989. *Nous et les Autres. La réflexion française sur la diversité humaine* (Paris: Seuil).

TRADITIONAL FOLK AND INDUSTRIAL MASSES

Irene Cieraad

Nowadays, terms like 'folk' and 'the masses' seem to be less widespread than before; and the reader may be startled at my contention that traditional imagery around these concepts is still influential in European culture.[1] That influence is not limited to a certain interest in 'folk culture' or 'mass culture' but reaches further — so far indeed, that it may involve core symbols of modern European culture. I use the term 'core symbols' advisedly, since the imagery around 'folk' and 'masses' lies at the root of European thought, be it in the field of social theory from the early nineteenth century onwards or in the arrangement of urban and rural space. This contention may not, again, seem obvious to everyone — not because the phenomenon in question is abstruse or complex, but rather because it is so foregrounded and ingrained that it escapes notice. And it is this very foregroundedness and self-evidence which leads me to believe that the matter at hand is a fundamental one indeed.

---

[1]   There is a West-European-centered trend to call West-European phenomena 'European' *tout court*. I am aware of this foregrounding but found it difficult to escape from it.

Origins

The imagery around rural folk and urban masses should be viewed against the historical background of Europe's industrialization and urbanization, and in the intellectual context of the late eighteenth, early nineteenth century. This period witnesses the decline of the traditional biblical notions of space and time. Various advances, such as those in geology, challenge the biblical notion of time and advance a different, secular chronology, without the inherent eschatological expectation of a Second Coming that will terminate history. In this controversial period, and amidst the social upheavals of industrialization and urbanization, the biblical juxtaposition of city and country receives a new charge, and is translated by the social élite into a contrast between a rural, traditional 'folk' population and a growing industrial 'mass' population in the cities.

The social élite thus develops an imagery of 'folk' and 'masses'; it is not a simple, unambiguous one and reflects the controversies amidst which it originated. The secular view of history has meanwhile gained the upper hand; but I conclude, from certain striking differences in the élite's image of 'folk' and 'masses', that the original controversies are still fundamentally influential in the shape of modern European notions of culture. I intend to corroborate this hypothesis; but it will be necessary, first, to give a clearer idea of the nature, background and development of the biblical notion of time and space; and, second, how the time controversy has worked its way into the imagery of folk and masses, both in nineteenth-century social theory and it what I call 'economic symbolism' and 'design patterns'. [2]

Urbs et orbis

I have deliberately spoken of a 'biblical' rather than a 'Christian' notion of time. Indeed there is an important difference between the Jewish and the Christian element which are both encompassed in the biblical phraseology. Scholars like Fabian (1983) do mention the enormous influence exercised

---

[2]   These two concepts will in turn be explained and illustrated through certain West-European trends in the arrangement of space.

on Western thought by the Judaeo-Christian tradition, but the polarity within that tradition is rarely taken into account; and this polarity does have its relevance for my subject. For the Judaeo-Christian tradition contains two, quite distinct, notions of time and space; these notions spread with Christianity and appear to come close to what Gouldner (1973) calls 'deep structures' within Western thought.

The two notions can be correlated with the Judaic and the Christian elements in the biblical tradition; the demarcation line is that between the Old and the New Testament.

The Old Testament reflects a fundamental distinction between inhabited and uninhabited space, between city and open countryside. [3] In the Judaic view, the city is a sacred place while the open country is profane. This view underscores Jewish distinctness and separates them from their neighbours, whose deities dwell in trees and mountains. The God of Israel is not a Tree God but a Domestic God who dwells among his people. Thus, as the people of Israel moves through the desert, their God inhabits a tent or tabernacle, and as they settle down He is given a fixed abode in a specially constructed temple at Jerusalem.

Those who live in the wild, profane open spaces, who inhabit the country or what we would call 'free nature', are in the Old Testament's view considered unclean. Shepherds and fishermen, who play such a prominent role in the New Testament, are held in contempt. The etymology of words like *pagan* and *heathen* (Lat. *pagus*, Eng. *heath*) in many European languages still contains this old Jewish view of the 'country folk', those who dwell in the wilderness. [4]

This Jewish notion of space has its repercussion in a notion of time. Concentrating on the city as a sacred centre, and on the temple, and on the Holiest of Holies as the most sacral centre within the temple, entails a notion of time where none besides the Jewish people can share in that sacred history in which they are the Chosen People. This concentration on the centre as an 'exclusive, shared property leads to what I call the

---

[3]   This sacralization of the city can be observed in other Asian religions.

[4]   The adjoining, non-Jewish tribes are *hors catégorie*; the earliest Greek translations of the Old Testament use the blanket term *ethnikos* for all non-Jews jointly. A similar connotation (the conflation and cognitive dismissal of all that is foreign or uncouth) is still at work in the current usage of terms like *ethnic* and *ethnicity*.

centripetal, *exclusive* aspect of the biblical (Jewish-Christian) notion of time.

To this centrist world-view of the Old Testament, the New Testament adds a concentric dimension (Fabian 1983: 26-7). It makes a less rigid distinction between city and country, *urbs* and *orbis*. Jesus chose fishermen to be his apostles and ordered them to disseminate his ideas among foreign nations, *ethnikoi*. This missionary urge is whole alien to the Jewish tradition. In the New Testamental scheme, history can be shared by everyone. The conversion of all people will mark 'the fullness of time' and prepare the Second Coming. Neither time nor space is exclusive, and the Christian tradition adds to the Jewish, exclusive, centripetal tendency an *expansive*, centrifugal one — which has found expression mainly in the missionary enterprise.

These two tendencies co-exist in the Judaeo-Christian tradition. The centripetal, exclusive one finds expression, not only in the perceived superiority which believers derive from their contract with Christ's promised salvation, but also in the persistent allure of the sacral centre — be it manifested in the medieval crusades, in pilgrimages to Rome, or in attendance at Sunday Mass. These are so many instances of that centripetal tendency to withdrawal into the own identity. The centripetal and centrifugal moments (or, in other words, the 'exclusive' and the 'expansive' moments) typify the vicissitudes of the Judaeo-Christian tradition in the west, one or the other, alternately, being dominant.

This alternating preponderance is exemplified in the history of European Christianity. Its expansion from the Mediterranean area northward is counterbalanced by the growth of exclusive, close, ascetic monastic communities; monastic orders were to play an important role in the stratification of church dogma. The various crusades which are instigated from the eleventh to the thirteenth century are also centripetal in nature: their aim is not only to repulse Islam, but especially to conquer Jerusalem and to establish a Christian centre there.

Another example of the centripetal, exclusive tendency is provided by the anti-heretical drive of the late medieval church authorities protecting their uncertain Rome-centred authority by rigidly excluding ('excommunicating') and persecuting rivaling teachings, which seem to find their strongest support in rural areas.

A similar spatial dichotomy, albeit in secular shape, can be registered in the eighteenth century. In the Enlightenment opposition between the rational and the irrational, the city counts as the locus of reason and science whereas the countryside is seen as a benighted area of ignorance and superstition. [5] In the secularisation of the Christian notion of time, the centripetal tendency to my mind seems to be paramount. Despite the Enlightenment idea that all men are born equal, and ought to share equally in the universal resource of (secular) time, the endowment with Reason is elevated into a mark of exclusiveness and superiority. The elect initiates of Reason in their academic environment feel little urge to spread their Enlightenment beyond their own social sphere. The result is a clinical, 'objective' separation from nature, the prime object of research in the eighteenth century: nature and all that is connected with it (peasants, 'savages') is regarded from a critical distance; accordingly, the separation between city and country, between centre and periphery, becomes more pronounced. Rural areas and their inhabitants are thus effectively 'rusticated', isolated, set apart as benighted fringes uninvolved in the Enlightenment. [6]

Although eighteenth-century rationalization and secularization were important and radical changes, they were for a long time restricted to a small circle of scholars (Hampson 1968: 130, 180-195, 252; Charlton 1984: 7, 16). A Christian notion of time, I am sure, did persist and fed an important counter-current in the Romantic movement. A well-known harbinger is Rousseau, who, as a convinced Protestant, doubts the primacy of reason. Following him, the pre-romantic literati incline towards a more 'involved' and celebratory attitude to nature.

In the wake of romanticism, which primarily affects a new, bourgeois élite in the early nineteenth century, the centripetal and secular notion of time is overshadowed by a centrifugal tendency. Nature is

---

[5]   My use of the term 'countryside' is overly general and should be differentiated if space allowed. Within the European situation, a distinction persisted into the nineteenth century between the attitudes towards wilderness (forests, mountains, moorlands) and towards the cultivated countryside.

[6]   Rational thought in the eighteenth century is characterized, according to Lemaire (1976) by an appropriation of time and history by the bourgeoisie. However, Hampson (1968: 233) maintains that this appropriation of time and belief in progress was prevailed in a narrow aristocratic élite rather than in the bourgeoisie.

revered as a divine force, 'naturalness' is the highest value, and all that nature stands for obtains a positive valorization. This attitude may be couched in a religious vocabulary or in a humanist one, and is reflected in a huge civilizing mission, in the ideal of 'improvement'. The highest achievement of civilization is the spreading of its boons to all mankind.

This romantic manifestation of the christian idea of time the city counts as profane, whereas the countryside with its artless, rustic inhabitants becomes 'Nature as God created it'. The romantic notion of God reverts from a domestic to a natural one; a true cult of nature, with mystical elements, is in evidence (Lemaire 1970: 31-9); and in the process, the artless, rustic countryfolk shares in the rising appreciation of the divine Nature which surrounds them. Their innocence, their closeness to the earth and to the vicissitudes of nature, becomes a powerful topos in nineteenth-century literature, art and scholarship. However, this new image of nature (and of human groups associated with nature: peasants, shepherds, women, children) is not without a history of its own.

Country life

In Christian doctrine, well into the seventeenth century, nature as well as man is considered sinful and 'fallen', as a result of that bitter moment when Adam and Eve, in the garden of Eden, sinned against God's command by eating of the Tree of Knowledge. That trespass resulted in their expulsion from the Garden, that spot of perfect, pure and uncorrupted nature. From that moment onwards, no more harmony can exist within nature, or between man and the natural world. This notion of Original Sin, based on Old Testament material, is complemented by the New Testament idea of redemption, which in the Christian tradition has served to tone down the idea of corruption in man and in nature. The point is a thorny one and led to doctrinal dispute; and the Reformation, with its rejection of confession and indulgences, took a harder line, closer to the Old Testament notion of Original Sin; the more lenient, anthropocentric attitude surfaces most clearly in sixteenth-century humanism and from there gradually gains ground; its echoes can be found in eighteenth-century Christian thought (cf. Hampson 1968: 102-7).

Eighteenth-century anthropocentrism initially emphasizes the balance between man and his inner nature, his emotions and passions, and later on stresses the balance between man and his (natural) environment (cf. Charlton 1984: 22,25). Paintings from the period typically show rural scenes with well-settled ladies and gentlemen who (sometimes in shepherds' dress) enjoy the countryside within the safe confines of their estates (Hauser 1975: 343-5). The atmosphere is dreamy, contemplative, and the pastoral topic often has amorous overtones.

This pastoral idyll is transformed, in the nineteenth century, to the idyllic 'village scene'. Central figure in such a scene is not the shepherd, but the settled peasant: he comes to stand for the good life in the country, in tightly-knit, closed village communities. That tight village community in turn becomes the nineteenth-century ideal of social harmony — a nostalgic ideal, obviously catering for deeply-felt needs in a restless social order that was still experiencing the aftershocks of the French Revolution. In that climate, the peasant's bond with his land becomes the nationalist symbol of historical 'rootedness'. Moreover, there is an economic aspect as well: the icon of the hard-working peasant (often found in nineteenth-century painting) symbolizes an economic reliance on natural forces of productivity. Each idyllic scene of harvests in golden sunsets bespeaks a sober businesslike realization of the importance of agriculture in a period of industrialization and urbanization (Charlton 1984: 38-9, 181-6).

All those lofty connotations which, from the late eighteenth century onwards, are vested in country life, become part of the image of rural folk and folk culture generally. The disparaging notions of countrydwellers (heathenish, primitive or benighted) are now outshone by a positive appreciation: a sense of tradition, harmony, piety, industriousness, a united, pure and artless 'folk'. The counterpart of that image is vested in the bourgeois élite's idea that city life is depraved, impious and un-natural — something which applies both to the decadent upper classes and to the uprooted mass of the proletariat, the pauperized slumdwellers. Rural 'folk' culture is given, in the course of the nineteenth century, a mobilising ideological function: a focus of identification for state nationalism, a point of reference for social harmony within the state. Especially in Eastern Europe, where an intensive process of state formation takes place in this period, national 'folk' culture furnishes a political icon of identity; accordingly, new and more combative qualities are added to the imagery in order to highlight the nation's indigenous folk nobility.

City life

Much as the 'folk' image is determined by its rural setting, so to the image of the 'masses' is influenced by an urban decor. At the same time (the late eighteenth and early nineteenth centuries) when the notion of the 'moral' folk emerged, a complementary image of the 'immoral' masses took shape, in a context of increasing industrialisation and urbanisation. As Raymond Williams showed in *Culture and Society 1780-1950*, the (initially neutral) concept of 'masses' gradually underwent a change for the worse. Five other key terms (industry, democracy, class, art and culture) also shifted their meaning, in what Williams considers a structural, non-fortuitous process (1958: xiii-xx, 295-312).

Thus, industry ceases to connote mere industriousness and comes to be applies to factories and industrialisation — that process which gathered a large labour force onto the work floor and into the cities. This concentration is called 'the masses' and the meaning of that term is pejorative to the extent that the process itself is disconcerting or threatening to the urban élites. In the course of the century, as these 'masses, developing into the labour class, the notion of class becomes increasingly conflated with that of the urban proletariat. Simultaneously, the idea of 'democracy' means 'power to the masses'; and it is against this background of industrialisation, urbanisation and a growing urban proletariat in the early stages of political organisation, that a shift in meaning in the terms art and culture should be viewed.

Art and culture become markers by which a bourgeois élite seeks to distinguish itself from the urban masses. Culture ceases to be a neutral term for the breeding and cultivation of produce, and becomes the exclusive marker for the élite's moral, intellectual and artistic refinement. Similarly, the term art shifts in meaning from 'accomplished craftsmanship' to the realm of inspired imagination; it is at this time, too, that the Arts gain their autonomous status and, no longer a mere commissioned commodity between patron and artist, stand somewhat aloof from the normal traffic of supply and demand. The nature of Art changes to an expressive one: spontaneous overflow of powerful feeling, the individual expression of individual emotion (cf. Hampson 1968: 199-203). Such exclusive and personal experiences and creations are gathered and displayed in the public art gallery or museum — likewise an invention of this period.

The image of the 'masses', determined as it is by the process of industrialisation, could quite naturally come to be applied specifically to factory workers. Caught in a simplified, streamlined mass production process, they seem to lose their individuality; and the negative and 'immoral' attributes begin to cluster: the wilful, variable and gullible masses; the superficial, materialist, passive, uncultured and godless character of the individualist amidst the masses (Huizinga 1945; Ortega y Gasset 1930). This view of man is the diametrical opposite of the ideals of élite culture: intellectual, active, committed, responsible and independent (Baudrillard 1981: 62). That, again, is a bourgeois ideal born of opposition against a decadent nobility. The bourgeois idea of culture is that it is innate only in potential, and that it requires life-long application. Hence related terms such as refinement or the German *Bildung*, widely used in the nineteenth century, connote an active process rather than an achieved state. Ironically, the traits ascribed to the masses (passivity and self-indulgence) has previously been attributed to the aristocracy.

The nineteenth-century image of the city as a moral abyss has a counterpart, however, in the continuing Enlightenment notion of the city as a mainspring of culture and civilization, bastion of reason and science, focus for artistic activity (Charlton 1984: 194-5). Bulwarks of bourgeois Culture appear as bastions against the rising tide of the masses: buildings such as museums, university buildings and even public institutions are given a dignified and imposing aspect, with turrets, monumental staircases, and high iron gratings. Architecture is historically eclectic — subtly underscoring the position of the bourgeois élite.

The dualistic image of the city indicates that the élite or its constituent sub-groups holds different views on society (with itself for central point of reference). Spatial divisions reflect the élite's hierarchical distinction according to mentality or state of enlightenment. Whether the distinction is that between christians and heathens, between the Enlightened and the Benighted, between the moral and the immoral, or between 'folk' and 'masses':[7] in all these cases the imagery is constructed by the élite. The spatial separation (and the sociocultural hierarchical division) is not always guarded with the same strictness; it can vary from period to period

---

[7]   Strictly speaking, the opposition between 'folk' and 'masses' is not a binary one, but part of a triadic constellation with the élite for a third partner. Relations in this triangle may be viewed differently by various groups within the élite.

and may be correlated with what I have called the 'centrifugal' and 'centri-petal' tendencies, which may coexist within different subgroups of the élite.

Reason and Romanticism

The intellectual élite's discovery of 'folk' and folk culture in the late eighteenth century typifies a romantic, expansive-centrifugal tendency in the élite's conceptualization of time. The élite, in its wish to identify with 'folk' values, marginalizes the city proletariat as uncultured masses; but by the same token it initializes a civilizing mission amongst that selfsame proletariat. This mission proceeds by presenting to the urban masses an image of the moral 'folk' as an ideal to emulate. There is, of course, a certain self-interest involved: disciplining the workforce and obtaining its political loyalty (Nijenhuis 1981: 13, 28).

That civilizing mission is alien to other parts of the élite in the Enlightenment tradition: here, people withdraw into their bulwarks of science and civilization: an exclusive-centripetal tendency which highlights the distance both from the 'folk' (considered vulgar and backward) and from the uncultured masses. Within this group there is a high degree of resistance against the egalitarian ideals of many civilizing initiatives.

Social theory as it develops in the nineteenth century reflects both attitudes. Gouldner (1973) likewise argues that this period witnesses the origin of two deep structures in the social sciences — termed by him the classicist and the romantic, respectively, in what I consider a parallel to my own distinction between an exclusive 'centripetal' and a more romantic and expansive 'centrifugal' tendency.[8] It may be useful to illustrate this distinction with reference to nineteenth-century theoreticians such as Tönnies, Durkheim, Frazer, Morgan and Marx.

---

[8]   To be sure, this distinction in my view is not so much a product of the nineteenth century (as Gouldner sees it), but rather a continuation of older patterns.

Decadence and progress

The German sociologist Ferdinand Tönnies distinguished, in 1887, between two social models: 'community' (*Gemeinschaft*) and 'society' (*Gesellschaft*). The former denotes social life in a close-knit, closed group, the latter stands for life in a differentiated framework. This typology is similar to the one made by Emile Durkheim in 1893, between mechanical and organic solidarity. Mechanical solidarity (however odd this might sound at first) is typical for social life in a close-knit community, a *Gemeinschaft*. This mechanical solidarity is replaced in a modern society (*Gesellschaft* in Tönnies' terminology) by an organic solidarity, adopted on the basis of mutual expedience.[9] Durkheim explains this shift from a far-reaching division of labour in nineteenth-century society, which, while increasing individual liberty, has eroded a common morality. Thus, the distinctions drawn up by Durkheim and by Tönnies describe not only societal differences, but also a historical process — in which the interiorized solidarity of the community is ousted by the individualist values (business-like, expedient) of modern society (cf. Lemaire 1976: 244-6). The net result, in moral terms, is a regrettable decline, an ethical price paid for industrial development and societal progress.

There is a deep structure in the notions of Tönnies and Durkheim which may (to recall Gouldner) be called romantic. Gouldner calls their theories reactionary to the extent that they chart cultural decay and glorify the past — although he exempts their resistance against growing rationalization (1973: 8). The nostalgia for the *Gemeinschaft*, the folksy and 'moral' roots of a coherent and harmonious living community, bespeaks a centrifugal, romantic notion of time: the folksy community is cherished as a primordial, a-historical phenomenon. It is still untouched by the march of history, with its decline, decay, and perhaps an apocalyptic sense of crisis and impending collapse associated with the rising masses.

That vision of history is opposed by a rational belief in cultural progress. Theories like those of Lewis Henry Morgan and Sir James Frazer

---

[9]   Durkheim's terminology invokes two opposing views of nature. The older mechanistic view sees nature as a perfect closed system, a divine clockwork; the more modern, atomistic view sees nature as subject to an inner evolutionary force (cf. Charlton 1984: 66-86). This divine connotation of the term 'mechanical' has by now disappeared.

provide us with examples of what Gouldner calls a 'classicist' deep structure. Morgan, for one, distinguishes seven stages of social development, from primitive barbarianism to the heights of civilization. He charts an increasing refinement leading from benighted darkness to civilized enlightenment. Frazer, too (in his famous *The Golden Bough*), sees cultural history as a grand development of the human mind, from superstition and religion to scientific thought. This history is written by the elect of rationality: they are the only ones who, in their exclusivist view, are 'up to date'. European folk culture is a survival, an atavism, a remnant of past periods. Rural 'folk' are, quite literally, 'backward'.

Johannes Fabian (1983) has recognized what he calls a 'denial of coevalness' in the ethnocentrist sense of Western superiority evinced by theories à la Morgan and Frazer. This denial of coevalness is widespread, I think, in nineteenth-century attitudes. Rural 'folk' are generally linked to the past; the urban masses connected with an apocalyptic future. [10] The folk community is vested with timeless characteristics, is placed outside history, and is de-synchronized from the 'modern' existence of the contemporary élite. Whether folk communities are denigrated for being backward, or else glorified for being unspoilt, in both cases they are depicted as isolated, sequestered in distant parts of the countryside. This correlation of spatial and historical marginality (reinforced as it is by growing state centralization in the course of the nineteenth century) can lead to something like internal colonialism (cf. Weber 1976). Fabian

---

[10]   This also holds for the theories of Karl Marx, even though these, on the whole, are a special case: Marx seems to embody both deep structures, romantic and classicist. There is, on the one hand, Marx's romantic resistance against the capitalist refashioning of life and of labour; there is, likewise, the nostalgic idea that there once was a past when people lived in harmony and solidarity with each other and with nature (cf. Gouldner 1973: 12). On the other hand, however, Marx does proclaim a belief in progress — he insists that bourgeois capitalist society is the highest social development so far, and holds out a messianic vision of the proletariat's victory over capitalism and the advent of communism. Gouldner fails to account for this curious combination of a romantic and a classicist deep structure. One might look for explanations in Marx's biography; suffice it to say here that Marxist theory is a conglomerate of many nineteenth-century historical and sociological tenets. Rural folk, in Marx's view, are backward, will contribute nothing to the coming proletarian revolution: his hopes are fixed on the urban labouring masses once they have developed class consciousness.

concludes, therefore, that the denial of coevalness is a political act, from which a mandate for political initiative is derived.

The polarity between classicism and romanticism, between centripetal and centrifugal attitudes, can be followed throughout the nineteenth century; it influenced the atmosphere within which early sociologists and anthropologists worked; and its repercussions can still be registered in the social sciences, e.g. in the debate between objectivism and relativism.

Economic spheres and economic symbolism

Economics, as an independent science, can be dated back to the eighteenth century; and the connotations of 'folk' and 'masses' have, from that period onwards, also obtained an economical dimension. As economics developed into the science of the optimum control of commercial traffic, it too became subject to the nineteenth-century friction between reason and romanticism. Thus, Marx's theory starts from an analysis of commodities, and distinguishes between their use-value and their exchange-value; the classless primordial community relied on a direct consumption-related production of commodities whose value was wholly use-oriented. Capitalist modes of production has privileged exchange-value over use-value, and it is this shift which determines the relations between élite and masses, between capital and labour. In this marxist sense, the masses become synonymous with exchange values (e.g., wage in exchange for labour), as folk notions are linked to non-commercial relations and a non-estranged, use-oriented mode of production. [11]

Nineteenth-century theory tends to identify 'folk' and 'masses' with different economic spheres; these spheres, gradually loosed from their theoretical context, obtain a symbolic currency: the economic symbolism around 'folk' is that of non-profit bartering and of useful subsistence production aimed towards the community's own needs; the economic

---

[11]   Again (to recall Gouldner's polarity, and the previous footnote) we see a combination of rationalist and romantic elements in Marx: Lemaire (1985) considers Marxist economics, and their emphasis on commercial exchange, an instance of that rationalism which inspired economic theories in general; while Marx's criticism of reification, of the estrangement of labour, and of exploitative commercial exchange, may count as 'romantic'.

symbolism around 'the masses' is that of mercantile, profit-oriented exchange, reified exchange values and the economic structures of a stratified *Gesellschaft*. Again, these distinctions have survived into the present, and in postwar consumer patterns each economic symbolism has been given its own design pattern.

Design patterns and the reform movement

The British anthropologist Mary Douglas (1978) has made explicit correlations between cognitive classification and spatial delimitation. She argues that spatial divisions mirror cultural distinctions, and uses the example of a house, which in each culture has its own compartmentalizations. These in turn (and their status in daily life) can be read as an expression of underlying cultural attitudes (thus, Douglas interprets the cleaning and polishing of demarcations as a symbolical emphasis on their demarcatory function).

Patterns in the compartmentalization of living-space may, then, be read as a design language expressive of cultural attitudes; and it may be fruitful to compare classicist and romantic design patterns to the deep structure polarity which has been the subject of the preceding pages.

That style which in the closing decades of the eighteenth century comes to be known as 'classicist' tends towards high-gloss materials and a shiny finish. Its outlines are, on the whole, straight and angular, and ornaments are on a flat plane, often in gold leaf, brass or veneer. The polished finish of materials and cloths such as silk or satin emphasizes smooth and hard qualities. The design pattern as a whole (which may, or may not, explicitly invoke classical examples) works towards self-contained, well-defined units, obviously satisfying, on the symbolical plane, a need for the rigid demarcation of spatial and social orders. The classicist style also connotes, in its economic symbolism, the exchange relations between elite and masses.

The romantic style is less severe and angular, and prefers round and curly or wavy outlines. Soft and 'warm', non-shiny materials like plush or velvet are used, and wood is given, not a high gloss but rather a natural finish. Ornament is heavy and often harks back to organic, living forms, especially flower-shapes; it is sculpted to an extent that contrasts sharply with the flat planes of classicist ornamentation. Thus, outlines are obscured both in the choice of 'fuzzy' materials and in the use of highly raised or sculpted ornament. The overall design pattern bespeaks a centrifugal notion of time; the economic symbolism reflects the élite's penchant for barter and use-oriented production.

Obviously both design patterns may be correlated with the deep structures previously discussed. The romantic style, especially, is close to the élite's image of folk art. Later in the century, 'craftsmanship' comes to be prized highly, and what is 'unpolished' has the values of honesty, usefulness and reliability. The reform movement (most famously exemplified in William Morris's 'Arts and Crafts') will continue this folksy element in the romantic design pattern.

The late nineteenth-century reform movement, based in the bourgeois élite, touched almost all spheres of social and private life. It advocated an improvement of taste and a revaluation of craftsmanship, opposed rigid and disciplinarian forms of education, advanced healthier ways of clothing and nutrition; but it also combatted iniquitous and unsanitary working conditions, fought for women's suffrage and emancipation. In its drive for 'mass education' or 'popular education' (the terminology is significant) one overriding concern becomes obvious: the immoral urban masses are to be given the moral quality of 'folk'. The reform movement's political and artistic achievements are considerable; but its romantic, idealist notions on purity, natural values and natural health were slower in spreading; until well into the present century, they were restricted to a small intellectual élite.

After the Second World War, increasing numbers of (especially) young intellectuals showed signs of impatience with the prevalent consumer mentality, the impersonal nature of society and its dependence on technology. Their return to natural or 'folk' values was marked by a renewed emphasis on personal human relations and on the link between man and nature. The design pattern that went along with this was, again, the romantic one, with a marked preference for soft, woolly materials, and for an unpolished finish. This post-war romantic revival, like the one in the last century, is of urban origin.

Trends

The nineteen-sixties were times of upheaval in most Western industrialized societies. Students (and to some extent, society as a whole) became more radical and progressive. The case of Amsterdam is perhaps exemplary: playful anarchists (the *Provo* movement) and Flower Power adepts propagate a romantic communism and militate against the city élite, against 'immoral' entrepreneurialism and commercialization in the inner city, against undemocratic decision-making (Van der Lans 1983). The reorganization of inner-city space is considered a matter of common concern, and the old community values (the authentic past; natural civic solidarity) are invoked in a playful and deliberately non-rational campaign for human liberties. The stance against exploitation and repression has an internationalist dimension, and a variety of shops offering third-world produce and other forms of idealistic development aid crop up.

This romantic, idealist attitude has had a marked impact on the city. More neighbourhood pubs and 'granny shops' (as second-hand curio shops are called), part of the pavement or sidewalks upturned to have shrubs or trees planted. The 'reform groceries', originally upmarket health stores, have become part of a broad vegetarian or wholefood movement, and the old reform ideals of harmony with fellow-men, nature, and the universe, have become 'New Age' issues. The familial values that adhere to so-called 'granny bikes', 'grandpa chairs', 'granny dresses' and 'grandpa glasses' do not only connote a pervasive nostalgia, but also an anti-consumerist notion of old-fashioned thrift and non-profit bartering. [12]

Many hippies and ex-*Provos* move to the countryside as from the late sixties — individually, communally, or with their family; they take their urban romanticism with them. They are young, richer in ideals than in wealth, and love to settle amidst authentic villagers in decrepit farm buildings. Thrift, rural isolation and self-sufficiency are glorified; they bake their own bread, spin their own wool, knit their own jumpers, generate

---

[12]   This is mere economic *symbolism*, of course, and empty symbolism at that; this much can be gathered from the old-fashioned, cosily nostalgic decorating in many restaurants and bars, which, while connoting similar anti-consumerist values, is in fact inspired by hard-headed commercial reasoning. This distorted use of design language has been criticized by Baudrillard (1981) as a consumerist code.

their own energy and heal themselves by natural means or with 'alternative' medicine. They get involved in environmentalist issues and animal rights; however this leads them into conflict — not only with the political and commercial powers who plan motorways and are responsible for technological projects, but also with the agricultural industry whose living space they share, and whom they accuse of a reckless disregard for the environment and the welfare of their livestock.

The result may be described as a fragmentation of rural space into different symbolic spheres, each with their own design patterns. Nature preserves lie adjacent to strictly planned-out commercial agricultural lands, which border plots of wholefood farmers lying next to square concrete-built industrial areas. It would be wrong to see this as a gradual urbanization or citification of rural areas: the pattern of fragmentation runs through both the country and the city.

Squatters, punk rockers, yuppies

The urban confrontation in the wake of the rusticated ex-hippies is marked by a new, more aggressively assertive generation. In Amsterdam, the squatter movement consists of students and unemployed young people; they conduct a bitter resistance against the projected metro, which they consider an elitist prestige project. Their rallying-cry is one of the old *Provo* ideals: the people's right to live in the inner cities; they campaign against the commercial demolition of old dwellings and the commercialization of the city centre, which they blame on the joint interests of the financial powers and the political élite. Their style, however, is less playful than that of the old *Provos*; their wearing of the *keffiyeh* seems to indicate a sense of solidarity with the combative stance of the PLO. Their ideals are less diffuse than those of the sixties, rarely invoke the notion of 'solidarity', and on the whole express themselves in concrete battle-cries of the 'Down with...' or 'Smash the...' brand.

The contrast with the *provo* and Flower Power movements is also apparent in the stylistic influence, from the late seventies onwards, of puck rock. Strident colours rather than the old earth tones; sharp forms rather than the old woolly outlines; Mohawk haircuts rather than avuncular beards; and a return to the streamlined, technologically-inspired shapes of nineteen-fifties design. This return to an emphatically urban design seems to be matched, demographically, by a returning urbanisation wave and a renewed settlement of the inner city.

The right to live in the inner cities is now generally acknowledged; but the ones to profit most from it have been young careerists, the so-called yuppies. Their preferred environment is not the house in the country, but the luxury apartment, which results in a trend towards gentrification of the inner cities. The yuppie lifestyle places extreme value on trendiness, on being 'with the times'; they exemplify the so-called 'me generation' in a set of values which I would describe as centripetal; and their design pattern accordingly favours a classicist register. [13] Generally, economic conditions have tended to favour a sense of competitiveness and a businesslike approach to human relations; the emergence of yuppiedom has gone hand in hand with a growth in the number of underprivileged and jobless; and the progressive ethos of the sixties and seventies has yielded to a widespread move towards conservatism.

The redistribution of urban space, like that of the countryside, has led to conflicts, and like the countryside, the economic symbolism of urban space has fragmented. We can recognize which is which from the various design patterns: a friendly, romantic and 'cosy' pattern in suburbs where gardens and parks encourage verdure and dwellings are often clustered around little courtyards. Interestingly, many large-scale suburban high-rise apartment buildings from the nineteen-fifties and sixties are now demolished and replaced by, or otherwise refurbished into, a more welcoming architecture; while a distinctly classicist pattern dominates the urban business centres, with much reflecting glass, shiny steel and white concrete. This fragmentation of differently oriented spaces into different design patterns has become a planner's automatism.

Conclusion

I have tried to outline a preliminary charting of a complex pattern of interaction between various polarities: centripetal and centrifugal; folk and masses; classicist and romantic design patterns. Those interactions have not

---

[13]   To be sure, some elements from the earlier romantic wave seem to persist: non-rational intuition is highly prized, and holistic ideas abound, witness many 'New Age' phenomena (cf. Gastelaars & Verbij 1987).

come to an end; and the polarity between centrifugal and centripetal can be traced back many centuries. In my view, it is a red thread throughout the history of christian civilization in the West. My main aim in the preceding pages was to correlate this polarity with two distinct notions of time which arose among the social élite in the eighteenth century: the secular Enlightenment view and the religious, romantic view. These notions of time shaped the élite's attitude towards two new social categories from that period: rural folk and urban masses. The élite's image of the 'folk' and the 'masses' has had a profound influence throughout Europe, and has ultimately led, I believe, to a pattern where those two have become alternating core symbols in European post-war culture. I call them 'symbols' because they do not contain any specific or real reference and have been divorced from the original spatial polarity and historical situation in which they originated. Already the terms themselves, 'folk' and 'masses', require inverted comma's, and they may drop out of usage altogether; but despite this ongoing erosion, the polarity between city and country may persist in the ongoing 'classicist'/'romantic' alternation of its concomitant design languages.

Sources

J. BAUDRILLARD, 1980. *For a Critique of the Political Economy of the Sign* (St. Louis: Telos Press).

D.G. CHARLTON, 1984. *New Images of the Natural in France: A Study in European Cultural History, 1750-1800* (Cambridge University Press).

M. DOUGLAS, 1978. *Purity and Danger: An Analysis of the Concepts of Pollution and Taboo* (London: Routledge & Kegan Paul).

J. FABIAN, 1983. *Time and the Other: How Anthropology Makes its Object* (Columbia University Press).

M. GASTELAARS & A. VERBIJ, 1987. 'Helden van onze tijd: De consistentie van de yuppie', in *Van totem tot lifestyle: Europese cultuur in ontwikkeling*, ed. K. Fohrbeck & H. Kuijpers (Amsterdam: Koninklijk Instituut voor de Tropen), pp. 116-24.

A.W. GOULDNER, 1973. 'Romantiek en classicisme: Dieptestructuren in de sociale wetenschappen', *De Gids*, 136: 3-26.

N. HAMPSON, 1968. *The Enlightenment* (Harmondsworth: Penguin).

A. HAUSER, 1975. *Sociale geschiedenis van de kunst* (Nijmegen: SUN).

J. HUIZINGA, 1945. *Geschonden wereld: Een beschouwing over de kansen op herstel van onze beschaving* (Haarlem: Tjeenk Willink).

J. V.D. LANS, 1983. 'De kultuur van het provoïsme', *Te elfder ure*, 27, 35: 730-64.

T. LEMAIRE, 1970. *Filosofie van het landschap* (Baarn: Ambo).

T. LEMAIRE, 1976. *Over de waarde van kulturen: Een inleiding in de kultuurfilosofie* (Baarn: Ambo).

T. LEMAIRE, 1985. 'De "homo economicus" tussen ruil en uitwisseling: Enkele beschouwingen rond de economische antropologie', *Antropologische verkenningen*, 4, 2: 77-106.

H. NIJENHUIS, 1981. *Volksopvoeding tussen elite en massa: Een geschiedenis van de volwasseneneducatie in Nederland* (Meppel: Boom).

J. ORTEGA Y GASSET, 1930. *La rebelión de las masas* (Madrid: Revista de Occidente).

E. WEBER, 1976. *Peasants into Frenchmen: The Modernization of Rural France, 1870-1914* (Stanford University Press).

R. WILLIAMS, 1958. *Culture and Society, 1780-1950* (London: Chatto & Windus).

FREUD'S PHYLOGENETIC NARRATIVE

Raymond Corbey

> In diesen wie in vielen anderen Hinsichten lebt der Mensch der Vorzeit ungeändert in unserem Unbewussten fort.
>
> Sigmund Freud, 1915

In much of the secondary literature on otherness/alterity a psychoanalytic frame of reference is present, more or less explicitly. The fierce nature — uncontrolled, aggressive, lascivious — attributed to others such as the medieval wild man or nineteenth-century 'savages' is usually explained in terms of 'projection' or similar impulses which are held to govern the behaviour of those who cherish such images of others. Interestingly, the psychoanalytic paradigm which is used to explain structures of alterity seems itself to be implicated in those selfsame structures. My aim in this paper is to lay bare the role of alterity in the architecture of psychoanalytic theory, and to reflect upon the strange circularity of a theoretical perspective which itself, to a certain extent, seems to be tainted by the phenomenon it purports to explain.

    We shall have to deal with some analogous, interconnected or convergent themes and ideas in late nineteenth- and early twentieth-century anthropology, archeology, folklore studies and philosophy. But first let us take a look at the persistent concern with the archaic/primitive in Freud's thought.

Freud on the archaic

Throughout his life Freud maintained a keen interest in archeology and cultural history. Not only was he widely read in these fields, and a fanatic collector of antiquities; his bent towards prehistory was, as Paul Ricoeur once remarked, one of the most tenacious tendencies of his thought. The human soul, according to Freud, carries many traces of what befell to our prehistoric ancestors. The terms *archaisch, prähistorisch, primitiv* and *urzeitlich* abound in *The Interpretation of Dreams* (1900), as well as in his *Three Essays on the Theory of Sexuality* (1905).

Freud's most important work on cultural history is probably *Totem and Tabu - Some Points of Agreement between the Mental Lives of Savages and Neurotics* (1913). Many of the building blocks of this work were present as early as 1900.[1] Here, Freud launches his famous thesis of the primal patricide. In the prehistoric horde, the sons murdered and ate the father who dominated them and monopolized the women of the group, thus gaining access to these women, their sisters and mothers. But out of remorse over this terrible deed — for they had not only hated but also loved him — they refrained from intercourse with the women of their group/totem, and from killing their totem, the substitute or surrogate of their dead father.[2] What became taboo here corresponded to the two crimes of Oedipus, and to the two primal wishes of the male child: killing the father and marrying the mother. Thus originated social order, law and religion.

Apart from being influenced by Haeckel's biogenetic law and by the theory of survivals, Freud was a convinced Lamarckian, who believed that the memories of this tragedy were inheritable as acquired characteristics, and thus became part and parcel of everyman's psychological make-up. Contemporary 'primitives' or 'savages', for him, represented an early phase in the development of humanity: he regarded them as contemporary ancestors. As such they were comparable to the early phase of

---

[1]   This contention is based on a careful investigation of Freud's early writings by I. Wallace in his *Freud and Anthropology. A History and Reappraisal*, New York 1983, p. 51.

[2]   *Totem und Tabu*, in the *Standard Edition of the Complete Psychological Writings of Sigmund Freud*, London 1953 ff., 13: 141-3. To be referred to hereinafter as *SE*.

individual development: the child, with its characteristic sexual inclinations and world view. In addition, primitives, prehistoric or contemporary, were comparable to another case of arrested development: the neurotic. Neurosis is an atavism, a case of regression, not only ontogenetically, but also phylogenetically. All three, the primitive, the child and the neurotic, Freud holds, are characterized by a deficient sense of reality and by belief in the omnipotence of thought.

In 1983 an unknown manuscript by Sigmund Freud was found among the papers of his friend Sándor Ferenczi. It concerns a sketch for an *Overview of the Transference Neuroses*, as it is entitled, written down by Freud in 1915, two years after the publication of *Totem and Tabu*. [3] The second part of this manuscript, never published and never intended to be published, is highly interesting in the present context. In this second part, which in a letter to Ferenczi Freud called his 'phylogenetic fantasy', [4] specific causal connections are postulated between several types of contemporary neuroses and the experiences of mankind during the harsh, anxiety-provoking ice ages which put an end to its previous paradisiacal existence. Problems in the psychosexual development of the individual reflect what happened in correlating phases in the development of prehistoric humanity. Many of the characteristic emotional reactions, sexual peculiarities and coping strategies of neurotics were once effective adaptations to the severe, traumatizing living conditions, natural and social, of primal times: the cold, scarcity of food, persecution and castration by fathers, the killing of fathers. In ontogeny, phylogeny still manifests itself.

In Freud's later publications this lamarckist point of view keeps appearing again and again. In his *Introductory Lectures to Psycho-Analysis* (1916/17), for instance, he remarks that it is very well possible that everything that is told as a fantasy during analysis today — child seduction, the awakening of sexual excitement through watching the parents having intercourse, the threat of castration — was once, in the earliest days of mankind, real. In *Group Psychology and the Analysis of the Ego* (1921), mass movements are interpreted as a revival of the power struggle in the primal horde, with the figure of the father/leader, with

---

[3]   S. Freud, *Übersicht der Übertragungsneurosen. Ein bisher unbekanntes Manuskript* (ed. I. Grubrich-Simitis), Frankfurt 1986; also available as *A Phylogenetic Phantasy. Overview of the Transference Neuroses*, (ed. I. Grubrich-Simitis, transl. A. & P.T. Hoffer), Harvard University Press 1987.

[4]   *Ibid.* (1986), p. 90. The letter is dated July 18, 1915.

whom all the group members identify, as the key to social cohesion. 'Just as primitive man survives potentially in every individual,' Freud holds, 'so the primal horde may arise once more out of any random collection; in so far as men are habitually under the sway of group formation we recognize in it the survival of the primal horde' (*SE* 18: 123).

Again, in *The Future of an Illusion* (1927), he tries to understand the institution of religion in terms of neurotic remorse over the murder of the primal father. In *Civilization and its Discontents* (1930), a work that stresses the importance of the aggressive instinct and interprets culture as a struggle to control this instinct, he explains the excessively strong aggressive reactions of children to the first major instinctual frustrations and their correspondingly strong super-ego by pointing out that they are 'following a phylogenetic model and [are] going beyond the response that would be currently justified' (*SE* 21: 131). But especially his last work (his 'psychoanalytic novel', as he once called it), *Moses and Monotheism: Three Essays* (1939), represents a last and firm recapture of the phylogenetic plot of *Totem and Tabu.* 'The behaviour of neurotic children towards their parents in the Oedipus and castration complex', Freud writes here, 'abounds in such reactions, which seem unjustified in the individual case and only become intelligible phylogenetically — by their connection with the experience of earlier generations' (*SE* 23: 99). And: 'The essential point, however, is that we attribute the same emotional attributes to these primitive men that we establish by analytic investigation in the primitives of the present day — in our children' (*SE* 23: 81-2). Among the instinctual wishes 'born afresh with every child' he stated earlier, 'are those of incest, cannibalism and lust for killing'.[5]

The predicament of primitive man

Now that we have seen in outline how Freud's views of the wild nature and dramatic experiences of prehistoric man function in his interpretations of human behaviour, let us have a look at some backgrounds to these views.

In the nineteenth-century imagination, primal man had very peculiar

---

[5]   'The future of an illusion', *SE* 21: 10.

characteristics. In his *Primitive Marriage* (1865) for instance, McLennan, one of the evolutionary anthropologists whose ideas Freud knew and was influenced by, held promiscuity, even to the point of incest, to be normal during the first stage of the evolution of mankind.[6] As men were aggressive and violent, and women usually depraved, primitive marriage was (and still is among contemporary primitives) no more than a kind of rape. What is punished in civilized countries as crime was and still is customary among savages. McLennan's ideas on tribal or prehistoric others were by no means exceptional. They can be found in the work of other evolutionists like Edward Tylor, John Lubbock or Herbert Spencer, and indeed constituted a received view of the period.

The predicament of primitive man was one of impulsiveness and lack of self-control, of passing directly from impulse to gratification. Intellectually, the primitive mind was inconsistent, childish, confused, deficient in foresight, inclined to embroider facts with phantasies. Civilization was only possible on the basis of steering and regulating, or even repressing man's rude primary impulses. Evolutionary progress implied the domestication of man's bestial nature, the taming of the beast within, the triumph of reason in the transcendence of brute creation. Mary Midgley has shown convincingly how negatively the animal, man's primary other, has been stereotyped in most of western thought; animal categories used in nineteenth century discourse were no exception.[7] Animals have always been 'good to think with', as Lévi-Strauss put it, and in principle can have many meanings; in the case outlined here, they were a paragon of wickedness. As Darwin jotted down in an early evolutionary notebook, commenting upon the instinctive origin of mankind's evil passions: 'The devil under form of Baboon is our grandfather!'[8]

The monstrous primal man who is so prominently present in Freud's theorizing about human behaviour has a long pedigree. He shares many features with the monstrous Plinian races from antiquity such as the headless *Blemmyae* or the dog-headed *Cynocephali*, living on the margins of the known world, with characteristics that are the inverse of those of

---

[6]   J.F. McLennan, Chicago 1970.

[7]   M. Midgley, *Beast and Man. The Roots of Human Nature*, London 1980.

[8]   Quoted by G. Stocking, *Victorian Anthropology* (New York/London 1987), p. 222; the remark dates from 1838.

normal people; or with the medieval wild man and wild woman, ferocious beings situated deep in the forests and thought to give free rein to their aggressive and sexual instincts; or with the missing link of eighteenth century natural history, *homo silvestris* or *caudatus*, half man, half ape. All these imaginary others were contrasted with normal men: they inhabited the sphere of wildness outside the civilized world, often had animal characteristics, and generally their behaviour was uncontrolled. The same goes for primitive man, prehistoric or contemporary, in the nineteenth-century imagination, still living in that state of savagery from which the ascent to modern - white, middle-class, male - civilization had started.

Primitive man, moreover, was equated metaphorically with other social categories: not only, as we have already seen, to neurotics, and madmen in general, but also to peasants, labourers, criminals, prostitutes and women generally. People of these categories were held to be governed more by impulse, to be less capable of rational thinking, to be more like animals and closer to nature or to the natural beginnings of mankind, phylogenetically and ontogenetically. Many authors associated prostitution with essential femininity and saw it as an atavism, a form of behaviour once normal among all women. Typical physical characteristics of prostitutes such as the form of the ears, face and genitals were perceived as archaic, and as parallel to that of black African women. [9] The discourse defining these mutually connected categories as 'others' and excluding them from proper humanity was, of course, a strategy of subjection and power. Peasants, women, the 'inferior races', workers all stood in a subordinate, often exploitative hierarchical relationship to white middle- and upper-class males who dominated politics, the economy and discourse.

Thus the nature of man's primitive other was in accordance with a nineteenth-century discourse on savagery and civilization, on wildness and control, a discourse that played a substantial role in the constitution of psychoanalytic theory. In Freud's theorizing, a stereotypical wild other, now internalized, in fact still roams the inner landscape of the human psyche, the wildness within, as he once roamed the wilderness without. His aggressive and promiscuous nature may have contributed considerably to

---

[9]   See S. L. Gilman, 'Black bodies, white bodies: Toward an iconography of female sexuality in late nineteenth-century art, medicine and literature', in *'Race', Writing and Difference*, ed. H.L. Gates (Chicago/ London 1986), pp. 223-61.

Freud's hobbesian view of man:

> After all, we assume that in the course of man's development from a primitive state to a civilized one his aggressiveness undergoes a very considerable degree of internalization or turning inwards; if so, his internal conflicts would certainly be the proper equivalent for the external struggles which have then ceased. [10]

Archeology and folklore

There are two more specific cultural interests Freud took inspiration from in his theorizing on human behaviour: archeology and folklore.

Freud's study and his adjacent consulting room were crammed with antiquities - Egyptian, Greek, Etruscan, Roman, Asian, African. He was an avid collector, who used to set down new acquisitions before him on the dining room table during family meals, so that he could touch, study and enjoy them. The statues of mythical figures which surrounded Freud and his patients on the couch not merely served decorative purposes, but provided him with clues, in the form of stories, dramatic plots, to the nature of his patient's problems. [11] 'Here in Freud's corner,' writes Rita Ransohoff, 'the mythological figures from Pompeii and the head of the Roman citizen illuminate contrasting aspects of man: his impulsive animal nature and the civilizing influence of conscience and law. Here is a suggestion of the images of the id and the superego, two aspects of Freud's hypothesis of the structure of the mind.' [12]

Freud was convinced that everything once formed in the mind would survive or leave traces in one way or another in deep 'layers' of the psyche. He was a great admirer of Heinrich Schliemann, who heroically delved into the debris of ancient Troy, and often compared the analyst's work to the archeologist's laborious interpretation of excavated prehistoric

---

[10] 'Analysis terminable and interminable', *SE* 23: 244.

[11] See Marianna Torgovnick, 'Entering Freud's study', in Id., *Gone Primitive. Savage Intellects, Modern Lives* (Chicago/London 1990), pp. 194-209.

[12] 'Captions to the photographs', in E. Engelman, *Berggasse 19. Sigmund Freud's Home and Offices, Vienna 1938* (Chicago/London 1981), p. 59.

layers. [13] Archeological metaphors are pervasive in psychoanalysis, the archeology of the soul, structuring its discourse, its conceptual space. They suggestively communicate, as Donald Kuspit argues, authoritative core distinctions like the ones between surface and depth, manifest and latent, adult and infantile, civilized and uncivilized, historic and prehistoric, fact and fantasy, more and less fundamental. [14]

Another area of interest Freud took cues from was folklore. During many years he was an enthusiastic reader of the journal *Anthropophyteia*, devoted to folklore, especially of a sexual and scatological nature, and in 1913 he wrote a preface to the German translation of Bourke's *Scatological Rites of All Nations*. [15] I think a careful investigation of his interpretations of anthropological material of this kind would show that from the outset they were laden with the selfsame theoretical viewpoints on human behaviour they were meant to support. Folklore, Freud states in his preface to Bourke's work, 'shows us how incompletely the repression of coprophilic inclinations has been carried out among various peoples at various times and how closely at other cultural levels the treatment of excretory substances approximates to that practised by children.' [16] Here he attempts to explain cultural variability in terms of an opposition between civilized adults controlling an urge of the postulated type and childish primitives giving rein to it.

But theories of such phenomena as liminality, taboo, purity, transgression and inversion — as developed in British symbolic anthropology of the last three decades by such authors as Mary Douglas and Victor Turner — throw a completely different light on the reasons why in different cultural contexts variable categories of things, situations, behaviours may be forbidden or impure — primarily on the *cultural* plane, not on that of man's psychological make-up. German culture especially, as Alan Dundes has shown, is very rich in anal expressions, jokes, insults and

---

[13]   See for instance *SE* 23: 259-260.

[14]   D. Kuspit, 'A mighty metaphor: The analogy of archaeology and psychoanalysis', in *Sigmund Freud and Art. His Personal Collection of Antiquities*, ed. L. Gamwell & R. Wells (New York/London 1989), pp. 133-51; esp. p. 135.

[15]   Wallace, *op. cit.*, p. 47.

[16]   *SE* 12: 337; quoted by Wallace, *op.cit.*, p. 48.

curses.[17] Freud, however, mistook the many utterances of this type he came across in his practice for evidence of an underlying anal inclination, and even postulated the existence of a typical anal-erotic character.[18] In fact, anal expressions are a typical example of a powerful symbolic repertoire adopted from borders, margins and edges. What is culturally 'low' and excluded from official discourse is an effective means of parody, subversion and inversion.[19] Time and again Freud was confronted with phenomena from the rich sphere of folklore and popular culture, as analysed so eloquently by Bakhtin in *Rabelais and his world*. The suppression of that sphere was not a psychological mechanism, but a political one, an act of censorship, a strategy of power.

Freud's arguments in this field suffer from a fundamental *petitio principii*. On the one hand, folklore, mythology, ethnology etc. are supposed to deliver evidence supporting the psychoanalytic view of human behaviour, while on the other hand Freud holds that mythology and the universe of fairytales are incomprehensible without taking into account the sexuality of the child as understood by psychoanalytic theory. His evidence, in other words, from the very beginning seems to be constructed in terms of the theory it is to support.[20]

Philosophy of life

It is neither possible nor necessary in the present context to consider or even to mention all influences on Freud's interpretations of human behaviour; but we should take a brief look at one important current at least in nineteenth-century thought, one which steered Freud's views of human

---

[17]   Alan Dundes, *Life is like a Chicken Coop Ladder. A Portrait of German Culture through Folklore*, New York 1984. Dundes' monograph remains tied, however, to a psychoanalytic perspective, and does not apply theories developed by symbolic anthropologists to scatological expressions.

[18]   Thus his 'Character and anal eroticism' (1908), *SE* 9: 169-75.

[19]   P. Stallybrass & A. White, *The Politics and Poetics of Transgression*, London 1986; and cf. Kathleen M. Ashley, *Victor Turner and the Construction of Cultural Criticism: Between Literature and Anthropology*, Bloomington 1990.

[20]   See C. Lévi-Strauss, *La potière jalouse*, Paris 1985, pp. 252 and 256; and cf. his criticism of the way Freud interprets myths, pp. 248-249.

motivation: the *Philosophie des Lebens*, and especially Nietzsche and Schopenhauer.

The precise extent to which Freud was influenced by Nietzsche is controversial, but both authors interpret human morality as the outcome of a tragic conflict between the pressures of civilization and the demands of instinct, between the social and the biological, a conflict that has its repercussion in man's archaic bad conscience. Nietzsche's remark that conscious reason may be no more than a 'more or less fantastic commentary on an unknown, perhaps unknowable but felt text' [21] — that of our deepest impulses — might as well stem from Freud. In *Die Geburt der Tragödie* Nietzsche, like Freud, postulated an era of wild otherness at the beginnings of mankind, preceding the civilized Apollinian period: the era of the sexually unrestrained, amoral Dionysians, still one with nature, symbolized by the chorus of half-bestial satyrs in Greek tragedy.

A passage called 'Traum und Kultur' from Nietzsche's *Menschliches, Allzumenschliches* (1878) highlights some of his ideas on this point, and their great similarity to views held by Freud:

> The brain function which is most strongly restricted by sleep is memory: not that it stops completely - but it is reduced to a state of imperfection, as, in the earliest days of mankind, it may have been with everybody even when awake in the daytime. Arbitrary and confused as it is, it continually exchanges one thing for another on the basis of the most superficial similarities [...] and even now travellers observe regularly how strong is the savage's tendency to forgetfulness, and how [...] from sheer debilitation, he produces lies and nonsense. But we all resemble this savage [...] The complete clarity of all dream images, which is contingent on an unconditional belief in their reality, reminds us again of the state that primeval man found himself in, in which hallucination was an extraordinarily frequent phenomenon that now and then simultaneously held whole communities, whole peoples in its sway. Thus in sleep and dream we go once more through the daily business of early mankind. [22]

---

[21]   F. Nietzsche, *Werke in drei Bänden*, ed. K. Schlechta (München 1969), 1: 1095.

[22]   Nietzsche, *op. cit.*, I: 453-4; and cf. Kim Holmes, 'Freud, Evolution and the Tragedy of Man', *Journal of the American Psychoanalytic Association*, 31 (1983): 187-210.

In an addendum from 1919 to his *The Interpretation of Dreams* (1900), Freud concurs with Nietzsche's view that in dreams man's innate archaic heritage manifests itself:

> We can guess how much to the point is Nietzsche's assertion that in dreams 'some primaeval relic of humanity is at work which we can now scarcely reach any longer by direct path'; and we may expect that the analysis of dreams will lead us to a knowledge of man's archaic heritage, of what is psychically innate in him. (*SE* 5: 548-9)

According to both authors, primitive man survives under the thin layer of civilized morality, although Freud, unlike Nietzsche with his idea of the *Übermensch*, never wanted man to overthrow civilized self-control, merely to moderate it. An analogous interpretation of the human condition is to be found in the philosophy of Arthur Schopenhauer, who sees the conscious intellect as but a weak servant of man's proper nature: mighty, blind, irrational, insatiable *Wille*. Schopenhauer substantially influenced Nietzsche, and was regularly quoted approvingly by Freud. In fact, Freud is one of many thinkers who were influenced by the romantic climate of opinion of the *Philosophie des Lebens* which, in reaction to the rationalism of Enlightenment authors, somehow always stressed the nonrational, the emotional, the unconscious: *das Andere der Vernunft, Leben, Wille*. This was one of the great themes of the period, worked out in different directions by philosophers contemporary to Freud, such as Ludwig Klages and Max Scheler. [23]

For our present purposes it is not so very important to precisely reconstruct the - very complicated - lines along which ideas were handed down and came to feed into one physician's brilliant attempts to make sense of his clinical observations. Thus, there is much discussion, even to the point of futility, on the origins of Freud's concept of the *Es*, and the role of a wide range of authors including Schopenhauer, Nietzsche, Eduard

---

[23]   Cf. O. Marquard, *Transzendentaler Idealismus - Romantische Natur-philosophie - Psychoanalyse*, Dinter 1987, a very detailed study on the philosophical backgrounds of psychoanalysis.

von Hartmann, Groddeck and Klages. [24] Similarly, it is very difficult to ascertain how Darwinian ideas came to Freud — directly or via Nietzsche and several other mediating authors. More important for us are certain aspects of the *general* structure of a nineteenth-century discourse on man and reality by which psychoanalysis was influenced. We already inquired into the role of the wild primitive Other in Freud's view of man. Here we see another way in which Freud's idea of 'wildness within' was strengthened: many nineteenth-century authors with whom he was well acquainted (and who articulated the *Zeitgeist* within which he worked) stressed the nonrational, wild, creative, mighty 'impulse' or 'life' in man.

Indeed, the two ideas were connected: that of the wild primitive within and that of the blind impulse within, both in Freud and in nineteenth-century thought. This is evident in the case of Nietzsche's notion of dionysian life, and also from the pervasive association of prehistoric or contemporary 'primitives' with impulsiveness and lack of restraint. A nine example of the theme of wildness within is a comment upon developments in Germany written in Paris in 1934 by an anonymous German *Exil*-intellectual:

> It is true that the wild, the bestial, the wild colours of the drives have evened out, worn off, and have been polished up and subdued in the course of the centuries, in which society has quelled age-old urges and impulses. It is true that increasing refinement has made him more serene and noble, but all the time the animal spirit sleeps at the bottom of his being. There is still a lot of animal in him [...] When the graph of life curves downward to the red line of the primitive, the mask drops; naked as in the old days he breaks loose, primeval man, the cave-dweller, in the total profligacy of his unleashed drives. [25]

---

[24]   See B. Nitzschke, 'Zur Herkunft des "Es"', *Psyche* 37 (1983): 769-804, and several reactions to his interpretation in *Psyche* 39 (1985): 97-178.

[25]   Anon., *Naziführer sehen dich an*, Paris 1934; quoted by K. Theweleit, *Männerphantasien*, Reinbek 1987, 2: 25.

Psychoanalysis as fiction

Let us recapitulate. We are inquiring into structures of alterity in the heart of the very same theory that is often invoked to explain such structures: psychoanalysis. As a convinced lamarckian, Freud assumed the nature and experiences of prehistoric man still to be relevant for an adequate understanding of the everyday behaviour of modern man. Primitive/primal man still lives within us. But this primitive man is truly 'primitive': a sort of monster, lascivious and violent. In fact he is, as we have seen, a stereotypical wild other from a nineteenth-century discourse on civilization and progress. This discourse, as variably as it may have manifested itself, in one way or another essentially operated with polar opposites: culture and nature, men and women, white and black, adult and child, man and beast, the rational and the emotional, contemporary and primal society. All the mutually associated categories that were subsumed under the second pole of these oppositions were regarded as impulsive, wild, uncontrolled. Freud's interpretations underwent similar, convergent influences from archeology and folklore, and from a romantic discourse on 'life', which stressed the blind impulse (*Trieb*) within, and opposed it to the controlling instance of the human intellect.

'Master of narrative, builder of myth': that is how George Steiner has characterized Freud. [26] Indeed, the psychoanalytic theory of human functioning possesses a pregnant narrative structure. It is a myth, a *muthein* in the sense of Aristotle's *Poetics*: a *mise-en-intrigue*. Myth is often defined as the primary way in which men interpret themselves symbolically, as a traditional narrative which explains how things are now in terms of what happened at the beginnings of times. Freud's origin myth tries to make sense of the intricacies of present-day human behaviour by narrating about primal times when savage men still lived in hordes and murdered their fathers to gain access to their mothers and sisters, then out of remorse.... These dramatic occurrences, he holds, still put their mark upon the soul of modern, only superficially civilized man.

Freud's *Es*, I suggest, is an avatar of the imaginary, wild Other, who now inhabits the wilderness within just like the monstrous Plinian races once inhabited the wilderness without, the wild periphery of the

---

[26]   *The Sunday Times*, 6 September 1987.

civilized world. The dramatic struggle between the *Über-Ich* and the *Es*, which is to be civilized, controlled, domesticated, is nothing but a counterpart of the equally dramatic colonialist 'civilizatory' offensive of imperial empires subjecting dark-skinned peoples defined as wild, still-natural, contemporary savages, recipients of the good brought to them by white heroes in this narrated, imaginary world.

Women play a very passive and marginal role in Freud's phylo-genetic speculations. Moreover, he does not escape from that association of women with other categories of impulsive others (savages, ancestors, children, neurotics, the lower classes) which was so common in the last century. In the second of his *Three Essays on the Theory of Sexuality*, for instance, he links female nature with the polymorphously perverse disposition of the child, with prostitution, and with sexuality among the uncontrolled lower classes in general.[27] Freud despised the masses, looked upon them as unrestrained, unable to control their impulses, unlike the civilized elite he was glad to reckon himself among. In his letters, for instance one to Arnold Zweig in 1927, and in private conversation, for instance with Lou Andreas-Salomé in 1929, he often used the denigrating term *Gesindel*, rabble, for common people, as well as for the neurotic patients he treated.[28]

In *Die Frage der Laienanalyse* he calls adult female sexuality the 'dark continent' of psychology.[29] S.L. Gilman comments:

> In using this phrase in English, Freud ties the image of female sexuality to the image of the colonial black and to the perceived relationship between the female's ascribed sexuality and the Other's exoticism and pathology. It is Freud's intent to explore this hidden 'dark continent' and reveal the hidden truths about female sexuality, just as the anthropologists-explorers [...] were revealing the hidden truths about the nature of the black. Freud continues a discourse which relates the images of male discovery to the images of the female as object of discovery. (Gilman, *op.*

---

[27]   For an analysis of these associations, see S. Gilman, 'Freud and the prostitute: Male stereotypes of female sexuality in fin-de-siècle Vienna', *Journal of the American Academy of Psychoanalysis* 9 (1981): 337-60.

[28]   See P. Gay, *Freud. A Life for our Times*, New York 1988, note 4 to chapter 11.

[29]   *SE* 20: 212. In the original text the expression is in English.

cit., p. 257)

Did Freud himself not, we might add, once refer to his *Konquistadoren-temperament*? [30] All the mechanisms and tropes that generally govern the images of others at the period are present: women as seen by men, peasants or the lower classes as seen by the bourgeois, blacks as seen by whites. The attributes of the other constitute an inversion of one's own: we are rational while they are not, we control ourselves while they are impulsive, we are completely human while they are not, we are civilized beings while they are closer to raw nature. At the same time, a mechanism of exclusion is at work: the other is excluded from (what is seen as) proper humanity. Furthermore, others are equated metaphorically and metonymically with animals. And they often are categorically ambiguous, not altogether human, nor altogether animal, and for that reason invested with strong emotions, in the same way as the scatological.

The others inhabit, as we do ourselves, a discursively constructed imaginary world, a Bakthinian 'chronotope'. This semiotic space is divided into two spheres, that of civilized humanity were we live, and that beyond the boundary, the sphere of wildness, were they live. This chronotope provides the setting for stories in which we and the others are narrative characters, such as the story of Europeans who in the name of Civilization have to go among savages, or that of Christians who in the name of God have to go among the heathens. According to psychoanalysis, we all have to conquer and domesticate the wildness within, in the name of proper humanity. In colonialist discourse, white colonials go into the wilderness to cultivate it, bringing civilization. In Christian discourse, it is the missionary who heroically crosses the boundary between civilization and wildness in order to proselytize. In many tribal societies, the shaman/healer plays a similar role, as an exemplary mediator between this world and the other one, the one he travels through by virtue of his techniques of ecstasy. Again, the role of the psychoanalyst in psychoanalytic discourse is highly similar, as is the formalized, ritual context in which his activities take place. The analyst is a character in a dramatic narrative, who heroically penetrates into the dark, archaic, wild regions of the soul of his patient

---

[30]   S. Freud, *Briefe an Wilhelm Fliess 1887-1904*, ed. J.M. Masson, Frankfurt 1986, p. 437.

(internal foreign territory, *inneres Ausland*, as Freud put it, *SE* 22: 57) in order to conjure up and defeat evil forces, just as missionaries once penetrated into the Dark Continent to do the same thing. [31] Perhaps Freud's self-analysis is the finest example of such an undertaking. As to the dimension of time of the psychoanalytic chronotope: anyone who transgresses into the darkness of the unconscious leaves the here and now of historical time. This archaic world is there and then. It is governed by the primeval time of myth.

Here are some of the qualities Freud attributes to the Id: it is 'the dark, inaccessible part of our personality'; 'a cauldron full of seething excitations' (*voll brodelnder Erregungen*), 'no good and evil, no morality', chaotic, no space and time, no change (*SE* 22: 73 ff.). Helmut Stockhammer compared Freud's interpretation of the Id with Hegel's interpretation of the African continent and its inhabitants, and found many similarities. Both, Stockhammer concludes, are represented as raw, dark, inhuman, illogical, bestial, inaccessible, full of contradictions, negative, chaotic, incapable of development, low, timeless, sultry, cruel, explosive, perverse, fetishist, cannibalistic, unorganized, unscrupulous, godless, ecstatic, repulsive, capricious and unpredictable, fanatic, primitive, full of energy, blind, sensual, childish, closed, wild, and dark as the night. [32]

While Freud attempted to show up 'similarities between the mental life of neurotics and that of savages' (as the subtitle of *Totem and Tabu* reads), Lévi-Strauss has pointed out the similarities between the mental life of savages and that of psychoanalysts. Psychoanalysis, he holds, is not so much a sound strategy of scientifically explaining myth, as rather an authentic form of mythic thought itself, characterized by *bricolage*, the creation of narrative plots, and especially the overcoming of paradoxes and

---

[31]   The movement of the hero through narrative space is discussed by J. Lotman, 'On the metalanguage of a typological description of culture', *Semiotica* 14 (1975): 97-123. Cf. F.J. Sulloway's remarks on Freud as a hero-type in traditional Freud scholarship an biography: *Freud: Biologist of the Mind*, New York 1983, chapter 13.

[32]   H. Stockhammer, 'Schnappschüsse in Schwarzweiss oder: Wo liegt Afrika? Kolonialistische Denkformen in Hegels Geschichtsphilosophie und Freuds Metapsychologie', *Unter dem Pflaster liegt der Strand* 15 (1985): 125-58.

contradictions. [33]

Psychoanalytic interpretations of alterity

So what we seem to have here is a full-blown circle. A theoretical approach frequently invoked to explain structures of alterity itself contains such structures. Thus Wallace, a psychoanalyst and historian of psychoanalysis, in his monograph on *Freud and Anthropology*, holds that 'primitive' societies can be differentiated from contemporary Western societies 'in terms of their greater institutionalization of primary-process, in contrast to secondary process, modes', and that 'there is indeed an underlying commonality in neurosis and primitivity'. [34] Thinking and feeling in these societies, this means, are relatively unburdened by the demands of reality, time, order, or logic. In his classic book on *Wild Men in the Middle Ages* (1952), Bernheimer is prone to the same stereotypes. 'It appears that the notion of the wild man,' he writes, 'must respond and be due to a persistent psychological urge. We may define this urge as the need to give external expression [...] to the impulses of reckless physical self-assertion which are hidden in all of us, but normally kept under control. These impulses, which are strongest and most aggressive in the very young, are restricted slowly, as the child learns to come to terms with a civilized environment'. The wild man is exactly what we are, when stripped of 'all those acquired tastes and patterns of behavior which are part of our adjustment to civilization'. His life, and our essential nature, is one of 'bestial self-fullfilment, directed by instinct rather than volition'. The wild man's actions 'reflect to an absolute degree those impulses which make their compromise with the demands of reality. He approaches women with raw lust, or with bleak hatred'. [35]

Not even Mary Midgley, in her pioneering work on the interpre-

---

[33]   C. Lévi-Strauss, *op. cit.*, chapter 14. For a systematic comparison between the activities of the psychoanalyst and those of the shaman, showing many parallels, see his 'Magie et religion', in *Anthropologie structurale* (Paris 1974), esp. pp. 218-26.

[34]   E.R. Wallace, *op. cit*, p. 224.

[35]   R. Bernheimer, *Wild Men in the Middle Ages* (1952) reprint New York 1979, pp. 3, 4, 121.

tation of animals in traditional philosophy, escapes from this view of human nature. She sees man as 'a dangerous beast'. Man has always 'been unwilling to admit his own ferocity, and has tried to deflect attention from it by making animals out to be more ferocious than they are'. Her interpretation of early man is equally stereotypical: 'Let us consider the predicament of primitive man. He is not without natural inhibitions, but his inhibitions are weak. [...] He does horrible things, and is filled with remorse afterwards'. Her own, corresponding view of animal nature has strong primitivistic connotations, and, ironically, represents a lapse into the opposite of the negative traditional stereotype of animals she criticizes.[36]

These are just a few examples, but it would not be difficult to find many more. The wildness of the other, according to psychoanalysis, is an imaginary construct, a projection of a real wildness deep in ourselves on others. I put it that this wildness deep in ourselves is itself an imaginary construct, too, that an archaic, animal other within is hypostatized from the bourgeois self precisely to constitute that self by the repudiation and exclusion of 'low' and 'other' anti-values. Psychoanalysis, consequently, seems to be more interesting as a case than as an explanatory theory of alterity. Alterity is a discursive structure, and has slipped into psychoanalysis from hegemonic, disciplining cultural discourse: on culture and nature, man and animal, the civilized and the primitive, male and female, the ascent from wildness to civilization.

Things are not as psychoanalysis holds them to be, but precisely the other way around. Mythic themes do not well up from the depths of the human psyche to find their way into legends, popular customs, folklore, views of others and other kinds of human discursive behaviour; the rabbit which jumps out of this hat was smuggled into it first, when Freud constructed his model of the human soul under the influence of his wide readings in anthropology, mythology and folklore. Discursive structures such as the Oedipus plot found their way into the psychoanalytic narrative construction of a primal landscape within, characterized by heterogeneous space and allochronic time.

---

[36]   M. Midgley, *op. cit.*, pp. 28, 31, 40.

Conclusion

Freud with his fascinating high drama of human phylogenesis managed to knit together, and to impose form and order upon, many strange facts. His view of the human psyche to a considerable extent came about by the imaginative use of themes and material from myths, folklore, archeology and anthropology, and his supposedly purely empirical findings are heavily laden with a-priori preconceptions on this level; and these are central, not peripheral to the basic tenets of his theoretical work.

My primary aim in this paper was to show up structures of alterity in the very heart of a theoretical approach often invoked to explain such structures. A burning issue remains, which (stressing, as I did, the fictional and creative aspects of Freud's writings) I have addressed only indirectly: that of the scientific value of psychoanalysis. Freud's ideas on primeval man, apart from their methodological flaws, turn out to be speculative and outdated, and this reflects upon the validity of his theory of human behaviour. Frans de Waal's *Peacemaking among Primates* may be read as a cogent correction upon the traditional negative stereotype of the animal (including the animal within ourselves) as an impulsive, ferocious, brutish monster. The archeological metaphor has been criticized by Donald Spence as deceptive, unsupported by clinical evidence, and hermeneutically naive in suggesting the possibility of reconstructing historical truth from context-free, unequivocal data. And Gérard Mendel, to name but one more of many critics of psychoanalysis, has demonstrated the outdated character of crucial biological foundations of freudian psychoanalysis, especially its lamarckism. [37]

Freud's view of man and the (civilized) human condition is essentially a tragic one: man has fallen from nature, and can only maintain himself by denying his archaic heritage, by controlling the salacious, aggressive animal Other within. Modern man has to cope with his ineradicable animal nature. He is eternally afflicted by phylogenetic guilt, and therefore pays a high price for acquiring civilization. The world within

---

[37]   F. de Waal, *Peacemaking among Primates*, Boston 1988 (and cf. Midgley, *op.cit.*); D. Spence, *The Freudian Metaphor. Toward a Paradigm Change in Psychoanalysis*, New York 1987 (for a defence of the archaeological metaphor, see D. Kuspit, *op. cit.*); G. Mendel, *La psychanalyse revisitée*, Paris 1989 (along the same lines: Sulloway, *op. cit.*).

as Freud constructed it is intricately related to that of a nineteenth-century civilizatory discourse on races, sexes, classes and empire, and the wild other who inhabits this world within turns out to be an avatar of the colonial and sexual others constructed in this discourse.

Sigmund Freud: anthropologist of the mind, archeologist of the soul, master of narrative, builder of myth.

FROM SADE TO FASSBINDER:
AESTHETICS OF CRUELTY AND MALE LOVE
IN HOMOSEXUAL ARTISTS

Gert Hekma

Count D.A.F de Sade (1740-1814) initiated a literary tradition which expressed a fascination with violence and sexuality. He was a forerunner because he was the first to describe all varieties and differences in sexuality, and also because he considered cruelty [1] fundamental to social and sexual relations. Equally remarkable is his openness about pederasty and sodomy, and his defense of homosexuality in *La philosophie dans le boudoir* (1795). [2] In the western tradition no one had ever dared to be that open and radical about same-sex loves.

Sade may have heralded a tradition of literary presentations of homosexuality and violence; but the tradition did not emerge as such until a century later, in the generation of Oscar Wilde and Marcel Proust. Many authors with a 'gay sensibility' have been touched by it: Jean Genet, Pier Paolo Pasolini, Yukio Mishima, James Purdy, Joe Orton, Andy Warhol, Gerard

---

[1]   I use the term *cruelty* as in Antonin Artaud's *Theatre of cruelty*.

[2]   First published in 1795, translated as *The Bedroom Philosophers*. For Sade, see J.J. Pauvert, *Sade vivant* (3 vols.; Paris 1986-90). Cf. also A. LeBrun's essay *Soudain un bloc d'abîme, Sade* (Paris 1986).

Reve, Rainer Fassbinder. Younger writers such as Joseph Winkler, Tony Duvert, Hervé Guibert and Dennis Cooper continue to be allured by it. It is an independent tradition of interrelated citations. Fassbinder has filmed Genet's *Querelle*, citing Wilde's 'Each man kills the thing he loves'; Pasolini has adapted his *Salo* from Sade's *The 120 days of Sodom*, and so on.

Before going into the specifics of this tradition, I shall address some issues concerning homosexuality and society, homosexuality and violence, and literature and life. Discussing mainly homosexual violence, I do not deny possible connections between other forms of sexuality and cruelty. But violence in relation with male homosexuality has other historical backgrounds and other social contexts.

The history of homosexuality

Due to the influence of Michel Foucault, many researchers nowadays consider homosexuality a social construct rather than a natural essence. Not the biological origins of homosexuality are looked for, but the social transformations of same-sex loves and passions. Homosexuality itself is considered a neologism and a new, nineteenth-century social category. The body allows for the most diverse social forms which in no way correspond to physiological structures. [3]

Elsewhere I have analysed the social construction of homosexuality in nineteenth-century Holland. [4] Its conceptualization was initiated by homosexuals such as Karl Heinrich Ulrichs and Magnus Hirschfeld, and by psychiatric experts like Krafft-Ebing, Charcot, Binet, Lacassagne, Lombroso and others. Many sodomites and pederasts appropriated the new ideas of homosexuality as a legitimation for their sexual behaviours and erotic feelings. Being different was not only socially produced and individually accepted, some 'uranians' even participated very actively in defining homosexuality as a status of alterity. They hoped the medico-biological theory of homosexuality would give them a 'natural' or equal status in modern society, as had been the case in ancient Greece. Hirsch-

---

[3]   M. Foucault, *Histoire de la sexualité 1. La volonté de savoir* (Paris 1976).

[4]   G. Hekma, *Homoseksualiteit, een medische reputatie* (Amsterdam 1987).

feld even sustained this theory when it was against the interests of homosexuals to do so, as in the Eulenburg scandal.[5] And when Steinach developed a cure for homosexuals, Hirschfeld hailed this theory as an affirmation of his own views. Notions legitimating unequal treatment in equal cases have in the case of homosexuality not only been defended, but also been developed by homosexuals.

In medieval Europe, christian prejudices against sodomy (in general all sexual relations which did not intend procreation, in and outside marriage, often more specific homosexual behaviour) had made it a sin and a capital crime. In the Enlightenment, attitudes towards 'Socratic love' (Voltaire) changed: sins did not exist for a secular state, so sodomy could be decriminalized. The *philosophes* nevertheless found it a filthy topic and they preferred preventing homosexual behaviour by stimulating heterosocial relations. Only Sade defended homosexual pleasures, as he defended prostitution, theft and murder.[6] After the French revolution, sodomites and inverts had to stay in their underworlds because of the persisting social stigma. As importantly, sexual preference became, during the nineteenth century, a central part of personal identities through the efforts of psychiatrists and uranians. This process of individuation and sexualization culminated in R. von Krafft-Ebing's *Psychopathia sexualis*.[7] Now, one could be a born homosexual, as one could be a born criminal (Lombroso); the implication was that as a homosexual, one was member of an insane and asocial species.

---

[5]   I. Hull, 'Kaiser Wilhelm and the "Liebenberg circle"', in *Kaiser Wilhelm II: New Interpretations*, ed. J.C.G. Rohl & N. Sombart (Cambridge 1982), pp. 193-220; J. Steakley, 'Iconography of a Scandal', in *Hidden from History. Reclaiming the Gay and Lesbian Past*, ed. M.B. Duberman, M. Vicinus & G. Chauncey (New York 1989), pp. 233-263.

[6]   On the history of sodomy, see K. Gerard & G. Hekma (eds.), *The Pursuit of Sodomy. Male Homosexuality in Renaissance and Enlightenment Europe* (New York 1989). On the *philosophes* and sodomy: J. Stockinger, 'Homosexuality and the French Enlightenment', in *Homosexualities in French Literature*, ed. G. Stambolian & E. Marks (Ithaca 1979), pp. 161-185.

[7]   Published in Stuttgart 1886. It was annually reprinted in enlarged and revised editions over the next 10 years, and widely translated.

Homosexuality and violence

Social discrimination and prejudice influenced homosexual ways of life in many respects. In the first place, sexual preferences and escapades had to be kept secret. When a homosexual wanted to explore his sexuality, he had to do so in a world where others would not venture. For middle-class homosexuals, there were two ways to do so: going abroad (Paris and Italian islands, such as Capri and Sicily, were popular spots around the turn of the century) or entering the sexual underworlds of cottages and disreputable bars at home. Discrimination and criminalization drove homosexuals into an underground of petty thieves, pimps, and the like. In the large cities of the nineteenth century, homosexual and lesbian love flourished under the cover of prostitution. In this underworld homosexuals were exposed to three dangers: to meet their social peers, to be arrested by the police or to be deceived, blackmailed, robbed or bashed by their partners in this milieu. There was always the risk of physical or emotional violence in this underworld into which no straight man entered of his own accord. Even visiting prostitutes was less dangerous to heterosexuals.

This is my first point. In such a milieu, a connection between homosexuality and physical violence took shape. A double victimization: police persecution of homosexuals drove them into a subculture where they were even more exposed to violence — but where they also had their sexual opportunities.

There was a paradoxical side to this meeting of homosexual and criminal underworlds. It offered homosexuals also new sexual flavours and fetishes ('naughty boys') and gave them the unknown social opportunity to meet another social class outside fixed social boundaries. The homosexual underworld offered rare occasions for social unequals to meet on an equal footing, unhampered by the deadening paternalism characteristic of everyday encounters.

But the sexual attraction to naughty boys — soldiers, sailors, messenger-boys, butcher-boys, petty criminals — had also another background. The new theory of homosexuality was developed in accordance with ideas of sexuality as an attractive force between opposites. Therefore the homosexual, defined as a female soul in a male body, should be attracted to the real male — and wasn't the naughty boy a real male? Sexual difference was doubled by social difference, increasing the force of attraction. Also, maleness at the time was still defined in contradistinction, not so much to homosexuality, but to passivity. As long as the 'real male' kept up an outward appearance of activity, homosexual endeavours were not the threat they later became for him.

The novel-writing Marquis de Custine offers a case in point. He was victimized while cruising soldiers in Paris in 1828. He was bashed as he tried to seduce one among them, and was later found severely wounded. It was a great scandal throughout the Faubourg St. Germain, but Custine only became more conscious of his homosexuality. [8] He did not yet draw upon his homosexual experiences for his writing, however. At that time, August Count von Platen was the first poet to give in his poems cryptic expression to such desires; and he was more open in his diaries, published many years after his death. He became famous for his pen-fight with Heinrich Heine, one execrating the other for being, respectively, Jewish or gay. [9] Very different seems to have been the case of Heinrich von Kleist. It has been argued that his suicide can be partly attributed to the internalization of negative feelings concerning homosexual inclinations. He may have been the first victim of the individuation of homosexual desires and the sexualization of identities. [10]

Fiction and fact

The subculture of homosexuality and violence has often been described in literature. There are different ways to analyse the relation between fiction and the facts of life. Fiction can be seen as something autonomous, as an ideological, cultural superstructure determined by material reality, or, again, as standing in a relationship of interdependence, where fiction is both a product of social relations and an influential force upon them. Because of the relative autonomy of works of art, they are rather unreliable sources for

---

[8]   O. Gassouin, *Le marquis de Custine. Le courage d'être soi-même* (Paris 1987).

[9]   A selection from his diaries has been published recently as *Tagebücher*, ed. Rüdiger Görner (Zürich 1990). See also H. Fichte, *'Deiner Umarmungen süße Sehnsucht'* (Tübingen 1985).

[10]   James Steakley, 'Sodomy in Enlightenment Prussia: From Execution to Suicide', in K. Gerard, *op. cit.*, pp. 163-175.

sociology and history.[11] But art can also be considered an intense expression of social life, a complex and complete version of social discourses. For Dutch homosexual literature of the turn of the century, I have argued that the novels of Louis Couperus and Jacob Israël de Haan, part of the 'high art' literary canon, are more faithful and reliable as representations of contemporary homosexual ways of living than are the contemporary medical sources and gay shockers, which neglect to present the contradictions and extremes of homosexual passions. To be sure, such texts are worth researching — but it should be taken into account that they are more straightforward and generally fail to allow for inconsistencies. Consequently, literary sources (especially those with a dedication to the high standards of artistic realism) are a vital part of the data we possess of those times.[12] Certainly, this literature is intertwined with the biography of the author, the social context in which he lived, and the history and tradition of which he and his work are part.

The beginnings: Sade

It is strange to see how much attention is given to Sade as a heterosexual. When his biographer Pauvert concludes that Sade after his death sentence (for arson and sodomy with his man-servant Latour) did not go to Italy with his sister-in-law, as the myth has it, he asks the question with which lady he did escape to Italy. At the same time, he acknowledges the presence of Latour on Sade's Italian voyage. Thus, there was certainly a male lover whom Pauvert for some reason fails to consider a plausible sexual partner for Sade. Nevertheless, Sade's biographers are clear on his sexual preferences: Heine spoke of passive inversion, Lely of a homosexual without remorse and Pauvert sees Sade principally as a sodomite.[13]

---

[11]   Cf. J. Goudsblom, 'Problemen bij de sociologische studie van romans', in *Romantropologie. Essays over antropologie en literatuur*, ed. J. van Bremen, S. van der Geest & J. Verrips (Amsterdam 1979), pp. 1-18.

[12]   See my 'De benoeming van het onnoembare. Homoseksueel proza in het eerste kwart van de twintigste eeuw', in *Liber Amicorum A.G. van der Steur*, ed. F.W. Kuyper & B.C. Sliggers (Haarlem 1988), pp. 35-60.

[13]   See Lely, *Vie du marquis de Sade*, Paris 1965: 350-1; Pauvert o.c. 1, 47-48 and 265 where Heine's diagnosis is cited.

While, then, the biographers have formed a distinct impression of his sexual predilections, which also play a prominent part in his literature, they still keep looking for the women in his life. They pass over the very thing they acknowledge. When we consider Sade as a predecessor of an aesthetics of cruelty and sexuality, a central part in it will pertain to homosexuality. Libertines like Sade did not run into major problems in eighteenth-century France; nevertheless, Sade was imprisoned for a life time under both Old and New Regimes, because his crimes were a combination of violence, sodomy and blasphemy — each of them common crimes, but apparently not so in combination. Moreover, Sade never showed any remorse: he continued defending his 'nature'. The incentive for Sade to develop a literature and philosophy of cruelty and sodomy was certainly linked to his exposure to criminal prosecution and imprisonment, which ran counter to his ideas of an enlightened state.

Unlike the philosophers of the Enlightenment, Sade did not believe that human nature was fundamentally good and that only culture made man wicked. Nature is both good and evil, giving and devouring, and man has to acknowledge the just and unjust sides of life. Sade's heroine Justine, who wants to be good and looks for Christian honesty, suffers through the wickedness of man, whereas her sister Juliet, who indulges in good and evil, finds the joys of life. In Sade's work, violence is considered fundamental to social life, no matter how diverse its manifestations may be.

With regard to sexuality, Sade refused to deny the emotions in favour of reason; this, again, ran counter to the philosophical beliefs of his time. [14] By opposing reason and emotion, the philosophers of the Enlightenment perpetuated the mind-body split that was so engrained in western thinking, and rendered the status of emotions and sexuality highly problematic. This was a pitfall Sade aimed to avoid.

Sade is a typical transitional figure who could only come forward in the confusion of the Enlightenment. Not its liberal and libertine sides succeeded, but the puritanical and the repressive: Tissot with his theory of

---

[14]   P. Gay, *The Enlightenment. An interpretation 2. The science of freedom* (New York 1969), ch. 4:3.

masturbation, Rousseau with his pedagogical discipline and social contract. [15] With the tendency to restore 'bonnes moeurs', present from the beginning of the French revolution, but strengthened under Napoleon, the voice of Sade got lost. Or, to be more precise: Sade was hospitalized as a lunatic, his work was proscribed and burned as obscene. The reputation of Sade survived underground during the nineteenth century, and, as Mario Praz has indicated, did influence literary topics and styles. [16] But it was not until the fin-de-siècle that explicit literary renderings of sexuality and violence could be given again (Rachilde, Mirbeau) and Sade's work was republished.

Oscar Wilde: The Portrait of Dorian Gray

In gay literature of the late nineteenth century, violence became a prominent topic. Oscar Wilde's *The Portrait of Dorian Gray* can be read as an experiment in narcissism, i.e. to certain extent in homosexuality. When the painter Basil Hallward is finishing his portrait of Dorian Gray, Lord Henry comes in for a visit. The innocent Dorian is immediately seduced by this nobleman into a nightlife of dark vices. The first girl that falls in love with him commits suicide because he adores her only in the spotlights, and finds her completely banal off stage. Dorian Gray is wholly unaffected by his vicious and dangerous lifestyle and he does not show the outer signs of his escapades (as the then current theory of degeneracy would have it). [17] At the same time, his beautiful portrait begins to show exactly these signs, and is therefore hidden by Gray in a deserted and well closed room on the upper floor of his house. When the painter later urges Dorian to show him his portrait, Dorian shows Basil his ugly side and kills him. In the end, Dorian destroys his portrait; this is fatal to him, but the painting once again exults Dorian's pristine beauty. The signs of degeneracy are now on the body of the dead Dorian. Lord Henry, instigator of Gray's vices and murders, survives everyone. Evil still has its victory, notwithstanding the

---

[15]   T. Tarczylo, *Sexe et liberté au siècle des Lumières* (Paris 1983). This book contains an analysis of Tissot's work.

[16]   M. Praz, *The Romantic Agony* (Oxford 1970), ch. 3 ('The shadow of the divine marquis').

[17]   As regards theories of degeneracy and decadence, see J.E. Chamberlain & S.L. Gilman (eds.), *Degeneration. The Dark Side of Progress* (New York 1985).

suicide of the apparent impersonator of evil, Dorian Gray.

With hindsight, we may declare *The Portrait of Dorian Gray* one of the first gay classics: witness the relation between Lord Henry and Dorian Gray, certainly when seen in the light of Wilde's dictum 'Each man kills the thing he loves' (Lord Henry killed Dorian as much as Dorian killed himself); witness also the references to the criminal and gay underworlds which Dorian visited. [18]

Wilde and his times

Was the drama of Oscar Wilde his passive attitude? How he destroyed his social career for his lover, first by incriminating the Marquess of Queensberry, and then by not leaving England when he was losing his process? Or did he believe that a man of his social class and reputation could never be prosecuted for homosexual acts? Many others of his social class and his sexual inclinations had left England under similar circumstances by escaping to France. There were others who thought as Wilde did: for example, the advisor of the German Emperor, Prince Eulenburg, and his compatriot the steel magnate Alfred Krupp. Both ended in utter disgrace. Both Krupp and Eulenburg's friend Kuno von Moltke started criminal procedures against their incriminators, and both lost. Krupp committed suicide in 1902, before the court heard the case. A year later, the Scottish general Hector MacDonald, 'Fighting Mac', did the same when he found that his reputation was dishonoured. He had to appear in court because of relations with Ceylonese boys. Thanks to the criminal proceedings against Wilde we know he entered the dark underworlds of London where he indulged in sexual escapades with lower-class messenger-boys. Eulenburg, Krupp and MacDonald also favoured the lower class for their sexual pleasures. The aristocrat Eulenburg did not yet need the underworld of prostitution and inverts — he could find his sexual partners still among the man-servants of his estate, as MacDonald found them among the native

---

[18]   R. Ellmann, *Oscar Wilde* (London 1987); H. Montgomery Hyde, *The Trials of Oscar Wilde* (London 1973).

population of Ceylon. [19]

There is a close link between the vices in the literature and the life of Wilde; the parallel is even more pronounced in the collective pornographic novel *Teleny*. Wilde had had his predecessors, the most famous example being the love-affair of the French poets Paul Verlaine and Arthur Rimbaud. It is assumed that an actual rape of the boy Rimbaud by soldiers, on his first voyage to Paris, inspired him to a rape-poem. Later he started a tumultuous relation with Verlaine, a married bisexual, ten years his senior. Everything ended in Brussels when Verlaine shot Rimbaud, wounding him slightly. In their poetry they expressed their violent love-affair. [20] In the famous 'yellow book' *A rebours* by J.K. Huysmans (1884), the Baron des Esseintes cruises a schoolboy in the streets of Paris. The *Chants of Maldoror* by Isidor Ducasse (Lautréamont) describe city-life and pederasty in a highly cruel manner.

The passivity of Wilde may be amazing, yet there are many more twentieth-century gay artists who courted disaster. Wilde is not an exception, but an example in this 'gay' tradition of living dangerously. Cruising has exposed many homosexuals to victimization, even to murder. They fell prey, often defencelessly, to their aggressors. It is remarkable that in such violent encounters it is almost always the gays, nearly never the aggressors, who are worsted. Of course, gays are more vulnerable, looking for sex, not for trouble, whereas their assailants initiate the violence. Pasolini's murder is as clear an example of this pattern as is Wilde's passivity in the face of impending ruin. [21]

Homosexuals have become passive victims, following a pattern they themselves have established. It was still remarkable that Wilde went to the courts after being libelled a sodomite. Krupp and Moltke did the same, but they had also to face defeat. Later on, no one labelled a homosexual ever dared to seek redress from the courts (assuming the qualification was felt to be grievous at all). So, Oscar Wilde's passivity facing his ordeal was in a way typical for the love that dared not speak its name. At the same time

---

[19]   For Eulenburg, see note 5. For Krupp and MacDonald, see A.L. Rowse, *Homosexuals in History* (London 1977), pp. 218-219 and 199-200. Also T. Royle, *Death before Dishonour. The True Story of Fighting Mac* (Edinburgh 1983).

[20]   H. Peyre, *Rimbaud vu par Verlaine* (Paris 1975).

[21]   See D. Bellezza, *Mort de Pasolini* (Paris 1983).

others started to speak out about this silenced eros.

Netherlands: Couperus and De Haan

Oscar Wilde was a trendsetter in many ways, and certainly so for the gay tradition of violence. Around the turn of the century, two Dutch authors worked in this vein. In the year that *The Portrait of Dorian Gray* was published, Louis Couperus wrote his second novel *Noodlot* ('Destiny'), the story of the fatal love of a queer for a straight man. The queer is murdered by his beloved who in turn commits a double suicide with his girlfriend. In *De berg van licht* (1904/5, translated into German as *Heliogabal*), Couperus retells the story of the androgynous child-emperor of third-century Rome; the tale does not shy away from the cruel and homosexual side of Heliogabal's life. [22]

Much more explicit was Jacob Israël de Haan (1881-1923). His first novel *Pijpelijntjes* (1904, 'Pipelines', never translated) was so explicitly homosexual that De Haan lost his employment as a school teacher and as a journalist for the socialist daily *Het Volk*. His friend Arnold Aletrino, first (straight) defender of the homosexual cause in the Netherlands, bought the complete first edition of the novel and had it destroyed because he was himself recognizably depicted as a bisexual sadist. De Haan's second novel, *Pathologieën* (1908) followed the tradition both of decadent romanticism as of medical theories of degeneracy. A young man, René, discovers his homosexual inclinations by reading his father's medical books, is sent away, because of his homosexuality, by his father. He moves into a boarding house where he lives the life of a decadent homosexual and sadistic painter. He sexually abuses and tortures the innocent Johan, who lacks the willpower to withstand his torturer and eventually commits suicide, in compliance with René's intentions. René's experiment with Johan succeeded much as Lord Henry's with Dorian Gray did. The scenes of sexual abuse and humilation are depicted surprisingly openly, given the historical context. Finally, De Haan wrote a Faust-like short story in which the first-person narrator tortures and sexually abuses a cowardly Jesus by

---

[22]   F. Bastet, *Louis Couperus. Een biografie* (Amsterdam 1987). Like Wilde, Couperus was a married man. His wife translated *The Portrait of Dorian Gray* into Dutch.

order of Satan.[23]

De Haan's literary expression of homosexual sadomasochism is an early example, not only of the use of medical concepts of perversion and degeneracy, but also of their transformation and transcendence. Couperus and De Haan went much further than the authors of the homosexual shockers of the day, who merely couched biological theories of homosexuality and emancipation in a more or less literary form, who stuck to conventions and accepted wisdom, and who even introduced chapters in which a medical practitioner or student rendered the exact content of Hirschfeld's theories. Couperus and De Haan transgressed these views by touching on pederasty and cruelty, forbidden topics for the gay shockers and in 'positive' medical literature. By trespassing the homosexual views of the time, Couperus and De Haan certainly gave a more truthful picture of gay life. It is impossible to assess to what extent their art reflected real-life experience; but they certainly expressed vivid, albeit forbidden fantasies.

Like Oscar Wilde, De Haan was later to become a passive victim, not in a sexual scandal, but in a political struggle. After the First World War, he emigrated to Palestine as a zionist; however, he soon became an ardent anti-zionist because of the contempt shown by zionist Jews towards Arabs and orthodox Jews. As a literary man and a journalist, De Haan had easy access to leading western dailies such as the London *Daily Telegraph* and the Amsterdam *Algemeen Handelsblad*, where he vented his criticisms of zionist aspirations in Palestine. Radical zionist groups threatened to kill him if he should stay in Palestine; De Haan stayed on, and in 1923 was brutally murdered by the zionist organisation Agudat Israël.[24]

---

[23]   R. Delvigne & L. Ross, 'De geschiedenis van de Pijpelijntjesaffaire', in: J.I. de Haan, *Open brief aan P.L. Tak* (Amsterdam 1983). The story 'Over de ervaringen van Hélénus Marie Golesco' appeared in *Levensrecht* (1907: pp. 105-11) and was reprinted in the collection of stories by De Haan entitled *Nerveuze vertellingen* (Amsterdam 1983).

[24]   Cf. J. Meijer, *De zoon van een gazzen* (Amsterdam 1965), and the special issue of the weekly *De Groene* (19 April 1989) devoted to De Haan.

After 1900

At the turn of the century there was confusion as to the meaning and moral value of homosexuality. On the one hand, a homosexual emancipation movement had started and male homosexuals like De Haan virtually flaunted their sexual preferences; on the other hand, new forms of repression and persecution emerged: new and more repressive laws were passed in Britain in 1885 and 1897, in Germany in 1871 and in The Netherlands in 1911. Some men were surprised to find that they were considered homosexuals or sodomites (Wilde, Eulenburg, Krupp) and, as such, liable to prosecution. In this confusion, new initiatives were possible, especially in the scholarly and the artistic fields: Magnus Hirschfeld, Sigmund Freud, Marcel Proust,[25] André Gide, Thomas Mann, Robert Musil, and little later the English war poets like Siegfried Sassoon, Wilfred Owen and T.E. Lawrence. In some social circles, a certain openness with regard to homosexuality became possible; yet even the surrealists, who rediscovered De Sade, had a strong dislike of homosexuality, although their peer René Crevel was openly gay.[26] Growing knowledge about homosexuality was not without its drawbacks. Criminal prosecution grew, public prejudices became deeper entrenched so that the notions of manliness and homosexuality became incompatible (leading to the disappearance of the 'naughty boy' type); and medical science developed new possibilities to prevent or cure homosexuality. The psychological effect of these developments on homosexuals who grew up in the beginning of this century was disastrous. Suicide became a prominent issue, not only in the gay shockers of those days, but also in the real life of homosexual men. Around 1900, most famous homosexual suicides came after a scandal: King Ludwig II of Bavaria, MacDonald, Krupp, colonel Redl.[27] This generation had no doubts as to the necessity of hiding one's sexual preferences. But the apparent openness which existed after 1900 made many

---

[25]   H.C. Halberstadt-Freud has made an interesting comparison between Freud's and Proust's theories of sadomasochism: *Het sadomasochisme: Proust en Freud* (Amsterdam 1977).

[26]   M. Carassou, *René Crevel* (Paris 1989).

[27]   On King Ludwig see Rowse, *op. cit.*, pp. 195-199; on Redl, see E.E. Kisch, *Der Fall des Generalstabchefs Redl* (1924, reprinted Stuttgart 1988) and G. Markus, *Der Fall Redl* (Wien/München 1984).

homosexuals more daring: witness De Haan in the Netherlands, Arnold Bronnen and Klaus Mann in Germany,[28] Maurice Sachs[29] and Crevel in France, Mikhaïl Kuzmin in Russia.[30] They came close to flaunting their homosexuality. Their candour is admirable; but most of them got entangled in emotional or political difficulties more or less connected with their homosexuality. Crevel and Mann committed suicide, De Haan and Sachs were murdered.

These problems continued after the Second World War. Openness was greater (as in Jean Genet's work), but at the same time the enormous threat of repression remained in force. Homosexuals were considered seducers of youth and (given the Cold War climate) traitors of their country.[31] More freedom was promised by the sexual revolution of the 1960s, which also involved gay men. At the end of the decade homosexual emancipation came in full swing after the Stonewall Revolution, when gay men resisted the routine control of a bar by the police. Gay emancipation had its reverse side. The level of queer-bashing (the haphazard beating-up of gay men) and gay murders (mostly the killing of older gay men by hustlers) seems to have risen. This does not vitiate the advances made in

---

[28]   U. Münch, *Weg und Werk Arnolt Bronnens: Wandlungen eines Denkens* (Frankfurt 1985); see also Bronnens *Septembernovelle* (Berlin 1923); F. Kroll (ed.), *Klaus Mann Schriftenreihe* (3 vols., Wiesbaden 1976-1979; three additional volumes are in preparation).

[29]   H. Raczymow, *Maurice Sachs* (Paris 1988); and see Sachs' *Sabbath*, originally published in French in 1948. From a Jewish background, Sachs became a Catholic and then a Presbyterian; he was married for some time, but preferred homosexual relations. He worked for the Gestapo but was killed, in 1945, by the SS.

[30]   See M. Green's Introduction in Kuzmin's *Selected Prose and Poetry* (Ann Arbor 1980). Concerning the renaissance of gay culture in Russia in the years 1905-1917, see S. Karlinsky, 'Russia's Gay Literature and Culture: The Impact of the October Revolution', in M.B. Duberman et al., *op. cit.*, pp. 347-364. The poet Ryurik Ivnev was sexually obsessed with destruction by burning: cf. G. McVay, 'Black and Gold: The Poetry of Ryurik Ivnev', *Oxford Slavonic Papers*, 4 (1971): 83-104.

[31]   See J. Costello, *Mask of Treachery. Spies, Lies, Buggery and Betrayal* (New York 1988); for the role played by MacCarthyism, cf. G. Chauncey, 'Paniek in de pers en vervolging van homoseksuelen', *Sociologische Gids*, 32, # 5/6 (1985): 371-393.

the western world with regard to homosexuality, but the level of anti-gay violence remains very high these days. Thus, in Amsterdam one in ten murders over the last decade was gay-related. [32] Perhaps the high level of violence is only a passing phenomenon in a time with great uncertainty and confusion about sexual roles and behaviours in the wake of the sexual revolution of the 1960s and the sexual panics (incest, child abuse, pornography, sexual violence) of the 1980s. Though it might be overly optimistic to expect that in the near future violence will cease to be connected with homosexuality, possibilities do exist to reduce the levels of violence or to change its contents and directions.

The description of cruelty in earlier gay works was reticent: Musil's *Die Verwirrungen des Zöglings Törless* (1906), De Haan's *Pathologieën* (1908), Pessoa's *Ode maritima* (1914), Proust's *Sodome et Gomorrhe* (1921/2) and Bronnen's *Septembernovelle* (1923). There is no question that the literary representation of acts of cruelty corresponded to the real-life experience of homosexual men, probably to a stronger degree than is the case with their heterosexual counterparts. Also, other socio-sexual situations were described without a heterosocial equivalent, as the boy's play and sexual degradation in Musil's boarding school. This literature of cruelty and homosexuality was not very sexually explicit, because the general reticence on sexual matters in literature.

Even in the beginning of the century, we can observe a certain prevalence in literature by gay authors of an aesthetics of cruelty, [33] more

---

[32]   F. van Gemert, 'Fatale seks', *Amsterdams Sociologisch Tijdschrift*, 17 #2 (November 1990): 169-192. On queer-bashing, see J. DeCecco (ed), *Bashers, Baiters and Bigots. Homophobia in American Society* (New York 1985); on murder: R. Senelick, 'Murderers', in *The Encyclopedia of Homosexuality*, ed W. Dynes (New York 1990); on serial murders: R.M. Holmes & J. De Burger, *Serial murder* (Newbury Park 1988).

[33]   Besides the aesthetics of cruelty, there was a tradition in which the beauty of youths was venerated. Proust and Gide are leading examples of this sadomasochistic and boy-oriented tradition. They had little understanding for each other's aesthetics, witness the following remark of Gide on a meeting with Proust: 'Lorsque je lui demande s'il nous présentera jamais cet Eros sous des espèces jeunes et belles, il me répond que, d'abord, ce qui l'attire ce n'est jamais la beauté et qu'il estime qu'elle n'a que peu à voir avec le désir [...]' *Journal 1899-1939* (Paris 1941), p. 694.

so than in the work of heterosexual novelists. As I have argued, this is certainly related to the fact that homosexuals found their sexual adventures in criminal subcultures, and that the gay world is a male one where violence and desire have been historically more pronounced than in female or heterosocial spheres. An additional important factor in the appearance of this homosexual aesthetics of violence was the growing body of medical literature on perversion and degeneracy, in which sadomasochism found a place next to homosexuality.

It is a strange paradox that with a growing mid-century repression of homosexuality under Stalin, Hitler, Pétain and MacCarthy, openness with regard to homosexuality also increased. It was in the middle of the Second World War, in Nazi-occupied France (Nazi-Germany being the first state in history to practise group murder of homosexuals) that the works of Jean Genet appeared; these were certainly a scandalous and, to contemporary standards, obscene depiction of homosexuality. In an underworld of sailors and criminals, travesty, homosexual desire and degradation take a central place. If Wilde had written that 'each man kills the thing he loves', Genet reverses this theme and addresses the desire inspired by murder (and transgression in general). [34] Genet was the homosexual and literary counterpart of a renewed Sadean appraisal by straight philosophers (Bataille, Klossowski). [35]

Genet's work has been pivotal in the gay tradition and in the tradition of the aesthetics of cruelty. Gay artists from the most different backgrounds continued in directions set by Genet: Pasolini in Italy, Mishima in Japan, Fassbinder in Germany, Reve in The Netherlands, Burroughs, Warhol and Purdy in the USA; Orton in England and Tournier in France. [36] The extremes of repression and liberation which gays

---

[34]   See especially his *Querelle de Brest* and *Journal d'un voleur*. On Genet see, among many others, A. Dichy and P. Fouché, *Jean Genet. Essay de chronologie 1910-1944* (Paris 1988) and J.B. Moraly, *Jean Genet, la vie écrite. Biographie* (Paris 1988).

[35]   G. Bataille, *L'érotisme* (Paris 1957); P. Klossowski, *Sade, mon prochain* (Paris 1947).

[36]   J. Lahr, *Prick Up Your Ears. The Biography of Joe Orton* (London 1978); S. Sheperd, *Because We're Queers. The Life and Crimes of Kenneth Halliwell and Joe Orton* (London 1989); H. Scott Stokes, *The Life and Death of Yukio Mishima* (New York 1974); D. Bourdon, *Warhol* (New York 1989), pp. 278 ff.; R. Katz,

experienced were a very fertile ground to develop an aesthetics of violence. But gay artists went further. They were fascinated and attracted to violence. Colette already had a gay man describing a hustler (who had murdered one of his clients, after the act) in the following terms: 'Il rayonnait de beauté, de malice, et d'une folie à son aurore'. [37] This fatal attraction has been highly typical of gay aesthetics: the boys and young men who radiate a certain frenzy are the celebrated ones. In his diary Joe Orton wrote down the assignment of his lover (and later murderer) Halliwell: 'You must use all Genet's subjects — beautiful young murderers, buggery, treachery, bent and brutal policemen and theft'. [38]

Recent deployment

The gay fascination with cruelty has since the sexual revolution become clearly expressed in the leather subculture, in which sadomasochistic rites, signs and practices play an important part. With the evaporation of many homophobic intolerances and prejudices since the sixties, the attraction of violence for homosexual men took a different turn, and has become almost officially formalized in S&M terms. [39] Traces of this specialized culture are to be found in literature: Pierrejouan, Reve, Townsend. [40] But aside from this trend, the more general tradition of cruelty is continuing in the descriptions of the problems and passions of gay love. The Austrian Joseph

---

Love is Colder than Death. The Life and Times of Rainer Werner Fassbinder (London 1987); and see also *Text + Kritik*, 103 (1989: special issue *Rainer Werner Fassbinder*).

[37]   *Ces plaisirs* (Paris 1932), p. 194.

[38]   *The Orton Diaries*, ed. J. Lahr (London 1986), p. 71

[39]   Cf. T. Weinberg & G.W. Levi Kamel (eds.), *S and M. Studies in Sadomasochism* (New York 1983) and A. Spengler, *Sadomasochisten und ihre Subkulturen* (Frankfurt/New York 1979).

[40]   C. Pierrejouan, *MS. Récit* (Paris 1979). L. Townsend is a prolific writer of gay S&M porn novels, and author of *The Leatherman's Handbook* (New York 1972); on Reve, see my 'De meedogenloze jongen', in *Eigenlijk geloof ik niets. Essays over het werk van Gerard Reve*, ed. V. Hunink, J. Paardekooper & P. Sars (Nijmegen 1990), pp. 51-64.

Winkler describes the terrors of coming out in Karinthia. [41] The French-
man Pierre Guyotat writes about the Algerian war as a stream of blood and
sperm. [42] Hervé Guibert has used sadomasochistic themes in *Les chiens*
(Paris 1982), and reworked the myth of the boy-seducer in *Vous m'avez
fait des fantômes* (Paris 1987). [43] In *Closer* (New York 1989) the American Dennis Cooper describes the excesses of fistfucking and suffering in
gay circles. In cinema Fassbinder, Patrick Chéreau and Stephen Frears have
addressed extremes of passion and love. Fassbinder's *Faustrecht der
Freiheit* and Chéreau's *L'homme blessé* relate the arrival and the horrific
experiences of a young proletarian in a gay milieu. Frears retells the story
of Orton, murdered by his lover Halliwell who himself subsequently
committed suicide. The works of this younger generation of artists indicate
that with post-Stonewall gay emancipation the problems regarding
homosexuality have not been solved — they have come to another stage,
to other contents and contexts, but not to a solution.

---

[41]   Cf. his *Menschenkind* (Frankfurt 1979).

[42]   *Tombeau pour cinq cent mille soldats* (Paris 1967).

[43]   In 1990 appeared his AIDS novel *A l'ami qui ne m'a pas sauvé la vie*,
which also portrays his neighbour Michel Foucault.

ALTERITY AS DEFECT:
ON THE LOGIC OF THE MECHANISM OF EXCLUSION

Machiel Karskens

Introduction

In his key work *Madness and Civilization*, [1] Michel Foucault describes an experience of madness which has the form of a partition between reason and unreason. I shall use Foucault's analysis of the dynamics of this partition as paradigmatic for the mechanism of social exclusion. My argument will be that the essence of this mechanism is what I term a *blocked privative relationship*. This postulate does not generally explain all processes of identity formation. I understand exclusion as an important, though not universal process of coping with 'otherness'. Against one of the currents in contemporary French philosophy I will argue that there are other types of opposition and other types of 'identity practice'. Therefore exclusion and privation should be distinguished from oppositions such as contradiction, contrariety, polarity and binary bifurcation. Finally I shall explain some of the risks resulting from a liberation of exclusion when this logic of privation is not recognized.

---

[1]   This book appeared in 1961 under the title *Folie et déraison. Histoire de la folie à l'âge classique*. The common title is now *Histoire de la folie* (=HF); I shall quote from the second edition, published in 1972. The English edition *Madness and Civilization* (=MC) (London: Tavistock, 1965) is a translation of an abridged version.

Madness as Unreason

In his analysis of the experience of madness in our culture Foucault contrasts the seventeenth and eighteenth centuries, called the Classical Age, with the preceding era, the Renaissance, and later times, the 'modern' age.

During the Renaissance madness was perceived both as a cosmic experience of the tragic and as a critical reflection on the limits of reason and reasonable discourse. In modern days madness is known and treated as mental illness. At the same time it is experienced as an intimate truth, a hidden dark side of the moon in each one of us. The Classical Age is characterized by the partition (French *partage*) of reason and unreason, where the unreasonable is excluded from the domain of the nor-mal=reasonable. This exclusion is performed by way of confinement ('le grand refermement'). Madness is only one kind of unreason. The madman is locked up, as are other unreasonable elements such as the libertine, the atheist, the pauper and the sexual pervert. Obviously this partition represents more than a neutral distinction. It has a moral, political and practical impact, which is implied *in this very type of distinction*. In my opinion it is first of all the *form* of this distinction that is responsible for its effects rather than the fact that, as most critics emphasize, reason is at stake here.

The point is not explicitly made by Foucault. Let us first present his analysis of this partition.

[1]   'It can be said [...] that until the Renaissance the ethical world beyond the partition between Good and Evil ensured its equilibrium in a tragic unity, that of fate, providence or divine preference. This unity now vanishes, being dissociated by the decisive partition of reason and unreason. A crisis of the ethical world commences which doubles the great battle between Good and Evil through the irreconcilable conflict of reason and unreason.' (HF p.120)

[2]   'Cultures like that of the Classical Age, in which many values were invested in reason, took with folly at the same time a maximum and a minimum risk. The maximum risk, because insanity was the most direct contradiction of all the things it justified. A minimum risk because it unarmed insanity completely and made it impotent. This maximum and minimum of risk accepted by the classical

culture [...] is exactly what the word unreason expresses: the simple, immediate reverse [...] of reason, [and] this empty form without content or value, purely negative, where nothing is figured but the imprint of a reason that has disappeared, which always remains the 'raison d'être' of what unreason is.' (HF.p.192)

[3]   'Unreason is in the first place that profound scission depending on an age of reason, which alienates the madman from his madness by making them strangers to each other. We can already grasp the unreason in this void [...] But unreason is more than this void [...] The perception of the madman in the end has as its only content reason itself [...] where one was looking for the positive plenitude of madness, one discovered only reason. This non-madness as the content of madness is the second essential point of unreason. Unreason means that the truth of madness is reason. Or rather quasi-reason. And this is the third fundamental characteristic [...] Because reason is the content of the perception of the madman, thus as a consequence it is affected by a certain negative index [...] [the] work of the negative cannot be simply the void of a negation [...] Other forces reign down there. Forces having nothing to do with the theoretical level of concepts and knowing how to resist them to the point of finally overthrowing them [...]' (HF pp.223-224)

[4]   'What we now know of unreason affords us a better understanding of what confinement was [...] It assumed its precise meaning in this fact: that madness in the classical world ceased to be the sign of another world, and that it became the paradoxical manifestation of non-being [...] The essence of confinement was not the exorcism of a danger. Confinement merely manifested what madness was: a manifestation of non-being [...] confinement thereby suppressed it, since it restored it to its truth as nothingness. Confinement is the practice which corresponds most exactly to madness experienced as unreason, that is as the empty negativity of reason [...] confinement cannot have any other goal than a correction (that is the suppression of the difference, or the fulfillment of this nothingness in death); [...] those options for death so often found in the registers of confinement [...] [are] the strict expression of its meaning: an operation to annihilate nothingness.' (MC p.116)

Unreason as privation

Let us discuss these traits of unreason in some detail.

In [1] Foucault speaks about another partition, presumably well-known: the one between Good and Evil. Despite this partition there exists a (tragic) unity, meaning that this division or rather opposition is not a fundamental gap. This much is known from daily experience: ordinarily we do not divide human beings in either good or bad ones. Many intermediate stages exist, even situations that escape this division. What is more, it is impossible in the christian cosmology, in which Evil is the reality of the Devil, to break reality into two distinct parts, because God acts as guarantor for the fundamental unity of reality. That is what Foucault refers to.

The dissolution of this unity is only brought about by the more decisive partition of reason and unreason, which are in irreconcilable conflict. Why is this? In my opinion, the logic of privation operates here in its exclusive way. By definition, the notions *reason* and *unreason* are mutually exclusive and irreconcilable. For unreason is defined as the *absence or privation* of reason, nothing more. This is confirmed by the second half of [2]: unreason as the purely negative, empty form, without content or value, and by the second characteristic of [3] describing folly as emptiness that can only have as its content reason itself. Also [4] analyses confinement from this point of view.

All this is in line with the logic of privation. According to that logic,[2] only the positive term can provide the relationship with content. The positive term must be a property or quality[3] that the subject (of

---

[2]   The term logic is not applied here in the usual sense of formal logic. In the formal logic of predicates it is not possible to distinguish between intrinsic and extrinsic properties of things or processes. As to the distinction between intrinsic and extrinsic, see note 3.

[3]   Aristotle speaks of habit (*hexis*) versus deprivation (*sterèsis*), see *Metaphysics*, X-4, 1055a33. The context of his analysis is contrariety as the maximum of difference. Privation is a subtype of contrariety. I use the term property in a broad sense to indicate every *real* characteristic of a being. I do not follow the whole of Aristotle's analysis describing every situation in which a word with the negating particle (alpha-privans) is used. I confine myself to the real, natural (*pephukos*) or intrinsic properties which beings (or processes) posses in themselves (*kath'heautou*), and their absence. These properties should be

predication) *ought* to have, but does not necessarily possess.[4] Furthermore, there is no middle way between the presence or absence of that property. In the case of privation as distinguished from other types of negation, the property must be a real, natural or intrinsic characteristic of the subject under consideration. In the scholastic definition a privation was therefore called a 'negation in the subject itself';[5] it is a real defect. On the strength of these distinguishing marks of privation one may conclude that in every use of privative speech the speaker wishes to point out the defect of a real intrinsic property of the being under discussion. Foucault clearly states that the culture of the classical age perceived reason as the essential real property (value) of man [2]. That is why the partition is experienced as fundamental [1].

The object, referred to by the privation, is a very complex phenomenon. The whole analysis of parts I and II of *Madness and Civilization* testifies to that complexity. As we have seen, the privated thing can only be conceived as the pure negation ('emptiness') of the property under discussion. But at the same time it remains a real thing — in contrast with other negative things which can be purely 'rational' (as in the case of 'Peter is not here'), or pertain to a positive state of affairs (as in the case of 'This rose is not red, but white'). As a real thing of its own, the deprived thing has its own characteristics even in relation to the absent property. For instance, a blind man is not only a man minus the faculty of seeing, but in relation to the absence of sight he possesses or has developed a set of dispositions and traits typical of his blindness. Now the

---

distinguished from all other ones, which are extrinsically ascribed. In contrast to Aristotle I maintain with Foucault and others, that a general and transhistorical theory about the real and essential properties of (human) beings is impossible. This entails that it is not possible to make an unambiguous distinction between intrinsic and extrinsic properties.

[4]   In *Categories*, X, 12a26-35 Aristotle emphasizes the normative aspect of privation: 'we rather use those terms of that which has not but should have teeth or sight [...]'. In this text he also clearly distinguishes this type of opposition from a *contrariety*, in which either a property, its opposite, neither of these or an intermediate quality can be the case (e.g. good-bad, health-disease, equal-unequal, white-black), from a *relative opposition*, in which both terms are correlatives (e.g. mother-daughter), and from *affirmative and negative statements* in which what is affirmed or denied need not to be in itself a positive or negative quality.

[5]   E.g. Aquinas, *Summa Theologiae*, I, 17 and 4.

problem is that these positive properties cannot be described properly as long as blindness is conceived only as the absence of sight. They are, as Foucault often puts it, 'reduced to silence'. Most characteristics of madness in the Classical Age (the first two mentioned in [3]) display this feature. When the positive property is valued as being essential, the situation of the deprived being becomes even more complicated. On the one hand a privation presupposes that both parts of the relation belong to the same species, on the other hand it now becomes impossible to acknowledge this in the deprived part while lacking the essential property. That is why madmen have so often been compared to beasts. [6] From this point of view the deprived being does not really possess an identity of its own. These are the roots for experiencing the deprived being as the totally other.

At the same time, however, the properties of the deprived thing remain a positive thing that cannot be negated. So they become 'strange forces' [3], which in their strangeness and inconceivability threaten the positive values of the property under discussion ([2] and the last part of [3]). In the end this threat may evaporate all positive contents of the original property. The second characteristic in [3] already indicates this by conceiving reason as non-madness. It shows that privation is a dangerous relationship which turns against itself. For if the positive property **P** under discussion is used exclusively in relation to its absence **non-P**, it also becomes impossible to develop its particular positive content. Only a **not-non-P** remains and this double negation can no longer be turned into an affirmation. In many situations of social exclusion these phenomena can easily be observed, as Foucault describes in the case of madness. [7] In these cases the privative relationship is *blocked*. As opposed to a dialectic relationship, where negation can function as a creative moment, a privative relationship tends to block itself. It becomes impossible to think positively either about the property (or value) under discussion or about its absence. The same holds for the practices, as we shall see now.

Finally, let us consider the role of exclusion in this logic of priva-

---

[6]   HF, esp. part I, ch.5.

[7]   A special case of this characteristic of privation is antisemitism as described by Sartre: Jews, in his opinion, are attributed all sorts of positive characteristics (intelligent, wealthy, powerful) which are a danger to mediocre men. The positive property denied here is mediocrity. See J.P. Sartre, *Réflexions sur la question juive* (Paris 1954), pp. 26-27.

tion. Understanding confinement as a particular form of exclusion, [4] explains that in Foucault's opinion exclusion does not function as an independent social phenomenon, but manifests on a practical level that the essence of privated things is nothingness. In this view exclusion is the practical manifestation of the logic of privation. It functions as *annihilation* in a double sense. Primarily, exclusion is the active execution of privative negation. It denies itself the property under discussion and thus annihilates the thing(s) or person(s) excluded by reducing them to **non-P**. In the second place, and this is emphasized by Foucault, it really annihilates the privated part as worthless. This point is also underlined by Sartre in his analysis of antisemitism. [8] For privation, as we have seen, is never a neutral operation, but will always value the privated part in a negative way. In this interpretation exclusion becomes one of the possible social manifestations — other ones are killing, correction and confinement — of an underlying conceptual partition, which operates according to the logic of privation.

Other quasi-privative relations

Why does the opposition *good-evil* [1] not establish a privative relationship? This opposition is a contrariety, as I showed in the preceding section. [9] In many theories, however, evil is conceived as the privation of good and not as a thing in itself. Thus the good has to become a real property of real things. The metaphysics underlying this assumption presuppose a fundamental unity of all beings. It is my assertion that 'good' first of all refers to the act of positive evaluation of the quality of a given thing and its properties, rather than to the thing itself or its properties. That is why good-evil in itself is not a privative relation *sensu strictu*

The same holds for the *true-false* opposition. It can be said that the falsehood of a judgement is a privation of an essential property of the judgement, i.e. its truth. This is correct, but holds only for the judgement as such, not for the state of affairs to which that judgement addresses itself.

---

[8]   Sartre, *op. cit.*, p.48.

[9]   See also note 4.

The state of affairs as such does not have truth as a real inherent property.[10] Only by hypostatising goodness and truth from transcendental
qualities into things in themselves or real properties, it becomes possible
to use these types of oppositions as privations. Foucault often does so,
when he speaks about oppression or exclusion of the false by the truth. He
uses this circumlocution to intimate that some forms of discourse, e.g.
scientific discourse, claim to be valid to the point of denying to other
forms the right to claim any truth at all.[11] Here, the dynamics of exclusion follows the same pattern that was analysed earlier with regard to the
opposition reason-unreason: truth is now conceived as a real and essential
property of discourse.

    The opposition between *self* (or *identity*) and *other* (or *alterity*) can
be analysed in a similar way. The other is not necessarily the privation of
the self, but only states a general un-alikeness of situations or things in
relation to each other. As Aristotle used to say: 'Everything in relation to
every other thing is either "the same" or "other"'.[12] When identity is seen
as a very special and unique quality possessed only by special kinds of
things — e.g. man in contrast with beast, or man as opposed to woman (as
exposed in De Beauvoir's *The Second Sex*), or people with identity cards
in contrast to gypsies or refugees — then it is possible to imagine alterity
as the absence of identity. In common parlance, however, 'other' used in
case of identity means another identity rather than its total absence. So it
is only in very particular cases that this self-other opposition can itself be
used as a privative relation.

    In sum: not all oppositions are privations, but it is possible to use
some oppositions in a privative way. If so, the opposite terms are seen as
the real property and its absence, and they are used in a process of
exclusion.

    However, this is not the same procedure as when all privative

---

[10]   Therefore I do not subscribe to the metaphysical theory of transcendentals,
where the one, the good, the truth and the beautiful as real properties of a being
can be transposed into one and other ('ens et verum, unum, bonum convertuntur').

[11]   I disagree with the interpretation that in stating a truth, the negation of
that truth is ipso facto *really* repressed or excluded from discourse. In this case
the *logical* relation of non-contradiction between a certain statement and all other
possible statements is confused with a real negative relation, in which case the
negated part must always be specified in relation to the topic under discussion.

[12]   Aristotle, *Metaphysics*, X.iii, 1054b15.

relations are valorized in such a way that the positive term is the good, the true or the self, and the negative term the bad, the false or the other. These valorizations make sense because privation concerns a property that the thing *ought* to have in order to be a 'good' or a 'true' thing. If this property is essential, it is can also be said that it constitutes the identity of the thing. What happens when this property is felt as a fundamental value, is shown in the fate of Reason in our culture; it can also be observed in many social groups' attempts to preserve their identity trough the process of exclusion as described above. There the general oppositions mentioned in the previous paragraph are interwoven in such a way that good, truth and self are also mutually identified in their exclusive identification with the property under discussion, which turns into the Good, the Truth and the Self. [13] As a result, not only the direct opposite of that property, but also *all* other things turn into privations of this one and only supreme being, unless they can be immediately identified with it. These other things in their turn will be identified with the primary privation itself. For instance: all types of non-rational behaviour are associated with unreason and madness (as per Foucault). The same can be observed in the case of properties of, for example, women, blacks, homosexuals or Turks, when they are all treated as mere privative negations of the properties of men, whites, heterosexuals or Dutchmen. [14] Under those conditions the vicious circle of blocked privation, as described in the foregoing pages, can take full effect. In the end the contents of both identities disappear in an endless game of reciprocal negations. This also is the case with the general privative relation between Self and Other mentioned by Foucault in the 1960s. [15]

---

[13] This is perhaps the origin of the theory of transcendental properties mentioned in note 10.

[14] I deliberately use different types of repressed groups or 'minorities'; the last example is the only one selected to give an example of a *cultural minority* as experienced by the Dutch. In fact a lot of so-called Turks in Holland are Kurds, who have fled from Turkey because of the repression of Kurdish culture there.

[15] See the introduction to *Les mots et les choses* (Paris 1966), and the articles on Bataille and Blanchot: 'Préface à la Transgression', *Critique*, 195-6 (1963): 751-769, and 'La pensée du dehors', *Critique*, 229 (1966): 523-546.

Let us sum up. In my opinion the logic of privation accounts for the following characteristics of a process of exclusion:

— the fact that the excluding part and the excluded part are conceived as irreconcilable;
— the fact that the excluded part is perceived in purely negative terms, having no property of its own but merely expressing the absence of the properties of the other;
— the valuation of these properties as good, vital, true, just or identity, i.e. as properties that one ought to have in order to be a real **P**;
— the fact that the properties of the excluded are experienced as strange, hidden, frightful and menacing;
— the fact that the properties of the positive part in their turn are experienced as a mere negation of these strange forces;
— the fact that exclusion itself (or confinement or annihilation) is executed as a social phenomenon.

Although these traits are easily recognized in various processes of social exclusion, I want to emphasize that a purely conceptual relationship of a very special character is operating here. For example: the fact that in the Classical Age all non-rational experiences and behaviour were conceived as *un*-reason was responsible for the phenomena of exclusion in that age. This is different from a situation in which, for example, rational and emotional behaviour are distinguished from, or even opposed to, each other, and are differently valorized. In the latter case the emotional a priori has its own characteristics, in the former case these characteristics are only the emptiness of reason, the 'hidden forces of negation' and their annihilating consequences. [16]

---

[16]   This also holds for the cases mentioned in the foregoing paragraphs. Thus the difference between man and woman in my opinion is primarily a polar opposition (from a biological point of view), which can be, and often is, treated as a privative one. In the case of blacks, homosexuals or Turks the privation is constructed from differences rather than oppositions.

Privation and exclusion as historically contingent phenomena

Thus far I have analysed the reason-unreason relation as a privative relationship. This accounts for several characteristics of the dynamics of exclusion as described by Foucault; it even accounts for the very process of exclusion. However, we should be wary of facile over-interpretation and generalization: not all types of social contrast or conflict can be seen in terms of exclusion and the logic of privation.

Foucault has stressed the important role of concepts (*savoir* and discourse) in cultures and social practices. As we have seen, this also holds for exclusion as a social practice itself. Foucault's technique of *conceptual bifurcation* in explaining historical phenomena has been seen at work in the case, described above, of the reason-unreason opposition. Other examples are the oppositions normal-pathological (in *The Birth of the Clinic*), self-other, true-false, conscious-unconscious (in *The Order of Things*), legal/normal/innocent vs. illegal/abnormal/guilty (in *Discipline and Punish*), heterosexual-homosexual (in *The Will to Truth*) and active-passive (in the last two parts of his *History of Sexuality*). Foucault treats all of these as binary oppositions and often discusses partitions created by them.

Some critics [17] have, not without good cause, pointed out that, in his hunt for binary oppositions, Foucault uses the structuralist technique of Lévi-Strauss. [18] However, I should like to stress that only some of these oppositions are privative relations — in which case they generate processes of exclusion — and that others work differently. The opposition between normal and pathological, for instance, is analysed as a radically novel way of coping with the old opposition between life and death. This opposition was formerly experienced as a privation (death as the absence of life); concomitantly, illness was conceived of as a privation of health. Conversely, modern medical outlook sees death as part of the life cycle, owing to the new scientific conception of the pathological as a *variation* in the physiolo-

---

[17]   Thus M. Cranston, 'Les "périodes" de Michel Foucault', *Preuves*, 209-210 (1968): 65-75, and Barthes in his review article of *Savoir et folie*, in *Critique*, 174 (1961): 915-922.

[18]   See C. Lévi-Strauss, 'L'analyse structurale', in Id., *Anthropologie Structurale* (Paris 1954, 1973), pp. 43-69.

gical processes.[19] Such an *inclusive opposition* between the normal and the pathological is an expression of a general tendency characterizing the modern era: to integrate otherness within the sphere of the self.[20] The same holds for the opposition between conscious and unconscious, even if the linguistic formulation ('un-') of this difference has a typically privative form. The freudian unconscious is not the absence of (the faculty of) consciousness in an individual, but the presence in the same person of consciousness *and* unconsciousness. Although the relation between those two is primarily negative (one of repression), they interact in a highly creative way. Moreover, they can both be analysed in their own operations.

This phenomenon of inclusive opposition shows that not every opposition or binary distinction can be analysed as a privative one. The importance of this point can be demonstrated in Foucault's works of the 1970s. In these he tried to develop a theory of positive power as a productive rather than repressive force; this is not possible when privative logic is used.[21] Another point suggested by these examples and confirmed by the last part of *Madness and Civilization* is the general thesis that the modern age is replacing exclusion by inclusion. This, too, is stressed in Foucault's later analysis of power, where the type of power relations prevailing in the pre-modern era (the repressive, juridical execution of power by the monarch) is contrasted with that modern disciplinary power which in every individual creates a trained body and a soul composed of the internalized mechanisms of correction and identity formation. Exclusion can easily be understood as a form of repression, but it is hard to combine with discipline. On the other hand, the analysis in *Discipline and Punish* shows that a combination of exclusion and inclusion is

---

[19]   Cf. my 'Biopolitiek en de gezonde mens', in *De gezonde burger*, ed. J. Rolies (Nijmegen 1988), esp. pp. 76-78.

[20]   This point is generally treated in *Les mots et les choses*, chapter 9.

[21]   The most important texts on this topic are: the beginning and part III of *Surveiller et punir* (Paris 1975), the two lectures of January 1976 published in *Histoire de la Sexualité, I: La volonté de savoir* (Paris 1976), chapter 4, sections 1 and 2; also the article 'The Subject and Power', originally published as annex to P. Dreyfus and H. Rabinow, *Michel Foucault. Beyond Structuralism and Hermeneutics* (Chicago 1982), pp. 208-226. An extensive treatment of Foucault's theories of power can be found in my *Waarheid als Macht* (*Te Elfder Ure* vol. 37/38, 1986).

responsible for the phenomenon of normalization. This process creates the identity or soul of modern man as the result of a constant process of control, differentiation and examination of the individual in relation to the established norms. [22] Apart from that, prison itself is a petrified expression of the survival of exclusion practices.

In sum, the privative relation and its social practice of exclusion seems to be a subspecies of the general feature of binary conceptual oppositions with their attendant social practices of identity formation. Foucault does not give a final account of the specific conditions responsible for the practice of exclusion, but seems to suggest that it is a survival of the premodern era.

Explaining exclusion: a methodological comment

The preceding section has shown that not every binary conceptual opposition results in exclusion. Foucault asserts in [4], that exclusion manifests a privative relation, 'an operation to annihilate nothingness'. Does this suffice to explain the phenomenon of exclusion ?

To begin with, not every privative opposition between a valorized property and its absence necessarily entails an exclusion, as the example of blindness shows. Furthermore, the appearance of excluding behaviour in all cultures is not sufficiently explained by the analysis of the underlying conceptual mechanism of privation. For it does not explain why some properties are experienced in this way, while other ones are not. The theory of privation only analyses the historical facts of exclusion. Foucault himself calls this type of explanation 'archeology' or 'diagnosis'. It describes the complex ties between a general sensibility, scientific knowledge, discourses and social practices, which together form the rationality of a given culture or a historical period. But it cannot account for the emergence of such a system, or for the occurrence and function of excluding behaviour as a general phenomenon.

Even the genealogical approach developed by Foucault in the 1970s

---

[22]   *Surveiller et Punir*, p. 201.

fails to satisfy. As Foucault himself puts it,[23] this approach describes the emergence of social phenomena out of the (social) practices and their mutations as a network of power relations. Power in general must be described as an organized set of actions restricting the field of actions of other actors; in the process it always tries to cope with differences by reducing them. Thence exclusion can be seen as one of the tactics of power, among other political tactics such as killing, submission, confinement, correction, discipline, normalization, persuasion and so on. Furthermore, the appearance of exclusion in the Age of Reason can be explained historically, as we have seen, by the type of power prevailing in that age. But that stills fails to account for the general appearance of processes of exclusion.

The historical, genealogical explanations given by Foucault would only suffice in two cases. First, if exclusion is confined to the privative relation between reason and unreason, that is to say, that it is confined to our western culture with its insistence on reason and its strong tie between reason and power (and there is enough evidence, I think, to consider such a limited application of the general phenomenon of exclusion overly restrictive). The second case presupposes that identity can only be moulded by a fundamental exclusion preceding it. This is the exclusion of the Other creating the Self. Foucault sometimes seems to suggest as much,[24] in accordance with other theories such as the transgression of Bataille, the foreclosure of Lacan and the *Seinsvergessenheit* of Heidegger. As I showed in an earlier section, this would amount to a sweeping generalization. In processes of identity formation the absence or presence of certain properties and their privative logic obviously play an important role. Nevertheless it is an fallacious generalization both to suppose that every opposition operating in this process is a privative one or could be reduced to one, and to hold that a concrete identity can *only* be formed by this play of oppositions.

So I conclude that Foucault's explanations take the fact of exclusion for granted and elucidate the conceptual mechanism involved in it and the historical conditions of its appearance. In combination they constitute a

---

[23]   See *Histoire de la sexualité*, II: *L'usage des plaisirs* (Paris 1984), pp. 17-18.

[24]   That suggestion is very strong in the 'Introduction' to the first edition of HF (p.7-9); the second edition has another Introduction in which this point is absent. See also the references to Bataille mentioned in note 15.

context-analysis of exclusion, resembling Foucault's 'analytics' of finitude, power and truth. Furthermore those other analyses prove, once again, that exclusion is not the overall mechanism responsible for all types of oppositions or conflicts.

Unmasking the exclusion: The privative traps of liberation

Foucault has never made it a secret that he intended to use his historical studies as a weapon (an ancillary context-analysis) in the struggles for power and liberation. This analysis and its results should be used as an instrument of liberation. The analysis of exclusion and especially the knowledge of the privative logic governing this process are, I think, very useful in that political struggle. They provide material and insights that are immediately applicable, much as the analysis of *Madness and Civilization* is used in the anti-psychiatric movement.

However, in my opinion their main function should be to prevent this struggle from being lured into the old fallacies of privative logic. As I pointed out, the dynamics of exclusion are characterized by fact that the privative relation is blocked. It becomes impossible to describe and experience in a positive way, either the properties of the excluded party, or the relevant property of the excluding party. This may also endanger the different tactics of liberation as well. One may try to achieve emancipation by proving that one is as normal as the excluding party (where 'normal' = any positively valorized P, e.g. reasonable, masculine, white, christian, human). This places one in the necessity of proving that one possess the denied property P; and it is obvious, then, that one is trapped in the definition and valorization of the opponent.

Another strategy of emancipation runs the risk of turning all the properties, except the central property, associated with the positive term of the privation into a mimesis. (Although unreasonable, a madman can also talk coherently; although not a person, a beast has identity; although not-white, a negro is smart; although not a man, a woman is strong; although not married, a homosexual can have a stable sexual relationship; etc. [25]).

---

[25]   This is an arbitrary sample of properties at stake in various exclusion processes.

More dangerous still is the opposite strategy of stressing one's own identity as the reverse of the properties characterizing the excluding party. Because this reversal is only experienced as negation, it is possible to create a world of reverse values, as Genet did in his *A Thief's Journal*. Moreover, the privation can simply be reversed without giving it positive content, as some radicalists do in stressing that whites, men, heterosexuals, etc. are inferior or should be extinguished. Also, one may stress one's own properties as strange or magic forces as mentioned by Foucault in [3]. In my view, Foucault's emphasis on otherness as a hidden truth beyond reason and ordinary language is a symptom of this type of strategy. The same applies to some feminist theories that stress the Otherness or mysterious forces of womanhood. In all these cases the liberating practice is perverted from the beginning, because it continues to be dependent on the definition and the block-up given by the privation.

As this privation is more generally defined and as more properties and values are associated with it, it will be more difficult to avoid these traps. I think it is necessary to counter these tactics of privation themselves, rather than the content of the privation. Theoretically this can be done by viewing the differences between things as instances of positive value, and by refusing to presuppose certain properties to be exclusively typical of a special group of things. Contrary to the ideas of Foucault and Deleuze during the 1960s, where it was held that thinking in terms of differences should rid itself of every contradiction or negation in general, [26] I maintain that careful distinctions must be made between different types of negation and that not all negations must overhastily be rejected as exclusions. I agree that a certain type of negation (namely, privation) should be avoided in thinking differences. In actual practice, the tactics of local resistance and the ongoing defence of one's own positive values and interests, are in my opinion the best method to break through the mechanism of privation and the processes of exclusion.

---

[26]   See G.Deleuze, *Logique du sens* (Paris 1966) and *Différence et répétition* (Paris 1968), and Foucault's reviews of these books: 'Ariane s'est pendu', *Le Nouvel Observateur*, 299 (31-3-1969), pp. 36-37; and 'Theatrum Philosophicum', *Critique*, 282 (1970). Cf. also his theory of events as expounded in *L'Archéologie du Savoir* (Paris 1969).

PHILOSOPHY AND THE MIRROR OF SEXUAL DIFFERENCE

Thea van der Kley

In this essay I take as a point of departure the position of a European philosopher between different discourses. My investigation concentrates on the differences in positions and conceptual schemes in feminist debates in Anglo-American and French texts. I will question the notion of the subject as a basic philosophical premise in both debates.

One can notice a peculiar similarity between the influence of recent French philosophy (often labelled Postmodernism) on Anglo-American feminist debates during the last decade, and the (equally) growing impact of analytical philosophy (logic, linguistics, philosophy of science) on the Dutch departments of philosophy, both on a textual and an institutional level. On the whole, knowledge is, like other aspects of Dutch culture, deeply influenced by Anglo-American ways of thinking. While studying social sciences I came to realize that 80% of the material to be studied was written in English. On the other hand, as a student of philosophy I became aware that almost 80% of the relevant literature was not of Anglo-American origin. When the primary focus on mainstream continental philosophy in Dutch departments of philosophy shifted to analytical philosophy, the whole faculty seemed to be split in two. Like a child, torn apart by divorcing parents, bound to both and raised by both, I began to wonder: where do they differ? When a similar dilemma arose in Dutch feminist debates as well (whether theory should concentrate on 'equality' or 'difference'), the split became an issue I could no longer neglect. There seem to be fundamental differences between these two traditions of thought. Instead of levelling them, it might be useful to focus on these differences where they are most noticeable: in the debates on sexuality. Would it be helpful to claim boldly that we are confronted with two different paradigms in a strict Kuhnian sense? [1]

From the sixties up to the eighties, Anglo-American and French feminist texts concerning sexuality were developed mainly within their own universe of discourse. [2] For the purpose of this paper my selection of texts is based on two decisions: I have limited my choice to texts from the mainstream reception of both Anglo-American and French studies in Europe; and I focus on those positions which present themselves as different only when compared to each other. I want to argue that, despite a great variety of inner differences on both sides, they share some fundamental assumptions which can only be made visible by confronting them with one another. 'Opposition' has recently been criticized as a strategy that involves meaning production, and a dichotomous approach risks the danger of a hierarchization of positions. [3] Even so, both 'bodies' of texts will be juxtaposed with respect to the following questions:

— Is there, due to a difference in theory-ladenness, a tendency to articulate markedly different positions in the exploration of the area of sexuality?

— Are these positions linked to different (hidden) conceptual schemes?

— Do these conceptual schemes bear on different (hidden) underlying philosophical premises?

---

[1]   'Strict', that is, as opposed to the widely criticized and even more widely persistent use of the word 'paradigm' in its vague and complex sense. By paradigm I understand 'some implicit body of intertwined theoretical and methodological belief that permits selection, evaluation and criticism', including explicit or implicit metaphysical beliefs (Thomas S. Kuhn, *The Structure of Scientific Revolutions* (University of Chicago Press, 1962), pp. 16-7).

[2]   I will not go into the recent mutual reception here, as this would require a different approach.

[3]   Mieke Bal, 'Language and its Motivations', in *Three Cultures* (The Hague: Universitaire Pers Rotterdam), pp. 31-43.

Stated Positions

Main Differences.

Schematically, the main differences may be outlined as follows: while Anglo-American feminists are shocked by the absence of woman's right to sexual pleasure, French feminism concentrates on the absence of adequate vocabulary to express it. Whereas the former undertakes a quest to reinstate and revalue the missing phenomenon, the so-called 'écriture féminine' is absorbed in descriptions of the sensual qualities of the individual female body. Female 'identity' is, by Anglo-American feminists, thought to be found in the forbidden area of sexuality (as outlined in the position of the libertarian feminists) while French feminists locate female identity in writing as an act of creation. While Anglo-American feminists are preoccupied with the (heterosexual) sex-gender system, and, in their attempts to analyse and to overcome it, become more or less defined by it, French feminists try to outline all those experiences which could not be lived due to barriers formed by linguistic phenomenon. The leading concept in Anglo-American feminism is 'sex and gender'. For French feminists it is *la différence sexuelle*.

Anglo-American Literature.

The 'classics' by Kate Millett and Germaine Greer partly uncovered and gave rise to the analysis of an objective view of both the female body and female inner experience, as well as the absence of cultural representation of female pleasure. [4] The overall response to this discovery has had an empirical character. The following may serve as representative examples: Mary Jane Sherfey's biological research on female orgasmic capacities; Shere Hite's well known (and widely criticized) 'nationwide study of female sexuality' to investigate the shared consensus of as many women as possible. Even the listing of titles appearing in a short period may be read as a sociological document: *Our Bodies, Our Selves, For Yourself, The Fulfillment of Female Sexuality, A Guide to Orgasmic Response, My*

---

[4]   Kate Millett, *Sexual Politics* (London: Virago, 1977 [1969]).

Secret Garden, Women's Sexual Fantasies.[5] The struggle to break away
from 'male-defined' sexuality, the many attempts to formulate and to return
to authentic female pleasure, is itself analysed as 'the tacit acceptance of
sexuality as identity and as the means to truth and liberation'.[6]

Only one step away from sexuality/identity on the personal level,
the framework can be found which organizes and restricts this undertaking.
Heterosexuality is analysed as a system on which social relations are
founded. Because they were translated early, the contributions of Adrienne
Rich (on compulsory heterosexuality) and of Gayle Rubin (on the traffic
of women) had a great impact on the Dutch feminist debates.[7] Rich's
point of view seems to be a condensed echo of the specific undertone
permeating many other studies, caused by the wide acceptance of
heterosexuality as the cultural norm.

French Literature.

A basic work of French feminist literature is Monique Wittig's *Les
Guerillières.*[8] This visionary book seems to anticipate many of the themes
that are later outlined in the texts of Luce Irigaray and Hélène Cixous.
Three features in this book are typical for *écriture féminine* as a whole: to
give birth to (to invent) another body, to create another myth, and to

---

[5]   Mary Jane Sherfey, 'On the nature of female sexuality', in *Psychoanalysis
and Women*, ed. Jean Baker Miller (Penguin, 1973), pp. 136-155; Shere Hite, *The
Hite Report* (New York: Dell, 1976); The Boston Women's Health Book
Collective, *Our Bodies, Our Selves* (New York: Simon & Schuster, 1972); Lonnie
G. Barbach, For Yourself; the Fulfillment of Female Sexuality. A Guide to
Orgasmic Response (New York: Jason Aronson Book Publisher, 1975); Nancy
Friday, *My Secret Garden. Women's Sexual Fantasies* (London: Virago, 1976).

[6]   Irene Diamond and Lee Quinby, 'American Feminism in the Age of the
Body', *Signs*, 10, # 1 (1984): 119-125 (122).

[7]   Adrienne Rich, 'Compulsory Heterosexuality and Lesbian Existence',
Signs, 5, # 4 (1980): 631-660; Gayle Rubin, 'The Traffic in Women. Notes on the
"Political Economy" of Sex', in *Toward an Anthropology of Women*, ed. Ranya
Rapp Reiter (New York: Monthly Review Press, 1975), pp. 157-210.

[8]   Paris: Minuit, 1970.

reclaim a position as a political, active person in history. [9] These features are realized by creating another language, another syntax, another grammar. From the very start, the denial of female pleasure is perceived as an effect of the exclusion of women from 'phallogocentric' discourse. It is felt that this repressed *parole de femme* (speech of/by a woman) should be articulated. [10] Hélène Cixous ponders over Grandfather Lacan's dictum that it is impossible for a woman to speak about her pleasure (*jouissance*), since what is not represented in language, does not exist. [11] Irigaray claims that woman's pleasure has to be unspoken, unsaid, because its articulation would threaten the very functioning of the Logos. The multifarious, non-ending pleasure of the female body, would, if outspokenly outspoken, unbalance the learned order of Unity and Identity. Women are separated from same-sex intimacies (mental and physical) to insure men's balance of power and to keep in place the phallogocentric universe in which they may function only in appointed places. [12] Not sexuality, but writing is the locus of change. [13] What has to be articulated is in the first place, the unspoken, censured 'narrative' of the female body. Along with female sensuality, a network of possible relationships and experiences are banned from reality. These impossible, imaginary relationships, female bonds, and mental fusions, are explored in a number of texts, the authors using every available style — litanies, psalmody, sermons, elegies, biblical metaphors — in order to undo (deconstruct) them as exclusive male options and to reinstate the forbidden female atmosphere. [14]

---

[9]   In my reading of French feminist literature I draw on interpretations (in Dutch publications) by Rina van der Haegen, Anjes Manschot Vincenot, Camille Montagne and Françoise van Rossum-Guyon.

[10]   Annie Leclerc, *Parole de Femme* (Paris: Grasset, 1974).

[11]   Hélène Cixous, 'Le sexe ou la tête?', *Les Cahiers du GRIF*, 13 (1976): 5-15.

[12]   Luce Irigaray, 'Pouvoir du discours/subordination du feminin' and 'Le marché des femmes', in Id., *Ce sexe qui n'en est pas un* (Paris: Minuit, 1977), pp. 65-82; 165-186.

[13]   Hélène Cixous, 'Le rire de la Méduse', *L'Arc*, 61 (1975: *Simone de Beauvoir et la lutte des femmes*): 39-54.

[14]   Luce Irigaray, *L'une ne bouge pas sans l'autre* (Paris: Minuit, 1979); Id., 'Quand nos lèvres se parlent', in *Ce sexe qui n'en est pas un*, pp. 203-207; Hélène Cixous, *Limonade tout était si infini* (Paris: Des femmes, 1983); Monique Wittig,

Conceptual Schemes

> *La différence sexuelle* versus sex and gender.

The leading concepts in Anglo-American and French investigations of the complex fields of sexuality differ. Moreover, both sets of concepts represent and refer to different epistemological frameworks. *La différence sexuelle* in French thought should be read in the context of contemporary French philosophy where 'la différence' is the fundamental metaphor. [15] Far more than presenting an extrapolation of a strict biological position — which is open to the reproach of essentialism — it has to be read and understood as a locus to decode and unbalance the existing production of meaning. In the style of Derrida, sexual difference (veiling polymorphic perverse positions of every human being) marks the edge (boundary) and possible rupture of philosophical logocentrism; it contains the strategy by which everything that seems evident can be 'deconstructed' and undermined. [16] In other words, the project of this philosophical undertaking is to undermine the social consequences of the production of meaning anchored in sexual difference. [17] *La différence sexuelle* is not a trivial empirical description, even less a (static) concept, [18] but a dynamic ontology without the involved classical claim for one (just One) Truth. One might compare its functioning with the blowing of the wind. 'Wind' can be hypostatized in language, but never in reality, 'blowing' can be measured, felt, foretold even, but you can never buy a box full of it.

With this metaphor in mind, we might perhaps say that, whereas the French are investigating the wind, the Anglo-Americans are occupied with its blowing. The distinction between sex and gender plays a dynamic, structuring role in Anglo-American theory. The meaning of the concept of

---

Le corps lesbien (Paris: Minuit, 1973).

[15]   Paul Laurent Assoun, ed. *Hedendaagse Franse Filosofen* (Assen: Van Gorcum, 1987).

[16]   Jacques Derrida, *Marges de la philosophie* (Paris: Minuit, 1972).

[17]   For an overview of difference as a concept, see Michele Barret, 'The concept of difference', *Feminist Review*, 26 (1987): 29-41.

[18]   Toril Moi, *Sexual/Textual Politics* (London: Methuen, 1985), p. 153.

gender is not fixed and seems to be changing with the development of this new and fruitful area of research.[19] Gender is usually traced back to Ann Oakley's *Sex, Gender and Society*.[20] Children who were seen as intersexed (often due to anatomically ambiguous external genitalia) adopted the gender identity ascribed by their parents, no matter what their 'real' biological sex was. This reaction stresses the fact that gender is a social construction. Many investigations from a social, cross-cultural and historical perspective try to outline and fix this premise.[21] In a way Simone de Beauvoir anticipated this idea, by declaring that women are made, not born. As in Oakley's sharp distinction between body and mind, nature and culture, gender carries the underlying assumption of a sexed body and an unsexed mind. Here an old rationalistic (Cartesian) inheritance seems to reach from the seventeenth into the twentieth century.[22] Joan Scott points to the often imprecise and different definitions of gender, including a range from persons ('women') to a system of relationships (*op. cit.*, pp. 1056-7). But whether gender is substituted for 'sex-role' or even 'sex', in all cases the shared assumption is that of an autonomous subject as a bearer of qualities 'a social category imposed on a sexed body'. This subject has a firm grasp of reality by defining the world, instead of being defined by it. In French philosophy, on the contrary, the subject is basically

---

[19]   For recent discussions, see Teresa de Lauretis, *Technologies of Gender* (Indiana University Press, 1987); Kathleen B. Jones and Anna G. Jonasdottir, *The Political Interests of Gender* (London: SAGE, 1988).

[20]   London: Temple Smith, 1972. Oakley in turn uses the insights formulated by Robert J. Stoller (*Sex and Gender*. New York: Science House, 1968), based on psychoanalytical descriptions of clinical encounters. In the footprints of Freud, Stoller refers to gender as "mental sexual characters" (p. viii).

[21]   Nancy Chodorow, *The Reproduction of Mothering* (University of California Press, 1978); Sherrie Ortner & Harriet Whitehead, eds., *Sexual Meanings. The Cultural Construction of Gender and Sexuality* (Cambridge University Press, 1981); Sandra Harding, 'Why has the Sex/Gender System Become Visible only now?', in *Discovering Reality*, ed. S. Harding & M. Hintikka (Dordrecht: Reidel, 1981), pp. 311-324; Joan W. Scott, 'Gender: A Useful Category of Historical Analysis', *American Historical Review*, 91, # 5 (1986): 1053-1075.

[22]   Kees Struyker Boudier, 'Van geslacht tot geslacht. Denken over seksualiteit', Unpublished thesis, Nijmegen University, 1985; Jean Grimshaw, *Feminist Philosophers* (Brighton: Wheatsheaf), p. 114.

seen as an effect, a product of language and culture. This means that the key to changing the world can be found in language, and less in changing patterns in social arrangements.

Circular versus linear discourse.

Language, the very tool of expression, plays a totally different part on the stage of these two discourses. On the French stage, the audience knows from the very start that the maid-servant is the leading lady. As for the Anglo-American stage, you never know; she might take over the plot some day. In French philosophy, language itself is no longer the vehicle of the drama, but the protagonist; it has left behind the linear discursive argumentative economy still predominant in Anglo-American thought. French feminists have broken with the habit of imposing their convictions on someone else, hence they no longer go by the rules which dictate the discursive game of power. Writing is seen as a process and this process is marked by a circular and deconstructive procedure. It is circular in the sense that one can start in the middle of a text and end whenever it feels right to do so. A theme may be approached from different perspectives, but not from a central question and not with the purpose to find an answer. Luce Irigaray's *Speculum: de l'autre femme* is an example of this approach. [23] Deconstruction contains a double strategy in which destruction of significance and construction of a new or other meaning is executed in one and the same gesture. As every textual position is just a knot in an intertwined textual system, there is no reason to refer to other texts, which are already, as it were, included in the texts one is writing or reading at the moment. [24] As the dominant framework for reflection, writing, teaching is the 'linear' one, this procedure is hard to describe. Being neither explained nor formalized, all texts are guided and judged by this invisible matrix. Opponents describe it as aiming at unity instead of plurality, fixed meanings instead of a multitude of meanings, instrumentality instead of diffuseness, closure instead of openness. The codes of linear discourse can be seen as the guard(smen) at the gateway of mainstream philosophy, with

---

[23]   Paris: Minuit, 1974.

[24]   This results in strange situations. Eric Blondel accused Derrida of 'borrowing' parts of his essay on Nietzsche without reference.

its claim of neutrality, objectivity, and truth. Sometimes it is identified with the analytic tradition in philosophy. In the words of Richard Rorty:

> Analytic philosophers, because they identify philosophical ability with argumentative skill and notice that there isn't anything they would consider an *argument* in a carload of Heidegger or Foucault, suggest that these must be people who tried to be philosophers and failed, incompetent philosophers. This is as silly as saying that Plato was an incompetent sophist, or that a hedgehog is an incompetent fox. Hegel knew what he thought about philosophers who imitated the method and style of the mathematicians. He thought *they* were incompetent. [25]

We touch on a problem with deep historical roots. Postmodern philosophical debates are in this sense an echo of the past. Feminist theory cannot escape from the powerful 'voice-over' of this echo. [26]

Sexuation du discours versus genderized vision.

The different styles or economies of language are, then, themselves conceptual schemes, since they have a great impact on the what, why, and how of chosen issues; they also structure that difference which I call 'sexed discourse' (*sexuation du discours*) as opposed to 'genderized vision'. The difference plays an important part in the 'theory-ladenness' of those two approaches: the Freudian reception which can be distinguished in the Lacanian version, versus the 'Americanized' Freudian (Object Relations Theory) approach. The connection between these two options, *sexuation du discours* and 'genderization of vision', lies in the fact that both analyse and use metaphors to criticize and provoke the 'phallogo-centric' 'male-biased' discourse, though they do this from different points of view.

---

[25]   Richard Rorty, *Consequences of Pragmatism* (Brighton: Harvester, 1982), p. 224.

[26]   Jane Flax, 'Postmodernism and Gender Relations in Feminist Theory', *Signs*, 12, # 4 (1987): 621-643. Linda Alcoff, 'Cultural Feminism versus Post-Structuralism: The Identity Crisis in Feminist Theory', *Signs*, 13, # 3 (1988): 405-436.

Let me first try to outline — in this limited space — what *sexuation du discours* stands for. It would take a book to elaborate on this critical approach to language in which Lacanian psychoanalytical insights operate alongside the highlights of French philosophy in an historical and epistemological sense.[27] Gender identity is acquired at the time that a child learns to speak and (from the Lacanian point of view) enters the Symbolic Order. As language structures and genderizes the unconscious, the unconscious is seen as 'sexed'. The claim of a neutral position is rejected as an illusion. The male unconscious bears the morphological marks of the male body. Language is marked by the dominance of the male libidinal economy whose characteristics are unity, linearity, self-identity ('le même'), teleology. This libidinal occupation and stage-managing of language is not admitted, but presented as 'human' and 'neutral'. There is not just an 'undercover' male sexual dominance in language that we, by repeating it, reproduce and reinforce. There is also a wish for One Truth, One Being, One Mind, One Symbol (the Phallus, or God, or classless society), all founded on the denial of the material (maternal) matrices. This wish is established in the form of the ap-propriation of the Symbolical in an epistemological disguise. The Logos is the *archê technê* (archetype) of a male-defined ontology.[28] But instead of opposing this *sexuation du discours*, *écriture féminine* dives into language and creates its own symbolism. This attitude is 'sex-biased' as well. Cixous creates (among many other inventions) the word *jouiscience* which combines *jouissance* (pleasure) with *science*. When Irigaray writes 'When our lips speak to each other/together', she refers to the mouth as well as to the female genitals.[29]

In French theory the lens of the morphological analogy with respect to the male body (Lacanian Phallus), language, and theory, brings into focus the deconstruction of leading metaphysical concepts: Truth, Being, Mind, and

---

[27]   Toril Moi is quite right in her mention of the 'heavy intellectual profile of French theory' (*op. cit.*, p. 96).

[28]   Luce Irigaray, 'Le langage "de" l'homme', *Revue Philosophique de la France et de l'Etranger*, 1987: 495-504.

[29]   Hélène Cixous, *Limonade tout était si infini* (Paris: Des femmes, 1983); Luce Irigaray, 'Quand nos lèvres se parlent', in Id., *Ce sexe qui n'en est pas un* (Paris: Minuit, 1977), pp. 203-217.

the analysis of dichotomy as the key model to meaning production, assuring the balance of power to one side.

The concept of gender seems to inspire another type of analysis. First, descriptions of gender-related values in science (power, control), subsequently a decoding of the genderization of metaphors in philosophy (for example, Nature as a bride) and of the metaphorization of gender characteristics, for example in biology. [30]

The received picture of metaphors stamped with feminine and sexual connotations can be reversed as well: hidden psychocultural gender-related aspects in the works of Plato, Descartes, and Rousseau, and their impact on epistemology, have been analysed in the context of object relations theory. [31] Thus, within the context of separation/individuation anxiety, Cartesian objectivism is 'explored as a defensive response to that separation anxiety, an aggressive intellectual "flight from the feminine" rather than (simply) the confident articulation of a positive and new epistemological ideal'. [32] It is hard to imagine what results the deconstruction of philosophy and 'the mirror of sexual difference' will bring in the future. Insofar as the connotation of gender referring to sex is not present, and, according to Teresa de Lauretis, totally untranslatable in any Romance language, [33] the 'genderized' vision may be a prerogative of Anglophone investigations.

---

[30]   Evelyn Fox Keller, 'Feminism and Science', *Signs*, 7, # 3 (1982): 589-602; Id., *Reflections on Gender and Science* (Yale University Press, 1985); Id., 'Language and Ideology in Evolutionary Theory. Reading Cultural Norms into Natural Law', in *Three Cultures* (The Hague: Universitaire Pers Rotterdam, 1989), pp. 17-31.

[31]   Jane Flax, 'Political Philosophy and the Patriarchal Unconscious: A Psychoanalytical Perspective on Epistomology and Metaphysics', in *Discovering Reality*, ed. S. Harding & M. Hintikka (Dordrecht: D. Reidel, 1983), pp. 245-282.

[32]   Susan Bordo, 'The Cartesian Masculinization of Thought', *Signs*, 11, # 3 (1986): 439-456.

[33]   *op. cit.*, p. 4.

Psychoanalysis: Lacan versus Object Relations Theory

Both Anglo-American and French feminist debates have been marked by a critical Freudian reception from the start. Both use psychoanalysis as a critical instrument for the benefit of women, although the users seem to wear different theoretical spectacles. Whereas French feminists refer to the Lacanian interpretation, many Anglo-American feminists are concerned with object relations theory. [34] Lacanian psychoanalysis does not offer much room for women: it is seen by feminists as the very epitome of the Western male power structure, with 'castration anxiety' as its crucial metaphor. Without women as supposedly castrated subjects, the myth would fall apart. When excluded from the Symbolic Order, the only place left for 'the feminine' is the Imaginary. One could object that *écriture féminine*, in the act of outlining the female unconsciousness, occupies the very locus which Lacan created for it. It is, as my 'Hegelian' (former) professor would say, a 'form of abstract negative relationship', meaning that the position is totally determined by what one opposes because other alternatives remain unexplored, even out of sight. [35]

Object relations theory postulates a developmental sequence in childhood with particular focus on the interrelationship between the capacity for sensuality and the development of object relations. The term is used to signify the belief that aspects of social relationships become internalized, become 'internal objects' for the self; the Freudian primacy on sexuality is rejected. The genesis of the subject is crucial: 'The process of becoming a self is one of drawing (such) boundaries, of differentiation and individuation, of learning both that one is a separate self and learning what sort of self one is.' [36]

---

[34]   Joan W. Scott, *Gender and the Politics of History* (Columbia University Press, 1983), p. 37.

[35]   'Relationship' is not the proper word. The Dutch *zich verhouden*, the German *sich verhalten*, the French *se rapporter à*, have no English equivalent that expresses a dialectic reciprocity.

[36]   Jean Grimshaw, *Feminist Philosophers* (Brighton: Wheatsheaf, 1986), p. 55.

The Subject at Stake

The striking difference, in my opinion, between the Lacanian interpretation of Freud and object relations theory as outlined by Chodorow — preceded by a postulated 'self' in ego-psychology — is that the former tears the subject apart, whereas the latter almost seems an inauguration of an autonomous subject, as a vehicle of qualities, close to the notion of 'substance' in traditional philosophy. Freudian theory is at the basis of both interpretations. [37] As a result of Lacanian theory the subject is seen as 'a network of imaginary identifications'. Whether in the concept of the 'mirror stage', where the child gets a first sense of coherence through identification with the image in the mirror, or in the act of speaking, where the unconscious may interfere with the imposed logic of the Symbolic Order, the subject is divided from its inner self. In many literary and philosophical French feminist texts this 'fragmented' subject is a point of departure. (Monique Wittig speaks of 'j/e'.) If there is anything that draws criticism from the Anglo-American side, it is this notion of a fundamentally split and 'fractured' subject. [38] On the other hand, the notion of an 'autonomous' subject as a coherent self underlying this criticism may be questioned as well. It is indeed, by observers from other cultures like Takeo Doi who investigated Japanese feelings of indulgence versus Western individualism: 'It is extremely difficult to have a self.' [39] It is also questioned by American philosophers. For example, Elizabeth Wolgast criticized the 'Atomistic view' (society as a simple collection of separate individuals) for having created a social myth of its own, involving 'the ultimate worth of individuals and the derivation of social values from them, the responsibility of individuals for their own actions, the value of individual freedom and independence and the right to pursue one's own

---

[37]   Paul Moyaert, 'Over het ik bij Freud en Lacan', *Tijdschrift voor Filosofie*, 45, # 3 (1983): 388-420.

[38]   Nancy Hartsock, 'Foucault on Power, A Theory for Women?', in *The Gender of Power*, ed. M. Leyenaar et al. (Leiden: Vakgroep Vrouwenstudies FSW/VENA, 1987), pp. 98-121; Barbara Christina, 'The Race for Theory', *Feminist Studies*, 14, # 1 (1988): 67-80; Linda Alcoff, 'Cultural Feminism versus Post Structuralism', *Signs*, 13, # 3 (1988): 405-436.

[39]   Takeo Doi, *The Anatomy of Dependence. Exploring an Area of Japanese Psyche. Feelings of Indulgence* (Tokyo: Kodansha International, 1973), p. 140.

desires.' [40] The analysis of society as a collection of separate individuals can only be made from the viewpoint that other ways of perceiving humankind, including another definition of the subject, are possible. Whether the concept of the subject is theoretically constructed (as fragmented) or derived from a set of moral values (as autonomous), the concept seems to locate the heart of a paradigm shift: the disconnected hinge between two separate discourses.

In this essay I have tried to turn my cognitive dissonance into an intellectual advantage. Considering the Anglo-American and French feminist theories as separate paradigms has been a fruitful approach to me. Now for the answer to my question:

I have tried to point out that there is an inclination to outline different positions due to a difference in theory-ladenness. In fact the field to be studied is so wide and complex, that one can only point out tendencies here and there. The major positions are linked with different conceptual schemes which guide selection and evaluation. 'Gender' and *la différence sexuelle* reflect the theoretical frameworks in which they are embedded. The very topic of sexual difference is already mirrored, and mediated, by conceptual and cultural representations. The conceptual schemes I have mentioned can be seen as basic patterns which express, reflect, and confirm the subject's attitude towards itself and the surrounding world. The notion of the subject, whether perceived as fragmented or as autonomous, acts as the underlying philosophical premise in both debates. This does not imply that it is taken for granted. To be more specific, the circular approach to language, for example, can only be *practised* by a subject who experiences itself as surfing on the waves of mighty cultural, political, and philosophical discourses, and not as master of the world. [41]

---

[40]   Elizabeth H. Wolgast, *Equality and the Rights of Women* (Cornell University Press, 1980), p. 141.

[41]   Research for this essay was supported by STEO at The Hague in 1988/89.

BETWEEN STRUCTURE AND CONTEXT:
SOURCES, SOURCE CRITICISM, AND ALTERITY STUDIES

Jean Kommers

> 1. Wir sehen und suchen weit
> 2. Durch viel Gefährlichkeit
> 3. Nicht ohne Krieg und Streit
> 4. Die abgelegne Leut
> 5. Und ihre reiche Beut.

Introduction

The above motto is from the engraved frontispiece (reproduced overleaf) of J.J. Saar's *Ost-Indianische fünfzehen jährige Kriegsdienste*, the second edition (1672). It reflects a seventeenth-century western colonial world- view in a nutshell. Peoples from afar are characterized as purveyors of riches, which, however, are not freely offered to the westerners but have to be fought for.[1] The Europeans take those riches as the proper reward

---

[1] There is a notable contrast between this type of frontispiece and those in compilations about firmly 'conquered' or dominated areas, e.g. the allegorical engraving in front of Baldaeus 1672, which symbolizes political relations rather than a warrior ethos. Although in the 1670s the two types coexist, Baldaeus's frontispiece points to the future: it symbolizes great promise as a result of good relations with mighty rulers in the East, whereas Saar's engraving symbolizes a more conservative tendency — which gives it its illustrative value.

for bravery, as a token of courage. Thus the European warrior ethos is both a condition for and a justification of the capture of oriental riches.

As such this device unifies a central value of the seventeenth century and an age-old myth. It also reflects the contents of the book: it characterizes Saar's fortunes. He was one of the many foreigners sent by the Dutch to fight for the commercial empire in Asia. Their share consisted mainly of *Gefährlichkeit* and *Krieg und Streit*. Sometimes they caught a glimpse of the *reiche Beut*, of the fabulous riches of an eastern despot or of the proverbial fertility of the country. But no more did these riches belong to the ordinary people in these far-off countries, than that they were available for the common soldiers employed by the East India Company. These men had to restrict themselves mainly to *sehen und suchen*. Yet their accounts contributed much to the consolidation of the myth, or even reinforced it. The descriptions pretended to be informative but were highly subjective. They show the other world from the European perspective which implicitly legitimizes the specific relationship with the other world. As such the motto articulates an image of the other world in a way that made it comprehensible and manageable for eyewitnesses like Saar, as well as for those who stayed at home. Yet it hardly covered the experiences of both groups. Eyewitnesses often became alienated from the western perspective after a lengthy stay in the tropics (Saar stayed in the East for fifteen years continuously); the readers' experience was limited to a single exotic element and an important oral tradition, which, however, we have lost for ever and which will always remain a mystery to us.

Nearly always the printed accounts of travels and adventures in strange lands were the result of 'mediation' (as a rule accomplished by the editors [2]) between both worlds of experience. In this process of mediation

---

[2]   Because of this — and of other aspects, specific to printed sources — bibliological accuracy is of great importance. As an example I refer to Peter Mason's recent article about Lafitau's *Zeden der Wilden*. In the absence of any mention of the first Dutch publication (by Van der Poel, 1731), Mason's reference to the Welbergen/Charlois edition gives the impression that this is the first one. At first glance this detail may look trivial, but seen as part of the history of the book it is important: in but seven years after the original edition, the enormous task of translating and producing the book had already achieved. Quantitative and qualitative details about the production of the two editions (and the relations between them) shed an interesting light on the way the book was received, or on the publisher's expectations (thus the first edition also comprised an issue of de-

cultural (and especially specific literary) conventions played a major role. This is one of the reasons why these sources may not be considered as a 'mirror', as a direct reflection of the author's mind and times. And even if it seems to be justified to use the concept of reflection, one needs to realize that, as a rule, the text reflects a time already bygone at the moment of publication. This 'conservative quality' is one of the dimensions of printed sources which deserve special attention in interpretation, particularly in interpretation serving the analysis of images.

A most illuminating example of that 'conservative quality' is offered by James Howell's *Instructions for Forreine Travell* (1642), a small book well-known for being the first English travel guide for the Continent, but which — alas — in anthropology never received the attention it deserves. Howell describes the discovery of an unknown people in the heart of Spain. It was a 'naked Savage people', living in 'a large pleasant Valley'. 'As simple and Savage they were, as the rudest people of the two *Indies* [...]' (Howell 1642: 134-5). Alva's falconers, who made the discovery, reported to their master that they had found a 'New World'. At first sight the way in which Howell explicitly links this newly discovered people [3] to the Indies seems to furnish us with an apt illustration of the seventeenth-century image of the Americas. Those recently discovered naked savages could adequately be represented as the cultural antipodes of the civilized urbane Spaniards by using the image of the American Indians, who after all were savages *par excellence*. Yet, in my opinion, such an interpretation would be false: Howell used the concept of

---

luxe copies on large paper, a detail not even noticed by Tiele 1884). Another problem is the way in which Mason conjectures a motivation behind the explanation added to the frontispiece: according to him, Lafitau had his doubts about the exegetic capacities of the readers. In fact such explanations of allegorical frontispieces were a mere convention, which existed far into the nineteenth century. As a rule, those explanations were not written by the author, but by the publisher, possibly with the aid of the artist. Although it seems certain that Lafitau had his hand in the technical explanations to the other plates, I doubt his role in the explanatory text to the frontispiece; that doubt is only strengthened when reading the original edition. (Mason 1990: 245).

[3]   They are described in terms of contrast with civilized people like the Spaniards: they are *Troglodites*, lack weapons and only have 'slings'; they worship the sun and the moon, their language is incomprehensible and they have swarthy complexions.

the Indies as a conventional term. As O.H. Green put it, 'almost a century after 1492, the word *Indies* had become a part of the vocabulary'; the meaning of the concept had widened very much and it could be used to designate something strange, something wonderful. The expression even acquired a religious connotation: the 'Divine Indies' (Green 1965: 27ff).

The importance of source criticism

Among anthropologists old ethnographic descriptions and travelbooks have a bad reputation. With the exception of ethnohistorians, anthropologists make little use of these sources for ethnographic research because of their reputed lack of reliability. If such sources are used, it is as a rule for the study of images about other peoples. It is revealing that old ethnographic texts, printed before the development of scientific anthropology, are generally considered obvious sources for the study of the formation of images. In those studies problems of interpretation, which often prove to be prohibitive for factual ethnographical analysis, no longer need — as the assumption goes — to bother the researcher. For the subject is not the 'factual truth' (difficult to find in 'unreliable' sources), but the 'distorted truth', which, it is assumed, presents itself directly to the reader. I think this idea is a little naive: spontaneous, 'direct' interpretation — even in the search for images rather than ethnographic facts — is destined to end in failure: psychologisms, anachronisms and images of images. A notorious example is Pott's book on the 'development' of Dutch images of foreign parts (Pott 1962). [4]

Besides this kind of research, aiming at the revelation of 'historical images' — as these once existed in the heads of the people - there is another approach which deserves our attention: it starts from the idea that the sources reflect the mentality of the people who constructed them. This

---

[4]   In criticizing Pott one has to keep in mind that his study was one of the first to return to those sources which were highly respected by earlier colonial historians, but which had fallen in oblivion after decolonization and its traumatic aftermath (following the independence of Indonesia) had caused serious stagnation in the development of colonial history. Even so, I refer to the book as an example of poor interpretation because of the influence it still has, especially in circles of ethnographic museums.

assumption that the sources give more information about ourselves than about the peoples and cultures described, is widespread to such a degree that Duviols (1985) thought a warning expedient:

> [...] il serait excessif, et en partie inexact, de ne considérer les récits de voyage que comme des documents sur l'histoire des mentalités européennes, ce qui limiterait singulièrement leur portée.

Those travel books not only form 'une source de rêves', but also

> une référence irremplaçable, le reflet d'un passé historique et anecdotique dont le sens nous échapperait en partie sans ces témoignages, approfondis ou superficiels, bienveillants ou méprisants, sur des événements historiques, sur des conflits politiques, sur la vie sociale et matérielle, enfin sur les moeurs et les croyances de peuples 'étranges', souvent à jamais disparus (p 13).

Harbsmeier, who argues in favour of the use of travel literature as sources for the history of mentality — indeed, he considers this type of literature as most appropriate for that kind of research - proves to be aware of the problems of interpretation connected with the specific use of sources (Harbsmeier 1982: 11). He notes that the originators of the use of travel literature for the sake of a history of mentality give one the suspicion that they

> [...] um sich der Mühe einer quellenkritischen Überprüfung des Wahrheitsgehaltes der Reisebeschreibungen entziehen zu können, oft Gewalt haben anwenden müssen, um die unüberschaubare Vielfalt der in den Reisebeschreibungen auftretenden Andersartigkeiten auf die binären Stränge einer Logik der asymmetrischen Gegenvorstellungen festnageln zu können. (p. 7)

In his article Harbsmeier aims at structural analysis, of which, by the way, he is an important advocate. Unfortunately he fails to address the problem of source-criticism:

> Aber wie auch immer man im einzelnen zu dieser Frage Stellung nehmen mag, so scheint mir doch erwiesen zu sein, daß der in diesen Arbeiten vertretene Zugang zu Reisebeschreibungen als mentalitätsgeschichtlichen Quellen einen wesentlichen Beitrag zur

Erforschung von der durch andere Quellen kaum erschließbaren
kulturellen Selbstverständlichkeiten zu leisten imstande ist. (p. 7)

I do not doubt this point at all, but it seems unwise to ignore the problem
or to assign it to separate cases. Some forms of external source criticism
are indispensable for the kind of research Harbsmeier proposes: for
example, those types which may help to determine the character and the
situation of the source. Before explaining this opinion in detail, I shall try
to indicate why source criticism is indispensable for the kind of structural
analysis Harbsmeier aims at. To phrase my argument simply: the less a
researcher realizes the quality, the character, and the historical position of
a source, the greater the risk that during the process of interpretation —
which often implies decoding, and (re)-construction — the researcher's
(theoretical) presuppositions will gain dominance. In particular in
structuralist analysis this risk is serious because of the intricate relation
between the 'mind of the author' and that of the researcher. In other words:
where does the construction of the historical author end, and where does
that of the interpreter begin?

Between structure and context: the image as research topic

In social contact, people tend to reduce the complexity of reality. This also
holds for the perceptions of the Other. In case of regular contact or of
frequent perception, simple stereotypical representations of that reality are
useful for conduct and serve the distinction between self and other(s).
During the process of contact this coherence affects observation in a way
that stereotypical representations become self-validating: one may think of
a tautological circuit.

In form as well as in substance, the representations originate under
the influence of structural principles, which may be postulated on a
paradigmatic level. By way of certain mechanisms (cognitive principles,
projection, metaphorical or metonymical relations) which influence the
structural principles, images or stereotypes are formed on a narrative
(syntagmatic) level: the level of social or theoretical discussion.

Both paradigmatic and syntagmatic analysis aim at the concrete
manifestations of the images, which, in turn, also validate the analysis. In
both cases those manifestations (I restrict myself here to printed texts) are

interpreted, constructed as a *case*, a research topic. Of course, those texts are not in themselves adequate units for analysis, but they are established as such from a specific perspective. The texts may not be considered as reservoirs of images which manifest themselves in an unequivocal way in those texts — a supposition often encountered in naive studies on images, such as mentioned above - but they contain elements which, when viewed from certain theoretical presuppositions, may be considered as indications for images. The image a researcher eventually takes from a text and uses as a unit of analysis or as an illustration always is partial and subjective. Much as the participant creates an image, which s/he considers as representative for reality, so too does the researcher construct — on the basis of narrative and iconographic manifestations — a case in point, a research topic which is considered as representative of the (historical) image.

A high risk of anachronistic interpretation is present if a structural-anthropological analysis pays insufficient attention to the specific narrative organization of the images. Starting from a theoretical perspective, a series of binary oppositions can be deduced by using a great variety of texts. Often the fact that those oppositions may be traced in the most diverse sources (sometimes from very different periods in time) is considered as an indication for the 'strength' of the method. Perhaps this is the reason for the idea that source-criticism is not very relevant to this kind of analysis. In this view source-criticism is a method for ascertaining the 'veracity' of the source; and to the structuralist this factual truth is not the most relevant quality of the source.

Even so, I think that because of at least two reasons the historical context as revealed in the narrative organization of the image deserves our attention.

In the first place there is the fact that the same (universal) structural principles which influenced the formation of the historical image may have an unnoticed effect on the construction of the image-as-topic. Of course, given the scientific character of the way in which the topic has been constructed, we may expect a certain restraint of the psychological mechanisms mentioned above; but the risk of circular reasoning remains unchecked as long as the exact relationship between the historical image and the image-as-topic remains unclear. The impression of tautology is particularly strong in research in which swift changes in level of analysis are combined with constant references to concrete historical manifestations of images, used as 'illustrations'.

My second reason to stress the necessity of attention for the historical context (in particular as regards the syntagmatic level) concerns the use anthropologists often make of structuralist studies of images: to gain an understanding of the development of mentality. In that type of research problems of periodicity and of representativeness often are underestimated. These problems are easily recognized in quantitative research, but in my opinion they may have serious methodological consequences in qualitative research too. Obviously the role of source criticism in the mentality-historical research of images differs from its more traditional purpose (i.e. ascertaining the veracity of the available information).

Some of the problems outlined here are technical ones, pragmatic rather than fundamental. Thus, in structural analysis it may be permitted to 'put aside' the exact status of a text. But as soon as the researcher wants to illustrate the effect of the structuring principles by using a specific text, the particular status of that text can no longer be ignored. This is, of course, particularly clear in syntagmatic analysis. Indeed one other reason why source-criticism is underappreciated in the anthropological study of image-formation is that in this branch of study the importance of syntagmatic analysis is underrated. [5]

Until the development of epistemological criticism (resulting, for instance, in experimental ethnography, cf. Van Maanen 1988: x) there was widespread consensus, especially among those anthropologists who were impressed by the notion of a 'crisis' in the social sciences, that texts about other cultures should be considered as tautological: as self-reproducing. It would be an illusion to think that the increase of the number of texts also meant a growth of knowledge. Focusing on the narrative aspect of ethnography it will be clear that this idea is untenable. One aspect is of particular importance for the study of the formation of images: the social dimension. Thus, to register variations in narrative structure and context, a series of texts — even if those texts seem identical in content — is more than mere reiteration. Indeed, on a social level the accumulation of texts may have given an impression as if they represent a growing body of

---

[5]   In this respect I fully agree with Corbey (1989: 82), who, in his important study on the European colonial image of Africa pays due attention to that level of analysis. In passing, I would like to add that recent ideas concerning experimental ethnography (because of the attention paid to ethnography-in-discourse) are very promising for the interpretation of old ethnographies.

knowledge. Therefore they are of importance for the conative dimension of the formation of images. In addition to this, a greater variety of texts permits — contemporaneously as well as *post hoc* — a greater 'symbolic load': a greater variety of (experienced) contents, and as a consequence more interpretations.

More fundamentally problematic than these 'pragmatic' issues is the idea that the image-as-topic is a construct of a construct. The scientific construct (the research topic) is an interpretation which pretends to decipher. But that deciphering always takes place within a social or ideological context which, in turn, inevitably affects the interpretation. Moreover, the topic is epistemologically linked with the 'scientific context', which in part depends on the social or ideological context. The researcher's social attitude (e.g. his or her social criticism) not only influences the selection, but also determines — at least in part — the perspective used.

The analysis of sources resulting in the identification or description of the topic is subject to many epistemological factors: to mention only the conceptual apparatus or factors determining the level of interpretation. For instance, the *topoi* which characterized fifteenth- or sixteenth-century descriptions of other cultures were strongly related to the memory-based topoi developed in the middle ages. The prominent position of the *memorabile* and the *insigne* in the early descriptions of the 'New Worlds' easily confuses present-day anthropologists, as does the specific qualitative character by which these descriptions distinguish themselves in a fundamental way from the modern type of (analytical/synthetical) ethnography. Incidentally, that is why it may be of interest to study topic-constructs borrowed from a period very different from ours, as I shall argue further on.

The interpretation of ethnographic sources not only depends on an adequate knowledge of the historical context, but also on a clear insight into the specific literary and epistemological characteristics, which qualify the source as representing a specific genre.

All this means that we should pay careful attention to the process of interpretation. Insofar as anthropologists are accustomed to pay special attention to methods of interpretation as part of their research on the formation of images, their attention is focused either on level their sources or on that of analytic procedure. The first case mainly concerns the 'direct approach', already qualified as naive (the assumption that the sources betray the images people once had 'in their heads', and which may be made manifest with the help of some form of psychologism). If source criticism is applied at all in this kind of research, it is mainly among ethnohistorians.[6] The second case mainly concerns 'analytical approaches'. These pay much attention to the interpretation process as set forth in various theories, but use the sources indiscriminately. As we saw in the case of Harbsmeier, source criticism is considered only incidentally significant. This kind of research also runs a risk of naivety: to underrate the importance of (external) source criticism in general implies the risk of overrating the force of theory, reflected in the opinion that the possibility to analyse indiscriminately an endless variety of sources from the most distant periods in history may be seen as an indication of the 'force' of the method used. In fact this 'force' results from ignoring problems concerning the interrelations among sources and problems of periodicity (*Quellenlage* and *Quellensequenz* to use concepts from the German tradition — see for instance Bernheim's classic handbook, 1908), or a question such as: to what kind of operations does to use a special type of source entitle us?

Interpretation decisively affects the process of topic construction; we may be sure that there is an inverse proportionality between our critical ability in interpretation and the uncontrolled influence of ideological or theoretical presuppositions and aspirations. Perhaps source criticism in the traditional sense may indeed be of limited use for structuralist research or for mentality history; but in an indirect way many of the very sensitive and ingenious procedures of source criticism may be of great value to explicitize qualities of a given case/topic which would otherwise remain unnoticed and therefore beyond control.

Relevant types of source criticism

It is not my aim to specify concrete techniques of source criticism. Instead, I would like to elaborate some implications of the foregoing argument. If we recognize the significance of source criticism for the study of image-formation, the question becomes: which procedures may be used, and in

---

[6]   Cf. Szalay 1983. Of course this does not mean that all ethnohistorians are naive! On the contrary: only a few of them use the 'direct approach'.

which way?

To define the 'topic' in another way: the topic is the source(-information) conceptualized according to ideological, social, and scientific values and perspectives of the researcher. Although as a rule the researcher will perceive the sources themselves as starting point for his or her analysis, at the very moment he or she locates the 'facts' and research units, the information becomes reconstructed under the values and perspectives mentioned. As this process of 'reconstruction' as a rule goes unnoticed (is 'unconscious'), it is very difficult to control: this would involve making explicit the exact operation of various relevant values and perspectives. This insight is essential in determining the required techniques of interpretation.

Because of the prominence of social/cultural influences (including 'scientific' ones) in the formation of the topic, it may be useful to start with an analysis of some 'topic-constructions' derived from another social or cultural context, e.g. from another historical period. Such constructs differ greatly from modern research with respect to social and scientific context, and differ from each other in one or more identifiable aspects. Such an analysis may best start with so-called secondary sources: works which are based on the same or on related 'primary sources', and which offer an interpretation from a specific social, ideological and scientific viewpoint comparable to — but different from — our own. On the one hand, such a study offers the possibility to distance us from unconscious tendencies or from social and epistemological influences upon our own studies, which may be difficult to comprehend and control from our own contemporary perspective. On the other hand, the confrontation with values and ideas unfamiliar to us may help us to ascertain the specific importance of the various influences mentioned. In this way we may identify the usefulness of certain forms of source criticism.

By way of illustration I mention two books which, in my opinion, would be very suitable for such a study. [7] Both are late-sixteenth-century works offering 'second-hand' descriptions of newly discovered worlds.

---

[7]   This suggestion stems from an analysis of sixteenth-century Portuguese and Spanish chronicles on which I am currently engaged. The aim of this research is to compare secondary descriptions of Western Africa and South America in order to explain differences in taxonomy and narrative structure manifest in those two descriptive traditions.

The first book is Osorio da Fonseca's *De Rebvs Emmanvelis* (1571), the most widely-read Portuguese book in sixteenth-century Europe (Bosch 1983: 50). Boies Penrose, the prominent student of the history of exploration, has called Osorio's chronicle well written, but devoid of anything new (Penrose 1952: 281). Indeed, the book is of little use for a student using the 'direct approach'. In his time, Osorio was well known as the Portuguese Cicero (Bell 1922: 209). His aim was to underline the significance and grandeur of Portugal, starting with the reign of Emmanuel I. Only little attention is paid to the internal history of Portugal: most of the chronicle is devoted to the overseas expansion. The story of military actions and nautical vicissitudes is interspersed with descriptions of the newly discovered peoples, in which Osorio also pays attention to the perceptions, attitudes and emotions of the discoverers. He took his information from a variety of sources. Even during the mid-sixteenth century an 'ethnographic tradition' concerning the description of the various regions was already taking shape, and chroniclers tended to use more and more the same 'corpus' of primary sources. Osorio too added little or nothing to the existing geographical knowledge. But he did more than only copying: he fitted the relations of conquerors and explorers into a specific historical framework, into a specific world view. This is evident in the ornamental language used by Osorio in describing the perceptions and emotions of the discoverers. As the book was widely read throughout Europe, it played a role in the formation of the image of the newly discovered areas in Africa, South America and Asia. The book was also important because at that time original literature about the discoveries was rare outside private collections (cf. Lach 1977: 39-48; Atkinson 1927; Borba de Moraes 1958). I have used the much augmented translation by De Senlis (1581), which has been reprinted many times (cf. Lach 1977: 25).

The other work, Jan Huygen van Linschoten's *Beschryvinghe* (1596) sharply differs in narrative structure from Osorio's humanistic chronicle. This book, originally a part of the famous *Itinerario*, contains the first Dutch compilation about America, composed of Spanish and Portuguese travelogues and histories, and of early descriptions, such as Thevet's (1558) and De Lery's (1578). With respect to the background and context of this book, I refer to the critical edition by Burger and Hunger (1934).

These two sources — being but two out of many possibilities — pretended to give 'true facts', to be used by scholars, politicians, and, in the case of Van Linschoten, by seafarers. As such we may consider them as compilations of historic topic-constructs. The contrast between the two works may help us to explicitize structural differences in the verbalizations of the images: differences to be explained by specific characteristics of the sources. Those characteristics depended on the social, ideological and scientific climate in which the authors worked. Now, to identify those characteristics in detail, source criticism offers a series of useful standard techniques. Techniques which may be used 'indirectly' ('heuristically') to ascertain what I have called the character and historical position of the source.

Thus, Osorio's book contains countless ornamental phrases, which according to the critique of reconstruction may be considered as 'interpolations' and as such may be regarded as negative indications for the 'value' (in the sense of veracity or of reliability) of the source. Of course, this conclusion is not relevant to the type of research we have in mind, but this form of source criticism may help the researcher to trace those 'interpolations', to evaluate them systematically from the point of view of a narrative analysis, and to relate them to other qualities of the source which are in fact relevant to this kind of analysis. For example, the ornamental phrases in Osorio's text (such as in the description of Da Gama's meeting with the lord of Goa — 1581 ed.: 39) often initiate digressions which shed light on the relation between Self and Other. If we choose to ignore this narrative dimension, we might agree with Penrose's aforementioned opinion; but his approach is of little use to the student of images and mentalities. On the other hand, syntagmatic analysis, departing from the insight that a work like Osorio's is much more than only the product of 'literary copying', may open up many perspectives unnoticed by scholars like Penrose. But even the most recent studies, where due attention is paid to a syntagmatic approach, exhibit a generic vulnerability to problems of interpretation. The dilemma between interpretative and syntagmatic naivety may be overcome if we take recourse to procedures such as analysing and contrasting historical topic constructs in order to find alternative ways of using traditional, but often ingenious techniques.

Conclusion

In an old textbook on historical research the aim of source criticism is defined as determining the 'moral' irrefutability of information (Philippen

1942: 59). Internal and external source criticism should fix 'the value' (the reliability, veracity) of sources. Evidently Philippen did not realize that 'the value' is only a relative quality, related to a specific idea of history. An alternative view on history would not make source criticism useless, but would lend it a new dimension, e.g. a heuristic one, as illustrated above. Of course, the significance of certain forms of source criticism for every kind of historical research is manifest. For instance, if we neglect semantic criticism or analysis of relations between sources, we inevitably will commit serious mistakes in interpretation (witness Pott 1962, that classic example of the 'direct approach' to image formation). My use of the concept of topic should not complicate the problems of interpretation unnecessarily. The main function is to stress one specific problem: the study of image formation is particularly vulnerable to social, ideological, and scientific values. Not only are images themselves often loaded with values (certainly in the case of images of the Other); research into those images is also unlikely to be wholly immune to, or free from, values. What is more, this (historical) research depends on sources, written in times in which those values were very different from ours. Therefore it is important to realize that what *we take for our starting point* in our analysis (the 'facts' or the 'historical images') *is already a construct,* a mid-way point between the historical facts — which always remain distant - and the structure which we ourselves impose through our analysing activity. This construct (our research topic) in its turn is the result of interpretative activities which often remain unnoticed ('unconscious'). Critical reflection upon this construct gives us an additional focus on the problems of interpretation. To reify the concept of image-as-topic, it goes without saying, would be a serious mistake.

Bibliography

G. ATKINSON, 1927-1936. *La littérature géographique française de la Renaissance; répertoire bibliographique* (Paris).
PH. BALDAEUS, 1672. *Naauwkeurige beschryvinge van Malabar en Choromandel, der zelver aangrenzende ryken, en het machtige eyland Ceylon* (Amsterdam).
A.F.G. BELL, 1922. *Portuguese Literature* (Oxford).
A.F.G. BELL, 1928. 'The Humanist Jeronymo de Osorio', *Revue Hispanique,* 73: 525-6.
E. BERNHEIM, 1908. *Lehrbuch der historischen Methode und der Geschichts-*

philosophie: mit Nachweis der wichtigsten Quellen und Hilfsmittel des Studium der Geschichte. (5. und 6. Auflage; Leipzig; orig. ed. 1899).

R. BORBA DE MORAES, 1958. *Bibliographia Brasiliana. A bibliographical essay on rare books about Brazil...* 2 vols (2nd. ed., revised, 1983; Amsterdam/Rio de Janeiro).

R. BOSCH, 1986. *Brasilien-Bibliothek der Robert Bosch GmbH.* Katalog bearbeitet von Susanne Koppel (Stuttgart).

A. V. BRAND, 1976. *Werkzeug der Historikers. Eine Einführung in die historischen Hilfswissenschaften* (8. Aufl.; Stuttgart).

R. CORBEY, 1989. *Wildheid en beschaving. De Europese verbeelding van Afrika* (Baarn).

R. CORBEY & P. V.D. GRIJP (eds.), 1990. *Natuur en Cultuur. Beschouwingen op het raakvlak van antropologie en filosofie.* Liber Amicorum Ton Lemaire (Baarn).

J.-P. DUVIOLS, 1985. *L'Amérique espagnole vue et rêvée. Les livres de voyages de Christophe Colomb à Bougainville* (Paris).

O.H. GREEN, 1965. *Spain and the Western Tradition. The Castilian Mind in Literature from El Cid to Calderón.* Vol.III (Madison & Milwaukee).

J. HAEKEL, 1970. 'Source Criticism in Anthropology', in *A Handbook of Method in Cultural Anthropology,* ed R. Naroll & R. Cohen (New York), pp. 147-64.

L.-E. HALKIN, 1966. *Eléments de critique historique* (2ième ed.; Liège).

L.-E. HALKIN, 1983. *Initiation à la critique historique* (many editions; Paris).

M. HARBSMEIER, 1982. 'Reisebescheibungen als mentalitätsgeschichtliche Quellen: Überlegungen zu einer historisch-antropologischen Untersuchung frühneuzeitlicher deutscher Reisebeschreibungen', in *Reiseberichte als Quellen europäischer Kulturgeschichte. Aufgaben und Möglichkeiten der historischen Reiseforschung,* ed. A. Maczak und H.J. Teuteberg (Wolfenbüttel: Herzog August Bibliothek), pp. 1-33.

J. HOWELL, 1642. *Instructions for Forreine Travell. Shewing by what cours, and in what compass of time, one may take an exact Survey of the Kingdomes and States of Christendome, and arrive to the practicall knowledge of the Languages, too good purpose* (London).

R. KLEINSCHMIDT, 1966. *Balthasar Springer: Eine quellenkritische Untersuchung* (Wien).

D.F. LACH, 1977. *Asia in the Making of Europe.* Vol. 2: *A Century of Wonder, Book Two: The Literary Arts* (London & Chicago).

JEAN DE LÉRY, 1578. *Histoire d'un voyage fait en la terre du Bresil, autrement dite Amerique...* (La Rochelle).

JAN HUYGEN VAN LINSCHOTEN, 1596. *Beschyvinghe van de gantsche custe van Guinea...,* ed. C.P. Burger Jr. & F.W.T. Hunger. Werken der Linschoten-Vereeniging, 39 ('s-Gravenhage 1934).

J. V. MAANEN, 1988. *Tales of the Field. On writing Ethnography* (Chicago & London).

P. MASON, 1990. 'Tout commence par la reproduction. Joseph-François Lafitau's *Moeurs des Sauvages amériquains comparées aux moeurs des premiers temps* voor beginners', in Corbey & v.d. Grijp 1990: 245-55.

J. OSORIO DA FONSECA, 1581. *Histoire de Portugal, contenant les entreprises navigations, & gestes memorables des Portugallois...* (Genève).

B. PENROSE, 1952. *Travel and discovery in the Renaissance 1420-1620* (Cambridge).

L.J.M. PHILIPPEN, 1942. *Beknopte methodiek der geschiedvorsching. Leidraad voor de leden der oudheidkundige kringen* (Antwerpen).

D.C. PITT, 1972. *Using Historical Sources in Anthropology and Sociology* (New York).

P.H. POTT, 1962. *Naar wijder horizon. Kaleidoscoop op ons beeld van de buitenwereld* ('s-Gravenhage).

W. PREVENIER, 1974. *Een overzicht van geschiedkundige kritiek* (Gent).

J.J. SAAR, 1672. *Ost-Indianische fünfzehen jährige Kriegsdienste und Wahrhafftige Beschreibung...* (Nümberg).

M. SZALAY, 1983. *Ethnologie und Geschichte. Zur Grundlegung einer ethnologischen Geschichtsschreibung* (Berlin).

P.A. TIELE, 1884. *Nederlandsche Bibliographie van Land- en Volkenkunde* (Amsterdam).

A. THEVET, 1558. *Les singularitez de la France Antarctique, autrement nommée Amerique...* (Paris).

ECHOES AND IMAGES:
REFLECTIONS UPON FOREIGN SPACE

Joep Leerssen

Bright echoes in the West: Tennyson's 'Bugle Song'

> The splendour falls on castle walls
>   And snowy summits old in story;
> The long light shakes across the lakes,
>   And the wild cataract leaps in glory.
> Blow, bugle, blow, set the wild echoes flying,
> Blow bugle; answer, echoes, dying, dying, dying.
>
> O, hark, O, hear! how thin and clear,
>   And thinner, clearer, farther going!
> O, sweet and far from cliff and scar
>   The horns of Elfland faintly blowing!
> Blow, let us hear the purple glens replying,
> Blow, bugle; answer, echoes, dying, dying, dying.
>
> O love, they die in yon rich sky,
>   They faint on hill or field or river;
> Our echoes roll from soul to soul,
>   And grow forever and forever.
> Blow, bugle, blow, set the wild echoes flying,
> And answer echoes, answer, dying, dying, dying.

This poem is part of a fairy-talish romance called 'The Princess' and counts among the favourites in the Tennyson repertoire; the poet exploits to the full his unique power of word-repetition, deploying verbal sonorousness in order to suggest moral loftiness or metaphysical profundity; an ideal poem to read out aloud. Its forum is the drawing-room, its setting a genteel picturesque valley, the locale of which is not further specified. It does not seem an obvious possibility to read this poem in any political sense; its verbal tissue, its actual content, offers hardly any clue whatsoever to see the poem in any other way than as a private, lyrical rhapsody. Indeed, in order to contextualize the poem, to see it in terms of its ideological presuppositions, we must look beyond its actual verbal contents and adduce circumstantial, historical information.

The actual locale of the setting (Killarney, in Ireland) was recognized as such, effortlessly, one evening in 1880 by Tennyson's faithful acolyte William Allingham, poet and Irishman. I quote from Allingham's diary:

> T. read us the 'Bugle Song'. I said, 'That's Killarney'.
> T. — 'Yes, it was Killarney suggested it. The bugle echoes were wonderful — nine times — at last like a chant of angels in the sky. But when I was there afterwards I could only hear two echoes, — from the state of the air. I complained of this and said, "When I was here before I heard nine." "Oh!" says the bugler, "then you're the gintleman that's brought so much money to the place!"' [1]

Second experiences are but echoes of the first, they never quite live up to the initial encounter; the echoes get fewer and fainter as Tennyson finds; and it shows the man in all his Victorian sternness that he can remark upon that and the 'state of the air' in such disgruntled terms, like a dissatisfied customer. The echo-as-merchandise undertone in this experience is echoed, aptly enough, in the flattery used by the bugler (purveyor to Killarney tourists of aural sublimity): Tennyson's poem has increased the tourist traffic to Killarney, it is that famous.

The poem effaces its own roots in the real world. It seems almost a matter of indifference whether the echoes 'fade on hill or field or river', as the poem lackadaisically puts it; what matters is not so much the state

---

[1]　*William Allingham's Diary*, ed. G. Grigson (Fontwell, Sussex: Centaur Press, 1967), p. 301. Killarney had been a sublime beauty spot for English travellers since the 1760s, and the practice of bringing out the echoes with a horn or trumpet had been long-established; cf. Leerssen 1986 pp. 76-9, 157.

of Ireland as the 'state of the air'. Bothersome, unaesthetic Ireland[2] becomes Elfland; what matters is not the state of that country but 'the state
of the air'; the poet fairly ordering the Irish echoes to live up to his elf-like
expectations: 'Blow, bugle, blow! Answer, echoes!' Even in Elfland,
Tennyson calls the tune. The poet laureate of the empire is also the great
poet of the imperative. Most of his famous 'quotable' lines contain
imperatives: 'Come into the garden, Maud', 'Breathe and blow, wind of the
western sea!' 'Ring out, wild bells, to the wild sky!' 'Break, break, break,
On thy cold grey shores, O sea!' To address the universe in this high-
handed fashion requires really the same voice that can boom out, on a
more military topic, 'Honour the light brigade! Honour the charge they
made!'

These echoes are English reflections upon foreign space. They are
the self-effacing literary transmutation of an intercultural confrontation; and
in that respect they belong alongside other literary articulations of national
identity and alterity: phenomena such as the use of regional or exotic
settings, of ethnically stereotyped stock characters or of historical material
from the national heritage. Seen in that context, the case of Tennyson's
echoes suggests the need for a unified approach, in the study of literary
texts, that takes into account, not only the text's verbal substance ('style',
'form', 'vocabulary') but also its historical context, the ideological
sounding-board against which it reverberates.

But by the same token the case of this poem suggests something
else as well: namely, that there does exist, *pace* Derrida, such a thing as
a delimitation between *texte* and *hors-texte*; indeed the articulation of this
delimitation (between what does and does not form part of the text's verbal
material) is the most basic thing performed by the text, much as the
exclusion of the Irish setting from this poem's text is one of its central
aspects. If texts (finite as they are) are themselves the result of a series of
decisions ('what to leave out', 'what to put in'), then the historical contextualization of literature is a necessary procedure in our critical analysis of
literary texts.

In the following pages I would like to present an approach in
literary studies which addresses precisely this point of intersection between

---

[2]   Tennyson in fact loathed Ireland, the skeleton in the British political cup-
board. Allingham's diary records many bigoted statements which are a far cry
indeed from the poem's celestial echoes. Thus: 'Ireland's a dreadful country! I
heartily wish it was in the middle of the Atlantic Ocean.' And again: 'Couldn't
they blow up that horrible island with dynamite and carry it off in pieces — a
long way off?' (Allingham, *Diary*, pp. 293, 297).

the text's verbal ('poetical') and historical ('ideological') properties, between the text as verbal tissue and the text as social act; an approach, therefore, which allows for an integrated textual and historical study of cultural and political imagery. That approach is known in German and French as *Imagologie*, 'image studies'.

Image studies: the institutional/methodological background

The topic, then, is stereotypes, clichés, images; more particularly, images of national character; ethnic prejudices and clichés; cultural stereotypes. For the present purpose, then, I define image studies[3] as 'the study of national and ethnic stereotype and of the literary representation of intercultural confrontation'. The source material on which the imagologist draws is centered, naturally enough, around the field of 'literature', by which we usually mean textual works of art; that source material is studied as to its representation of foreign cultures and nationalities. Marius-François Guyard (1951) defined the topic as *l'étranger tel qu'on le voit*.

The institutional background is that of comparatism as it was practised, especially, in France under the influence of scholars like Paul van Tieghem, Fernand Baldensperger and Paul Hazard: the men who founded the *Revue de littérature comparée* in 1921. To mention these names already indicates a radically *historical* interest in literature: Baldensperger's *La littérature: création, succès, durée* of 1913 is among the first works in this century to undertake a sociology of literature; Paul Hazard's *La crise de la conscience européenne* is among the forerunners of *histoire de mentalités*; and the same may be said of Paul van Tieghem's large-scale studies of multinational periods and trends in European literary and

---

[3]   I must preface these remarks with a caution: we all invent our past, our tradition; and to some extent the imagological 'background' which I chart here is my own projection. Also, if I speak of 'imagologists' in general, I refer to a small band and a rather tenuous tradition of scholars. Image studies has never been a mass movement in literary studies; and on both these counts the following sketch is a private family history more than anything else, and influenced perhaps by my own, subjective critical sensibility. It is for that reason that I speak of 'the' imagologist in the abstract (*mon semblable, mon frère*) as a 'he'. Yet again, these are not merely idiosyncratic, personal views dressed up into a private Trojan Hobby-Horse with a funny name: the ideas traced out here are more than just my own, witness other descriptions of image studies (usually written by comparatists for comparatists), cf. Dyserinck 1977 and 1988; Fischer 1981; Pageaux 1981 and 1983. See also the list of titles given on p. 252n. of Fischer 1983.

intellectual history. [4]

The historical contextualization of the text (as part of a period, a society, or a mentality) is common to these three scholars and the so-called 'French School' of comparatism which they led from the Sorbonne. When, after the Second World War, French comparatists tried to re-establish their activities, they attempted to salvage the cross-national study of literature à la Van Tieghem and Hazard from the institutional post-war chaos and from an incipient methodological conflict between stolid factualism and vapid aestheticism.

The answer was given by a second/third generation from Baldensperger's old Sorbonne department, when Jean-Marie Carré and Marius-François Guyard came up with the aforementioned notion of 'l'étranger tel qu'on le voit': the study of a particular type of literary topos (in this case: the 'image' of a certain foreign nation in a given corpus of literature), which would at the same time provide a precise historical focus and basis for textual study, and give insight, not only into a literary commonplace, but also into cross-national attitudes which shaped cultural self-awareness and the interaction between cultural traditions. Thus, a theme like 'the image of England in French literature' ideally not only charts a literary-historical tradition from Mme de Staël to Hugo, Dumas, Sue, and after, including both Jules Verne's Phileas Fogg and Baudelaire's combination of dandyism and spleen — by the same token, it would trace a French cultural attitude, from the Jockey Club to the *franglais* debate, a way in which a 'French' cultural identity was articulated through cross-channel juxtaposition. That, in turn, would shed light on some of the most fundamental determinants of international literary, cultural and even political traffic between the two countries from Waterloo to the *entente cordiale*.

Two tenets in image studies, which have been fundamental to the endeavour since it was first propounded as such, should be stressed. One is the shift from a traditional notion of existence towards one of perception or representation; the other is the differentiation of what traditionally counted as a single unit called 'identity' into a binary polarity between identity and alterity. Both these aspects are, of course, of their time and

---

[4]   It seems worth pointing out that Van Tieghem's work is not merely a development of interbellum *littérature comparée*; it gains fresh interest when placed in the context of Felix Vodička's outline of a possible programme for the historical study of literature (1976/1942). Vodička cites Van Tieghem's work as an example to emulate.

belong to the century-long French 'question de l'Autre' (Descombes 1979), the French philosophers' attempt to come to terms with post-Hegelian philosophy: the early imagologists are, after all, the contemporaries of Merleau-Ponty, Camus and Sartre much as the later ones like D.-H. Pageaux betray an affinity with Foucault and with structuralism.

Imagologists have made it a habit to stress, and to stress heavily, that they did not try, could not try, did not even want to try, to establish 'what such-and-such a national character was like'; on the contrary, they investigated 'how such-and-such a national character was perceived or represented' — a perception-representation by definition situated between 'l'étranger' and the 'on-voit'. This means, to begin with, that the imagological (i.e. comparatist, i.e. literary-critical) pursuit is a meta-discursive one, in that the images which one studies are seen as properties of texts, as the intellectual produce of a discourse: not as representanda, but as representamina with an imponderable 'truth value'; not as a measurably (un)faithful or (un)reliable item of information concerning a knowable objective reality, but rather as a textual construct. Imagologists have habitually emphasized that to speculate on the degree of validity of an image is nugatory, invokes imponderables and does not pose an answerable question: there is no saying how such-and-such a nation 'really' is, one can only study what other people have said upon that subject.

This is not merely a philosophical issue, reflecting tensions between ontology and epistemology;[5] in its own historical context it was also a political one. Hitler's genocides had been founded on the belief in an objectively real and operative ethnic identity and temperament, and national thought had in the immediately preceding decades shown its most horrifying implications. It is no coincidence that image studies were propounded most urgently in the early years of the UNO and the EEC: it was a time when national thought, ethnocentrism, chauvinism, had finally been carried to the point of sickening the world, when they appeared as the evil genius fanning most European wars of the last centuries, lurking behind the

---

[5]   The shift from essence to perception is a primarily ontological matter for Popperians like Dyserinck, who would classify images and stereotypes as objects of a 'world-3'; a primarily epistemological one for Foucaultians like E. Marc Lipiansky (1979), who would see images as 'objets discursifs' whose value is purportedly informed by their representing a social reality, but which actually depend wholly on the textual/discursive economy of an episteme. It should be pointed out that neither Popper nor Foucault are interested in the workings of the textual medium, and bypass this stage in their attempt to get at underlying attitudes or mentalities.

darker pages of colonialism and imperialism; and it is a fair assumption that many imagologists, in shifting the question of national character from the objective into the subjective field, in seeing it as a product of representation rather than as a datum of empirical reality, were actually hoping to debunk national prejudice, to render clichés, stereotypes and bigotry powerless by exposing them to the antiseptic of clinical, scientific investigation.

The shift from essence to perception logically implies that a monolithic sense of identity is fractured into the polar ambiguity of a difference between Self and Other. The structuralist shift (locating semiosis in patterns of differentiation rather than in units of identity) was at work here as in other disciplines, albeit without self-conscious recognition as such, and without the ritualistic invocation of the name of Saussure. Not only does *l'étranger* become *l'étranger*-as-perceived — but that *percipi* depends on an *on-voit*, an observer. Here as everywhere, it takes two to tango.

The point seems straightforward enough in practice: take texts about a given country (say, Germany), and survey them. How can a reading of the individual text, or a comparison between various texts, make historical sense if one does not take the provenance of the text into account, whether it is by a Swede or by a Russian, whether it is Tacitus' *Germania*, Heine's *Wintermärchen* or a piece of English or French First-World-War propaganda? The fact that the texts refer to an area which we call by one single name does not mean that they are cumulatively valid. Their common subject-matter is not a transhistorically durable, objective entity called 'Germany' but rather the set of changeable images of a hypothetical and historically variable Germany; in studying these images we must place them in their discursive environment. Indeed, it might be said that these images should be studied as textual properties, much as 'rhyme scheme' or the use of a first-person-narrator are textual properties.

Imagologists distinguish between 'auto-images' and 'hetero-images'. An image by its very nature signals an intercultural confrontation, an encounter between the text's domestic background and the foreign nature of the 'étranger' which that text describes. Mme de Staël's *De l'Allemagne* must be read in the light of its French, anti-Napoleonic background; thus, what Mme de Staël has to say about Germany would be the book's 'hetero-image', whereas her tacit presuppositions, or her explicit commentaries on French standards and attitudes, would constitute the auto-image — the reason, incidentally, why the first edition of *De l'Allemagne* was seized and destroyed by Napoleon's police in 1810. But to see texts of this kind as a locus of tension and interaction between auto- and hetero-image is more than just a *historical* mode of reading; it also means that imagologists radically rule out the possibility of reading such a text, referential and nonfictional though it be, in terms of 'correct' or 'wrong': an imagological reading is strictly *textual* in that it stays within the (inter-) textual confines of perception and representation. In this sense, Derrida's dictum *il n'y a pas de hors-texte* is more valid than I allowed for a few pages ago: [6] a latter-day reader cannot claim to have a patent on 'the true nature' of Germany and to gauge Mme de Staël's description against it.

The curious result of all this has been that image studies has tended to find itself between two stools: fellow-scholars in literary studies have tended to see the text as a *hermetic* medium and have denounced image studies for placing textual features under the aegis of social conditions and historical reality, whereas scholars with related interests in the historical or the social sciences have sometimes tended to disregard the representational, discursive aspects of collective attitudes and to treat representation as a *transparent* medium. The result has been, for a while, the marginalization of image studies within the comparatist discipline and within literary studies in general; [7] but by the same token imagologists may be in a

---

[6]   That is to say that the text's 'meaning' or reference is indistinguishably interwoven with the entire web of our semantic cognition; as opposed to the finite, clearly delineated outline of the text as the result of an enunciation, consisting of certain words to the exclusion of all others. This ambivalence already outlines the positions taken in the famous debate between Derrida and Searle.

[7]   Image studies has suffered from the decline of its progenitor, French inter-war *littérature comparée*. Traditional *littérature comparée* has been rejected as dry-as-dust positivism, preoccupied with atomistic 'facts', dates, biographies, labouring under intentionalist and essentialist fallacies. Traditional literary history of this kind came under attack from various quarters: from a post-Formalist and New Critical position (exemplified by René Wellek), from a hermeneutical position (exemplified by Hans Robert Jauss) and from a structuralist position (exemplified by Roland Barthes). The earliest of these was Wellek's: he distinguished sharply between those methods which deal with the properties of the literary text as such, and those which place the text in its extradiscursive (social, biographical, historical, philological...) environment. René Wellek's and Austin Warren's classic *Theory of Literature* dismissively opposes 'the extrinsic approach to literature' to the 'intrinsic study of literature'. That polarity has become both methodologically and institutionally ingrained; attacks by Barthes and Jauss on the biographical auctorialism of traditional literary history are both, in their respective ways, akin to Wellek's stance.

This ingrained polarity between literary poetics and literary history is, of course, diffractive. One way out of this jejune polarity is offered by a study of

position to offer a critical analysis of current practice in literary scholarship (cf. Leerssen 1988a) or in related disciplines — as the following example illustrates.

North and South (of what?)

Geert Hofstede's *Culture's Consequences* (1980), a sociopsychological investigation into the temperaments of IBM employees from various countries, measures a 'Power Distance Index' (PDI) as it can be differentiated by nationality. His contention is that there is a significant difference in PDI between people from Northern European (Germanic) cultural background and from a Southern European (Latin) one.

Hofstede's differentiation is not, however, a direct and cogent conclusion imposed by his empirically gathered data; it is, rather, an image (in the imagological sense) pre-existing his empirical fieldwork and governing his (sometimes laboured) interpretation of the data. The author himself acknowledges his conceptual indebtedness for this Germanic/Romanic North-South divide by referring to the work of the Belgian historian Henri Pirenne, a writer from the turn of the century much given to national/ethnic models of thought.

It is at this point that the imagologist can step in, and trace back the image whose echoes reached Hofstede by way of Pirenne. To do so means to explode Hofstede's claim that his temperamental North/South-differentiation is a 'zero-degree' representation of empirical reality, and exposes its ideological, discursively constructed nature. [8]

The image is this: the North of Europe tends to be more libertarian, more individualistic, more egalitarian and more democratic, as opposed to a more gregarious, hierarchically-structured and authority-dependent cultural tradition from the South. Furthermore, Northerners are perceived as more introverted and meditatively disposed, whereas Southerners are more extrovert, and with a comparatively amoral disposition combining the

---

literary reception, which may take place both at the textual level (reading experience) and at the social level (textual dissemination, reading practice, canonization); also, Dyserinck and others have argued that image studies can transcend, or at least side-step, the spurious distinction between the literary allure of a text and its extratextual (social or ideological) ramifications; cf. Dyserinck 1982, Leerssen 1991, Syndram 1991.

[8]   Cf. generally Leerssen 1988b and the ensuing exchange between Hofstede and myself in *Theoretische Geschiedenis*, 16 (1989): 358-365.

qualities of rationalism and sensualism.

That stereotyped polarity has been operative in political history (the absolutism of the Roman Empire and of the French and Spanish monarchies vis-à-vis the democracy of the Germanic tribes and the parliamentary systems of Holland, England and Scandinavia); in religious history (the moral authoritarianism of Roman Catholicism vs. the Reformation in the North of Europe — the Weber thesis fits this preconception); in literary history (classical and classicist traditions from the Mediterranean vs. the epic myths and legends of the heathen and medieval North); and it has been aligned with climatological circumstances (the sloth-inducing comfort of the lush South vs. the bracing cold discomfort of the wintry North).

This north-south distribution of temperamental stereotypes is a widespread and important European tradition drawing, ultimately, on Tacitus' *Germania* and including representatives like Montesquieu, Mme de Staël and Hippolyte Taine. Indeed it has become such an ingrained mode of viewing the world, that everywhere the opposition between North and South will tend to take on the aforementioned temperamental discourse. The opposition between Northern and Southern Ireland; between Northern and Southern Spain; between Northern and Southern England; between Scotland and England-as-a-whole; between Holland and Belgium; between Hamburg and Munich; between Germany and Austria; between Germany and Italy; between Milan and Palermo... the discourse of the north-south opposition is all-pervasive and can be repeated at almost random points on the map. Within The Netherlands, the North counts as more businesslike, less convivial and less jolly than the South; Friesland, in the extreme North, has from classical times onwards enjoyed (and cultivated) a reputation for rugged liberty and individualism, whereas at the opposite pole of the temperamental spectrum, The Netherlands' southernmost province of Limburg is frequently seen as being ruled from smoky backrooms by an impenetrable Catholic élite, while simultaneously having so jolly and convivial a temperament, and so unbusinesslike, that the epithet 'Burgundian' has been frequently applied to it.[9] But a village priest from the North of Limburg says this of his parishioners:

They are people who look before they leap. In their mentality

---

[9]   Given the interposition of Belgium and Northern France between Limburg and the area to which it is phraseologically linked, this nomenclature may seem odd. In Dutch, the term 'Burgundian' evokes a whiff of *La douce France* and Gabriel Chevallier's *Clochemerle*, as well as the colourful reign of the House of Burgundy described in Huizinga's *The Waning of the Middle Ages*.

they belong to Friesland rather than to South-Limburg. North-Limburgers are better business partners, and more reliable. [10]

All this is geographical nonsense — Limburg and Friesland are no more contiguous than Limburg and Burgundy; but the image makes perfect sense on the 'mental map', within the discursive commonplace that is shared by Mme de Staël, Henri Pirenne, Professor Hofstede and this parish priest. In other words, the similarities between such texts can be adequately explained from a commonplace grammar of representation, a conventional categorization. That explanation at the same time undermines these texts' claims to referential veracity and reliability, and allows us to see their inner tensions and contradictions.

That is not merely a dour cavil. It is part of the ongoing project of image studies, and points at its deeper importance. Image studies is not merely interested in tabulating textual typologies of various national characters as represented in literature — though that is an important enterprise. More than that, image studies wants to apply these individual typologies towards understanding the underlying structures of national imagery (e.g., the recurrent North-South distinction), and to demonstrate its *conventional* (as opposed to empirically referential) nature.

Image Studies as literary studies

The case cited above already indicates that images are expressed in a discursive continuum which ignores the division, imposed by critics, between 'Literature' (capital L, a verbal form of art) and 'the rest'. The stricture cited above (footnote 7), as made by Wellek and others, might therefore arise: what reason is there to pursue image studies as a branch of *literary studies*, if its topic straddles adjacent fields of study? Is this not a pursuit for the historian, the sociologist, the psychologist?

The question is a disingenuous one. It is usually asked, not to establish the best way of pursuing the topic of national identity and national culture, but to marginalize that pursuit in the institutional field of 'literary studies' proper, i.e. that institution which is based on the assumption of an essential difference between literature and the rest of

---

[10]   'Het zijn mensen, die de kat uit de boom kijken. Ze sluiten wat betreft hun mentaliteit eerder aan bij de Friezen dan bij de mensen uit Zuid-Limburg. Met de Noordlimburgers is het beter zaken doen, je kunt er beter van op aan.' (Quoted in De Ruiter & Paumen 1988).

human culture. Moreover, such an institutional division of labour seems tailored to serve the needs of those who, like 'literary scholars', are in continual need of territorial self-definition and of asserting the unique specificity and scholarly justification of their pursuit. This jealous concern for operational and institutional autarky is a sign of lacking self-confidence, and rather than creating the preconditions necessary for the actual study of literature, lures critics into counterproductive introspection and claustro-philiac theorizing.

But if we leave aside those implications, the question 'does not image studies address matters in anthropology, history, sociology, psychology?' might very well be answered in the affirmative. It would be strange had it been otherwise — almost all topics in human culture and civilization can be studied from a variety of approaches and disciplines; and in my own imagological work I have learned much from historians and anthropologists.

Even so I would argue that image studies is perhaps better placed in the institutional context of literary studies than elsewhere. In their permeation throughout the various textual genres and discursive fields, national stereotypes also operate in literary texts — in those texts commonly seen as the preserve of 'literary studies', i.e. those texts which are regulated by a certain set of poetical conventions and artistically valorized accordingly. Indeed we may assume, with Macherey, that the literary text, of all genres, is a particularly suitable subject for the critical study of ideological assumptions. It 'constructs a determinate image of the ideological, revealing it as an object rather than living from within it as though it were an inner conscience; the text explores ideology [...] puts it to the test of the written word' (Sim 1987).

This means that, if literary expertise is not the *only* prerequisite for the study of national images, it is certainly an indispensable one. 'Literary' texts, given the conventions under which they are constructed and under which they are read, are a medium of particular importance in the formulation and dissemination of national stereotype; recent publications in imagology have tended to stress the poetical and aesthetic status of images in the literary text (Leerssen 1991, Syndram 1991). Also, if image studies is more than the critical inventory of explicitly formulated national types, it will have to pursue the transmutations that such types can undergo when given 'literary' treatment; as in the case of Tennyson's lyricism.

This does not mean that the critic, like a modern Torquemada, vets the text for signs of the Cloven Hoof, or that it affords the critic a moral one-upmanship (indeed, 'authority') over the ideological benightedness of authors past and present; it merely means that we are given an angle of access, a perspective, towards what may be a central concern in many literary works in the Western tradition over the past century: the articulation of cultural identity. In many cases the values of the critic will differ (how could it be otherwise?) from those enunciated or implied in the text he studies; but that is incidental to the study as such. It may also happen that this approach (reading a text from an imagological perspective) opens the possibility of discerning, in positive terms, fresh aspects of the text's inner workings. I give an example from the one remaining point of the Eurocentric compass.

Dark echoes in the East: E.M. Forster's 'A Passage to India'

Mrs. Moore and Miss Quested, from the moment they set foot on Indian soil, evince a wish to see the 'Real India', as if the India that is there all around them is not real enough. Forster describes how the cramped attempts to flatter English exoticism cause embarrassment to all concerned: India, it is implied, should not be sought for in the colourful aspects that may amuse charmed tourists; the reality of heat, dust, oppression and incomprehension is there to see, and it is fond self-beguilement to think that a downtrodden colony is only a veil around the secret moonlit Taj Mahal of a better-than-real India. Indeed the one (better-than-)real India that is on offer locally lies in the Marabar caves, known only by vague reputation but vaguely agreed upon to be most remarkable. Miss Quested's quest for an India more colourful than her colonial fiancé can offer takes her to these Marabar caves, as her host Dr. Aziz becomes ensnared in a half-embarrassed and wholly embarrassing attempt to cater for English exoticism. What she finds is an echo: India only gives back the noise produced by its visitors, in such a way as to evoke blind sexual anxiety in Miss Quested and an overwhelming life-weariness in Mrs. Moore. Forster's description of these Marabar caves is an impressive piece of prose and evokes a notion of unattainable, self-enclosed otherness, an ultimate absence, a space which is untrodden, unperceived, filled only by its own emptiness:

> They are dark caves. Even when they open towards the sun, very little light penetrates down the entrance tunnel into the circular chamber. There is little to see, and no eye to see it, until the visitor arrives for his five minutes, and strikes a match. Immediately another flame rises in the depths of the rock and moves towards the surface like an imprisoned spirit: the walls of the circular chamber have been most marvellously polished. The two

flames approach and strive to unite, but cannot, because one of
them breathes air, the other stone. [...] The radiance increases, the
flames touch one another, kiss, expire. The cave is dark again,
like all the caves.
Only the wall of the circular chamber has been polished thus.
The sides of the tunnel are left rough, they impinge as an
afterthought upon the internal perfection. An entrance was
necessary, so mankind made one. But elsewhere, deeper in the
granite, are there certain chambers that have no entrances?
Chambers never unsealed since the arrival of the gods. [...]
Nothing is inside them, they were sealed up before the creation
of pestilence or treasure; if mankind grew curious and excavated,
nothing would be added to the sum of good or evil. One of them
is rumoured within the boulder that swings on the summit of the
highest of the hills; a bubble-shaped cave that has neither ceiling
nor floor, and mirrors its own darkness in every direction
infinitely. (Penguin edition, pp. 124-5)

This, then, is (in Forster's saturnine denunciation of English attitudes
abroad) the end-point of the Passage, the heart of a Real India. With this
description of a complete absence, an emptiness unperceived, an echo left
unsummoned by any intrusion of sound, he points out a paradox at the root
of all exoticism.

For what is exoticism? A fascination with what is different, a
desire to get in touch with otherness; and that desire is ultimately
impossible. Zeno formulated a paradox on the inability of ever moving
from A to B, given the fact that one would first have to cover the distance
to a mid-way point between A and B, or rather to a half-mid-way point
between A and that mid-way point, or rather... and so on in an eternal
regression; Derrida draws on a similar notion when he discusses the notion
of the 'meaning' of words, the referential relationship between signifier and
signified, arguing that an eternal regression of interposed mid-way points,
a continuous *différance* from one signifier to another, interposed one,
separates the world of language from that first-order reality which it
supposedly symbolizes.

It is curious to see how similar telescoping mechanisms of deferral,
the 'not yet quite there', are at work in exoticist discourse. The Really
Other Place is always elsewhere. To visit India might seem like an exotic
experience; but on setting foot in India, one has by that very act de-
exoticized the ground so trodden on — one has, in a way, appropriated the

part of India within one's purview, has made it less exotic by the mere fact of being present there. A Real India is an India without English people present, the India that is just around the corner, just beyond the horizon, the India one has merely heard about, from the reports of others, by rumour... A self-defeating exercise, then, to go in quest of that India, to go and Be there, see It! Indeed what Forster describes is, in a way, the ultimate Other, the Real India, the *Ding an sich*: there yet unsullied by being perceived, an *esse* without *percipi*, an *étranger tel qu'on ne le voit pas*, the hollow space that is an emptiness where exoticist desire loses and spends itself. [11] The patterns of expectation and experience which *A Passage to India* deals with are not unlike the issues that imagologists address when dealing with literary texts: What echoes? Upon whose ears? Upon whose silence?

Sources

V. DESCOMBES, 1979. *Le même et l'Autre. Quarante-cinq ans de philosophie française (1933-1978)* (Paris: Minuit).
H. DYSERINCK, 1977. 'Komparatistische Imagologie', in Id., *Komparatistik. Eine Einführung* (Bonn: Bouvier), pp. 125-33.
H. DYSERINCK, 1982. 'Komparatistische Imagologie jenseits von "Werkimmanenz" und "Werktranszendenz"', *Synthesis*, 9: 27-40.
H. DYSERINCK, 1988. 'Komparatistische Imagologie. Zur politischen Tragweite einer europäischen Wissenschaft von der Literatur', in *Europa und das nationale Selbstverständnis. Imagologische Probleme in Literatur, Kunst und Kultur des 19. und 20. Jahrhunderts*, ed. H. Dyserinck & K.U. Syndram (Bonn: Bouvier), pp. 13-

---

[11]   The source tradition ironized by Forster's treatment (a fact insufficiently appreciated by Said 1978) is the colonial adventure tale *à la* Kipling and Rider Haggard (regarding which, cf. Leerssen 1990). The narrative in such stories often gravitates towards the structure of the quest story, using topoi like penetration, rites of passage, treasures hidden in caves, death lurking in caves. A lot of caves, and time for Freudians to start salivating. Indeed a Freudian reading of such penetrations into the dark unknown appears enticing. However, I myself believe that this would mean to *impose* symbolism rather than to *decode* it. Sexual metaphors in a Freudian reading are metaphors applied by ourselves. They enable us to discern structural patterns in dissimilar phenomena; they add rather than strip a layer of symbolism. As a French wag put it: Freud said *C'est comme ça*; he should have said *C'est comme si...*

37.
M.S. FISCHER, 1981. *Nationale Images als Gegenstand Vergleichender Literatur-geschichte. Untersuchungen zur Entstehung der komparatistischen Imagologie* (Bonn: Bouvier).

M.S. FISCHER, 1983. 'Literarische Seinsweise und politische Funktion national-bezogener Images. Ein Beitrag zur Theorie der komparatistischen Imagologie', *Neohelicon*, 10: 251-74.

M.-F. GUYARD, 1951. 'L'étranger tel qu'on le voit', in Id., *La littérature comparée* (Paris: PUF), pp. 110-119.

G. HOFSTEDE, 1980. *Culture's Consequences. International Differences in Work-Related Values* (Beverly Hills: Sage).

J.TH. LEERSSEN, 1986. *Mere Irish & Fíor-Ghael. Studies in the Idea of Irish Nationality, its Development and Literary Expression, prior to the Nineteenth Century* (Amsterdam/Philadelphia: John Benjamins)

J.TH. LEERSSEN, 1988a. 'British Literary Critics and Continental Critical Theory', *Yearbook of European Studies*, 1: 59-84.

J.TH. LEERSSEN, 1988b. 'Over nationale identiteit', *Theoretische Geschiedenis*, 15: 417-430.

J.TH. LEERSSEN, 1990. 'Over exotische avonturenverhalen en Europese cultuurnor-men', *Forum der Letteren*, 31: 161-174.

J.TH. LEERSSEN, 1991. 'Mimesis and Stereotype', *Yearbook of European Studies*, 4: 165-175.

E. MARC LIPIANSKY, 1979. *L'âme française ou le national-libéralisme. Analyse d'une représentation sociale* (Paris: Anthropos).

D.-H. PAGEAUX, 1981. 'Une perspective d'études en littérature comparée: L'imagerie culturelle', *Synthesis*, 8: 169-85.

D.-H. PAGEAUX, 1983. 'L'imagerie culturelle: De la littérature comparée à l'anthropologie culturelle', *Synthesis*, 10: 79-88.

F.G. DE RUITER & M. PAUMEN, 1988: 'De kwade reuk van Ysselsteyn', *NRC Handelsblad*, zaterdag 27 februari 'Zaterdags Bijvoegsel': 1.

E. SAID, 1978. *Orientalism*. London: Routledge & Kegan Paul.

S. SIM, 1987. 'Interrogating an Ideology', *British Journal of English and Cultural Studies*, 10: 163-73.

K.U. SYNDRAM, 1991. 'The Aesthetics of Alterity: Literature and the Imagological Approach', *Yearbook of European Studies*, 4: 177-91.

F. VODIČKÁ, 1976 (1942). 'Die Literaturgeschichte, ihre Probleme und Aufgaben', in Id. *Die Struktur der literarischen Entwicklung* (München: Wilhelm Fink), pp. 30-86.

REREADING GILBERTO FREYRE: BRAZILIAN IDENTITY, BRAZILIAN ALTERITY AND THEIR IMAGES.

Ria Lemaire

In 1933 a young Brazilian sociologist, Gilberto Freyre, published a book entitled *Casa-Grande e Senzala*, which, at that moment, caused a scandal in Brazil. In 1933, Brazilian sociology and anthropology were still dominated by theories about race, colour and racial differences, which had been developed in the nineteenth century and which explained the differences between races and cultures in terms of biology and genetics. This complex of biological thinking was based on the presupposition of the white race's biological and cultural superiority and the inferiority of Blacks and Indians. Miscegenation of these three races, as the main source of the Brazilian population, was considered as an evil, as a degenerating biological process which had in Brazil produced an excessive number of mulattoes and *caboclos* (or *cafuzos*, i.e. 'inferior, weak, degenerated beings'), known as *sub-raças*. These sub-races were considered as the main obstacle to Brazil's economical and cultural development. Whitening (*bran-queamento*) was officially propagated and socially and politically stimulated as a strategy to rid Brazil of the odious part of its population. Gilberto Freyre was a child of the traditional white elite of landowners of the sugar-plantations in the North-eastern part of Brazil. As a member of that white elite, he originally shared its world-view, as he tells us in the preface of the first edition of *Casa-Grande e Senzala*: [1]

> Once, when I was already far from Brazil for more than three
> years, I saw a group of Brazilian sailors — mulattoes and cafuzos
> — in the soft snow of Brooklyn. They gave me the impressions
> of being caricatures of human beings. And to my mind came the
> words I had read in a book on Brazil by an American traveller,
> a book which I had just finished reading: 'The fearfully mongrel
> aspect of most of the population'. This was the result of mis-
> cegenation. (p. LVII)

Unlike most of the male children of the Brazilian elite of landowners, who
traditionally pursued their studies in Portugal or France, Gilberto Freyre
belonged to the first generation of young Brazilians who left Brazil to
study in the United States. There he became a student of Franz Boas, a
choice which produced a veritable earthquake in his intellectual life, as he
learned with Boas to consider racial differences no longer as biologically
determined, but primarily as products of social, geographical or cultural
influences:

> It was the study of Anthropology, oriented by professor Boas that
> revealed to me the true value of the negro and the mulatto. I was
> taught to consider as fundamental the difference between race and
> culture, to discriminate between the products of purely genetical
> relations and the products of social, cultural and environmental
> influences. (pp. LVII-LVIII)

The young scholar Freyre used the culturalist theories of Boas for a very
original and comprehensive enterprise: the development of a general theory
for the description and explanation of the origins of the Brazilian nation
and national identity as a product of the biological and cultural miscegenation of three races: white, black and Indian. The title and the subtitle of the book reveal his culturalist assumptions: 'The manor-house and
the slave-lodges — The formation of the Brazilian family under the regime
of patriarchal economy', combining cultural, social, political and econo-

---

[1]   Gilberto Freyre, *Casa-Grande e Senzala: Formação da família brasileira
sob o regime da economia patriarcal* (Rio de Janeiro: Maia e Schmidt, 1933).
Quotations are translated from the 25th edition, which Freyre oversaw himself
shortly before his death (Rio de Janeiro: José Olímpio, 1987).

mical elements.

In this book, Freyre presents the Brazilian nation and culture as the product of a harmonious, peaceful, secular miscegenation, a *confraternização* as he calls it, of races, under the direction of the Portuguese. For historical reasons, which Freyre describes amply, the Portuguese were free from the racial prejudices current among other European nations. As a result, they effected a policy of miscegenation in their colonies (*lusitanização*), which has shaped modern Brazil: a racial democracy where Blacks and mulattoes have every opportunity for social and economic well-being. Freyre argues that, if sometimes in Brazil we are confronted with forms of discrimination that could be considered racial, this is not what it looks like. In fact, discrimination in such cases is not based on race, but on economic or social, that is: class differences.

The title of the book is, in that sense, very expressive. Two elements of culture: the manor-house, *casa grande*, in which lives the powerful, white landowner, and the *senzala*, the small, poor buildings where the black slaves are lodged. Two cultural products to represent the economical, political and racial structure of society. In that sense the English, French and Italian translations (*The Masters and the Slaves*, *Maîtres et Esclaves* and *Padroni e Schiavi*) are inept. The German translation is better (*Herrenhaus und Sklavenhütte*), though it could have been more expressive, opposing the one, large and high manor-house to the many small, lower slave-lodges (*Herrenhaus* vs. *Sklavenhütten*).

The book contains five chapters. The first gives a general description of the colonial system that the Portuguese created in Brazil, with its monoculture of sugar in extensive plantations, the sugar-mill, the chapel, the food, the quality of life, sexual life, the polygamy of the Portuguese patriarchs in a basically patriarchal context. The second chapter describes the influence of the Indian in the formation of the Brazilian family and culture; the many contributions of Indian women in the process of miscegenation, biological as well as cultural, and the relatively unimportant contribution of the Indian males. The Portuguese male colonizer is presented in the third chapter, where Freyre enumerates all his individual, cultural and historical antecedents and predispositions for polygamy and miscegenation with women of other races. Chapters four and five deal with the contribution of the black slaves, mainly women, in sexual matters and in the Brazilian family.

Freyre's book brought a fundamental and radical revision of the racist and biologist presuppositions current in Brazilian society and scholarship at the time. It presented and propagated miscegenation as a positive, highly valued and undeniable factor in the construction of the Brazilian state and national identity. It rehabilitated the despised races, showing their fundamental contributions to Brazilian culture. To the white, intellectual elites it brought a new, revolutionary, but painful and threatening vision in their pursuit of national identity, which since the independence of the Latin-American nations ($\pm$ 1820) had been one of the main themes and obsessions of their cultural life and literature.

The history of the reception of Gilberto Freyre's book is a fascinating one. Its international reputation is enormous, unassailable and uncontested. Both in Europe and in the United States, it is considered as one of the fundamental contributions to the study of racial problems. The English and French translations have gone through about twenty editions. Freyre was given honorary doctorates at three European universities (Sussex, Münster and the Sorbonne). The book was translated or prefaced by famous scholars such as Roger Bastide, Fernand Braudel, Lucien Febvre, Roland Barthes, Ortega y Gasset, and translated into many languages. It also received many rewards, such as the Anisfield-Wolf (1957), the Aspen Prize (1967) for 'notable individuals and their exceptionally valuable contribution to human culture in the humanistic sectors' and (in 1969) the international literary prize La Madoniña (Italy) for having described 'with incomparable literary lucidity social problems, giving them human warmth, optimism, goodness and wisdom'. These two quoted phrases show a feature which is common to all the outstanding readers/critics who, everywhere in the world, have discussed *Casa-Grande e Senzala*: a sociological/anthropological/historical study of a specific geographical area in a well-delimited historical period is transformed into a piece of universal wisdom and integrated in the traditional white, European humanist discourse and its general, essential truths about mankind, the world, human nature. As Ortega y Gasset tells us, Gilberto Freyre is 'not only an anthropologist, but a philosopher of universal importance' (Quoted in *Casa-Grande e Senzala*, p. XC).

The reception history of *Casa-Grande e Senzala* in Brazil is a very different and extremely controversial one. For more than fifty years, a controversy has been raging between those who admire his study and those who detest it. Generally these positions can be related to a series of political and cultural assumptions and positions in Brazilian public life. Thus, the discourse of the Brazilian modernist movement (1922) of the industrial centre of the country, São Paulo, considered Gilberto Freyre as a more or less reactionary representative of the elites of plantation-owners in the North-Eastern part of Brazil; and it was thus opposed to the more traditional discourse of the regionalistic movement of 1926, in the North-Eastern part of Brazil, which saw Freyre as an excellent, as the best, theoretician of Brazilian society. The division which continues to separate, both economically and culturally, the rich southern part of the country and the poor northern part, is the basis of the controversy, which also involves different leftist and conservative positions. The consequence is that *Casa-Grande e Senzala* has been read, for more than fifty years already, within this complicated political, ideological context.

Reading Freyre nowadays, we are thus confronted with a prefab frame-work of reader-conventions and attitudes. As a literary historian, living in Europe, the international reception of the book pushes me towards that traditional attitude of respect and admiration which these universal human insights and eternal truths require from scholars and students in the humanities. In Judith Fetterly's terms, I will be an 'assenting reader'. [2] At the same time, as a scholar in Brazilian literature and culture, while I admire the well-written, literary portrait of a characteristic period of Brazilian history, I feel a profound despair when I consider its controversial interpretations. As I am not a sociologist, nor an anthropologist, nor a historian, nor a Brazilian, I am unable to discover who is right and who is wrong; I am thus obliged, once again, to be an assenting reader. But as a woman and a feminist, I feel disgusted and suspicious, in spite of my admiration for the beautifully written book. Reading it as a theory on harmonious miscegenation of races, and examining it from the perspective of what harmonious practices, as Freyre describes them, might have meant to women, I am confronted with a system of interrelated — and a rather *un*harmonious — practices which imply, for women (white, black, Indian and mulatto), various types of violence, such as abuse, rape and murder, by white males.

---

[2]   The concepts of the 'assenting' and 'resisting' reader have been worked out by Judith Fetterly in *The Resisting Reader* (Indiana University Press, 1978). Jonathan Culler has shown their importance as a strategy for deconstructionist reading in the chapter 'Reading as a Woman' in *On Deconstruction* (1983: 43-64).

The methodological and theoretical question thus raised by my 'reading as a woman' can be formulated as follows: how can I get rid of a double set of scholarly reader-conventions (the international one and the Brazilian one) and discuss this theory of Brazilian identity in a different way, or on a different level. Or, how can I ground, methodologically and theoretically, my spontaneous reaction as a resisting (feminist) reader? And shouldn't we, finally, after more than fifty years of controversial discussions in Brazil and after the shocking discovery that a first, stock-taking 'reading as a woman' already demonstrates convincingly the falsity of the international humanist consensus, field the hypothesis that something is fundamentally wrong in their presuppositions?

One of the strategies of a rereading of *Casa-Grande e Senzala* has been suggested by the author himself, who has frequently repeated that, first of all, he wanted to be a good writer and not a sociologist. And that is, through all the controversial discussions, a point on which all the critics agree: Gilberto Freyre is an excellent writer. As the jury of the Anisfield-Wolf award said: 'the best work of literature and science on race-relations'. Thus the Brazilian critic Fábio Lucas has characterized the book as a 'saga'; Richard Kaufmann, a German critic, as a tale; and the *Nouvelle Revue Française* as an epic. If we adopt this point of view, the question is no longer that controversial one: does this theory correspond to reality? Is it valid or not? It puts the discussion on a level where, provisionally, reality or validity do not matter, but where we focus on the text itself, its structures and strategies. The question then is: what sort of *representation* does Gilberto Freyre give of colonial Brazil, what sort of images did he choose to create Brazilian identity, and, related to this: to present alterity? Since *Casa-Grande e Senzala* tells a story about the origins of the Brazilian nation and identity, I have decided to read it as a myth, as one of the links in that long chain of 'mitos fundadores', origin myths, that Brazilian culture has produced since Romanticism and Independence. This decision implies a rereading from at least two perspectives: rereading it as a narrative, which enables us to apply various methods and insights elaborated for literary/textual analysis, and rereading it as a myth, which offers the possibility of asking a series of new questions, neglected until now in the discussions.

Reading the narrative

Reading *Casa-Grande e Senzala* as a narrative obliges the reader to distinguish various levels in the text and various types of 'writers' in the construction of the book. The first level we are confronted with is the book as a whole: text, narrative, history.

The text has been created by the Author (with capital letter, as Freyre presents and represents himself as of the second edition) and includes, in the case of the 25th Brazilian edition, the cover, the dedication, 668 pages, including 95 pages of introductions and prefaces, 115 pages of notes, the bibliography, indexes and the narrative itself: i.e. the title and the five chapters (336 pages).

The narrative, in turn, is the product of a narrator and his subjective, very specific processes and activities of selection, organization and aesthetic transformation of the history; and the history consists of the set of data, facts, and documents gathered by the sociologist and which he included in the text/book in the form of a huge amount of notes (115 pages in very small characters), of photographs, drawings, maps, plans (of houses) etc.

These basic distinctions allow for a variety of approaches, such as: the analysis of each text-genre separately (the narrative, the prefaces, the notes), or a cross-text approach in various directions. Thus we can investigate the processes of transformation of the history into a narrative, or the relationship of the prefaces and the narrative, or the textual and ideological strategies by which the Author of the prefaces tries to influence the reader-reception of the specific representation of Brazilian identity, created by the narrator in the narrative.

Let us concentrate on the narrative itself, keeping in mind our purpose: to reread *Casa-Grande e Senzala* as a myth of origins, based on harmonious miscegenation of races and cultures (that is: the transformation — by the white, male Portuguese — of the Others, such as Indians and blacks, into real Brazilians; the transformation of the alien cultures' alterity into constitutive, integrating elements of a new national identity). Our first question concerns the representation of the roles and positions of the various types of contributing subjects/actors/races. Thus the first step is the inventory of answers to questions such as: who is the narrator? How does he create other narrators, for instance, inserting quotations of historical documents or sociological studies, or quoting song-texts: and if so, what is their function? What sort of vision do they present? Or again: who are presented as actors and what types of actions, behaviour are ascribed to them? Are there specific categories of actors we can distinguish?[3] Drawing up this inventory reveals a specific actantial structure, in which we need to distinguish, not only in terms of race, class and gender, but also of age, as per the following scheme:

white race:	— male	- young promiscuous male
		- married, polygamous male
		- old widower
	— female	- young virgins
		- married, monogamous women
black race:	— male	(undifferentiated)
	— female	- young negress
		- adult concubine of white males
		- old nanny
Indians:	— male	(undifferentiated)
	— female	(undifferentiated)
mulattos:	— male	(undifferentiated)
	— female	(undifferentiated)

Reading the myth

After having thus established the actancial *dramatis personae*, we can proceed to the level of the reading as a myth. Our point of departure will be the definition of myth as given by Richard Slotkin in his *Regeneration through Violence* (1973). According to Slotkin, myth is 'a narrative formulation of a culture's world-view and self-concept, which draws both

---

[3]   The methodological and theoretical framework for this type of analysis can be found in Mieke Bal's *Narratologie* (1977), and, for this specific aspect (the actantial scheme), in 'Éléments d'une narratologie critique: Modèle de base', in *Femmes imaginaires* (Utrecht/Paris, 1986: 70-88).

on the historical experience of that culture and on sources of feeling, fear and aspiration deep in the human subconscious and which can be shown to function in that culture as a prescription for historical action and value judgment' (p. 294).

What sort of prescriptions for historical action and value judgements does the myth's narrator propound with regard to the roles and positions of the various categories of subjects, whose alterity (according to the theory of harmonious miscegenation) has been subsumed into (a Brazilian) identity? Are the Brazilian identities of these categories of (social and cultural) Subjects comparable and equal to each other? And is their representation a demonstration of harmonious participation? Do they confirm Freyre's theories concerning the absence of racial prejudice in the Portuguese males, or concerning the harmonious 'fraternization' of races and cultures in Brazil? As a matter of fact, they don't. In Freyre's representation, the mulatto is exclusively the product of sexual intercourse between white males and black women. Black men and white women were excluded from these practices of 'harmonious miscegenation', which by Freyre himself are generally represented as violently exclusive against white women and black males and aggressively sadistic against the women (black and mulatto) who had to submit to them.

Reading the myth as a woman

As the basis of my resisting-readership is to be found in my being a woman and a feminist, I can now, with the help of Slotkin's definition of myth, transform my initial distrust into a methodological and theoretical question: Which are the elements of Freyre's 'narrative formulation' that can be shown to function 'as a prescription for historical action' directed at women and as a 'value judgement' of their contribution to the creation of a Brazilian identity?
This general problem will have to be specified in at least three specific questions from the perspective of women's Brazilian identity:

1. What are the characteristics of the specific division of labour (sexual labour and other types of labour) between sexes, races, classes and age-groups in Freyre's representation of Brazilian identity? Why, for instance, are there no widows in the actancial scheme as outlined above? Did they not exist? Or has their history, well-known by the sociologist

Freyre, been written out of the narrative by the narrator? And if so, why?

2. What can we criticize in the 'scientific' (sociological, anthropological, historical) explanations given by Gilberto Freyre of women's behaviour and positions in Brazilian colonial society?

3. What sort of freyrian imagery ('feelings, fears and aspirations') can we detect in the rhetorics of his extremely persuasive and seductive discourse, in its literary tropes such as images, metaphors, comparisons, enumerations, repetitions etc.?

The approach outlined here raises a few further questions. Does Freyre's *representation* of biological and cultural miscegenation give a justificatory basis to his socio-anthropological *theory* of harmonious miscegenation? And if not, what sort of 'identity' or 'identities' is he constructing? Is this Brazilian identity merely a rhetorical, ideological 'image', which by its persuasiveness and seductiveness hides (on the level of representation? on the level of theory? on the level of social reality?) more subtle, and for that reason even more oppressive, forms of alterity?

I want to stress once more that, if we proceed in this way and look at the text as a literary representation, we bypass the controversial question of its theoretical validity in the controversial sociological/anthropological/ historical sense of the Brazilian debate, as well as the question of its universal truth as it is attributed to it in the humanist consensus. These will come back in an ulterior phase of the analysis, and in very different terms and conditions, in two interrelated groups of questions:

— why, in the thirties of our century, this specific myth of origins as a product of harmonious transformation of alterity into identity?

— what could be the explanation of the world-wide success of the myth? To which 'sources of feeling, fear and aspiration deep in the human subconsciousness' of humanist male scholars worldwide did it and does it appeal?

CONTINENTAL INCONTINENCE:
HORROR VACUI AND THE COLONIAL SUPPLEMENT

Peter Mason

I

Continental incontinence: Yes, of course, but whose?

II

The name America appears for the first time in 1507 on a map of the newly discovered lands by Martin Waldseemüller. As Waldseemüller explains in chapter IX of the accompanying text to the map (*Cosmographiae Introductio*, dating from the same year):

> non video cur quis iure vetet ab Americo inventore sagacis ingeni
> viro Amerigen quasi Americi terram, sive Americam dicendam:
> cum et Europa et Asia a mulieribus sua sortita sunt nomina. [1]

Why is it that these continents are named after *women*? To put the question

---

[1]   I do not see why anyone should rightly object to calling the country America after Amerigo [Vespucci], its wise discoverer: for both Europe and Asia are named after women too.

more irreverently, what is it about the thrust of colonial penetration which demands a female victim (Virginia, Florida, Cuba, Africa, Asia...) to open up to its importunate demands? For time and again colonial discourse on America yields the *topos* of a woman's body waiting to be appropriated by the (European) man. Sir Walter Ralegh talked about the 'glad feet' of the English trampling over 'smooth Guiana's breast', and in exhorting his fellow countrymen not to ignore the colonial challenge posed by Guiana, Lawrence Keymis (1596) used an even more extravagant metaphor when he wrote:

> Let it bee farre from us to condemne ourselves in that, which so worthilie we reproove in our predecessors; and to let our idel knowledge content it selfe with naked contemplation, like a barren womb in a Monasterie.

Peter Hulme (1985) has already discussed some of the problems raised in this colonial onomastics by the fact that the virgin Guiana, 'a countrey that hath yet her maydenhead', as Ralegh put it, was being courted by England, which was itself a 'maid' under the virgin Elizabeth. Besides the long visual tradition of allegorical representations of America as a woman of one sort or another (see e.g. Joris de Zavala 1983), we might see a *reductio ad absurdum* of this *topos* in the description of America by an anonymous author cited by Humboldt who speaks of

> a female form, long, thin, watery, and at the forty-eighth parallel ice-cold. The degrees of latitude are years - woman becomes old at forty-eight. (cited in Gerbi 1973: 417).

This *topos* is one of the threads running through the following remarks. It is therefore strategically appropriate to begin with the first images of the *women* of America, the naked females exposed to the gaze of the male European intruder (ill. 1), who stand in a relation of metonymy to the continent itself.

Waldseemüller's attempt to rule out objections to the derivation of the name of America from Amerigo Vespucci is so emphatic because he is aware of the rival claim to the discovery of the continent by none other than Christopher Columbus. Still, history gave him the benefit of the doubt and it is the accounts of various voyages to America by Vespucci, illustrated by woodcuts, that created the most persuasive early image of the

ill. 1

New World in the mind of the European public, rather than the drier accounts of Columbus' four voyages.

Both the chronology of Vespucci's voyages and the authenticity of the documents relating to them are matters of scholarly dispute. For present purposes, we follow the Latin text known as *Mundus novus*, probably published in Florence toward the end of 1503 or early in the following year, and the Italian text published some two years later known as *Lettera di Amerigo Vespucci delle isole nuovamente trovate in quattro suoi viaggi.* [2]

Vespucci's comment on the Amerindian women requires quotation *in extenso*:

> Mulieres (ut dixi) et si nude incedant et libidinossime sint, eorum tamen corpora habent satis formosa et munda, neque tam turpes sunt, quantum quis fortan existimare posset, quia (quoniam carnose sunt) minus apparet earum turpitudo, que scilicet pro maiori parte a bona corporature qualitate operta est. Mirum nobis visum est quod inter eas nulla videbatur que haberet ubera caduca et que parturierant uteri forma et contractura nihil distinguebantur a virginibus, et in reliquis corporum partibus similia videbantur, que propter honestatem consulto pretereo. Quando se christianis iungere poterant nimia libidine pulse omnem pudiciciam contaminabant. Vivunt annis centum quinquaginta, raro egrotant, et si quam adversam valitudinem incurrunt, seipsos cum quibusdam herbarum radicibus sanant. [3]

---

[2]   Waldseemüller published a Latin translation of this work in 1507 under the title *Quattuor navigationes A. Vesputii* together with the introduction to cosmography, a globe and the map.

[3]   The women, as I have said, go about naked and seductively, but their bodies are attractive and clean enough. Nor are they as shameless as one might perhaps suppose, because the fact of their being well filled out makes their shamelessness less apparent, since it is covered for the most part by their excellent body structure. We were surprised to see that none of them had sagging breasts and that those who had given birth did not differ at all from virgins with respect to the shape and size of their bellies. The same is true for the other parts of the body, which I shall gloss over for decency's sake. When they had the opportunity of having intercourse with Christians they were driven on by excessive lasciviousness and threw all decency to the winds. They live to the age of one hundred and fifty, are rarely ill, and if they do run into bad health, they cure themselves with roots. (Vespucci 1984: 104; Italian version *ibid.*: 134-135).

As one of the first portraits of Amerindian women, the text already deploys a combination of (very!) direct observation and moralizing interpretation. The comments on body complexion, fleshiness and tautness have an initial impact suggesting first-hand (whose hand, one wonders?) perception, but the references to libido bear an obvious moral message: judging by Vespucci's standards (and we shall see later on what the European standards were like), these women were excessively lascivious.

Well, what did Vespucci expect to find there? Apparently not the idyllic relationships supposed to characterise an earthly paradise which coloured Columbus' first perceptions of the New World, at any rate. One answer might be: the two stock themes which were present in European narratives of the (Oriental) other from the Middle Ages on — a social life of lascivious sensuality combined with a political regime marked by inherent violence (Kabbani 1986: 6). Another answer, closer to home, is: people resembling the Wild Man and Wild Woman of the European imaginary, who were also noted for their lasciviousness. [4] This suggestion is confirmed by a detail in the text: Vespucci's surprise at the firmness of the breasts of the women can only be explained if he expected to see the hanging breasts which were a feature of the Wild Woman in many European accounts (cf. Bucher 1981).

The lasciviousness of the women is portrayed in negative terms because it implies that the women wear the men out with their sexual demands. This *topos* goes back to what is perhaps the earliest Greek writer to have come down to us, the Boiotian farmer-poet Hesiodos (*Works & Days* 705; *Theogony* 593ff.). One of the most eloquent statements of this view, which displays a particularly striking similarity to the text of Vespucci, can be found in the case of the Indian women described in the *Epistola ad Aristotelem*, dealing with the campaign of Alexandros the Great against king Poros and with the wonders of India:

> Quae ignaros regionum homines in flumine natantes aut teniendo
> in gurgitibus suffocabant aut tractos in arundineto, cum essent
> specie mirabiles, in affectu suo avide victos rumpebant aut

---

[4]   Ruel la Forte, the wife of the giant Feroz in the *Wigalois*, could age a man prematurely with just one night of sex (Lecouteux 1982, II: 103). Her equally demanding male counterparts are illustrated in Gaignebet & Lajoux 1985: 120-127.

veneria exanimabant voluptate. Quarum nos duas tantummodo
cepimus colore niveo, similes nymphis, diffusis per terga
capillis. [5]

This detail from the Alexander romance presents the same fatal combination that we find in Vespucci: beautiful women who destroy men by
wearing them out sexually (literally 'taking their breath away').

The danger to the male is explicit in Vespucci's account of the
devices used by women to satisfy their desires:

Alius mos est apud eos satis enormis et preter omnem humanam
crudelitatem. Nam mulieres eorum, cum sint libidinose, faciunt
intumescere maritorum inguina in tantam crassitudinem ut
deformia videantur et turpia, et hoc quodam earum artificio et
mordicatione quorundam animalium venenosorum, et huius rei
causa multi eorum ammittunt inguina que illis ob defectum cure
fracescunt et restant eunuchi. [6]

The ability to render men impotent was also a recurrent accusation levelled
against witches in Europe (Kohl 1987: 69). In fact, with their long hair,
familiarity with herbs and sexual proclivity, the Amerindian women of
Vespucci to resemble the witches of Europe. We can consolidate this
casting of the Amerindian women in the role of witches if we shift from
text to image. [7] In a series of three woodcuts to a German edition of
Vespucci from 1509, we see an episode from Vespucci's third voyage. A

---

[5] These women suffocated my men while they, ignorant of the area, were
swimming. (They did this) either by holding them in the eddies or when they
were caught in the thicket of reeds. Since the women were extraordinary in
appearance, the men, who were completely overcome with their fond feeling (for
them), the women treated violently or killed during sexual pleasure. We captured
only two of those. Their complexion was snow-white, (and) like nymphs their hair
spread over their backs (Boer 1973: 57. Tr. Gunderson 1980: 156).

[6] Another of their customs is monstrous and exceeds all human cruelty. For
their women, in their lust, cause the genitals of their menfolk to swell to such a
size that they acquire an ugly and deformed appearance. They do so through their
arts and from the poisonous venom of certain creatures. For this reason many of
the men become impotent and, unable to find a cure, are left eunuchs. (Vespucci
1984: 100).

[7] Compare the depiction of the Amerindian woman as a witch in the
frontispiece to Part 13 of the *Great Voyages*, printed in 1627.

ill. 2

ill. 3

young member of the crew goes ashore, attracted by a group of women who are displaying their sexual wares there. While he is engaged in discussion with one of them, an old hag armed with a club comes up from behind and beats him to death. In the third scene, a woman looks on eagerly as an arm and leg of the victim are chopped up on a butcher's block. Thus a new witch-like attribute is assigned to the women: anthropophagy.

Vespucci claimed to have seen evidence of anthropophagy when he wrote:

> Et item steti diebus vigintiseptem in urbe quadam, ubi vidi per domos humanam carnem salsam, contignationibus suspensam, uti apud nos moris est lardum suspendere et carnem suillam. [8]

Finally, the third of the woodcuts described above shows the woman tenderly gazing on the feast in store as she caresses her breasts and crotch. This is a detail which crops up again in the iconography of Amerindian women. In the illustrations to the encyclopedic work which De Bry began publishing in 1590, we see the same association between sexual self-gratification in a scene of an anthropophagous feast (ill. 2, based on earlier woodcuts from Hans Staden, where these auto-erotic gestures are absent). In another scene, depicting *zemi* worship (ill. 3), the women who flock to the ceremony are depicted in similar poses. And some of the prints, as Bucher suggests (1982: 75), may also imply (the fear of) anal penetration of the male victims by their female assailants (ill. 4). [9]

The earliest texts and iconography relating to the women of South America thus reveal a complex of anthropophagy, sexual licentiousness, sexual deviance and the use of potions. This all adds up to a picture which is isomorphous with the accounts and depictions of witches by Hans Baldung Grien, Dürer and others from the same period. Behind many of these representations it is tempting to see the fantasy of the *vagina dentata* lurking, an age-old representation of the dangers of sexual intercourse as

---

[8]   And likewise I remained twenty-seven days in a certain city, where I saw salted human flesh suspended from beams between the houses, just as with us it is the custom to hang pork. (Vespucci 1984: 102).

[9]   In this connection it is worth considering the possibility that the naked buttocks of an unidentifiable figure in the second of the three Vespucci woodcuts are those of the male victim.

ill. 4

ill. 5

constituting a deadly trap for men by women.

In this connection, one of the most horrifying features of the scenes of cannibal feasts in de Bry is the fact that the consumers are women and children. Their macabre *déjeuner sur l'herbe* implies an *éducation sentimentale* as well, for the adult women here serve to socialize the younger generation in the appropriate table manners — at least, this is one way of reading the action of the child on the left of ill. 5. There is a sexual division present here, for some acts are gender-specific. For instance, illustration 5 conforms to the rule that it is a male who delivers the fatal blow to the victim.[10] Moreover, Bucher (1982) has indicated how the various parts of the victim are distributed in accordance with the gender and age of the recipient: some parts of the body are only consumed by males, others are only consumed by females, etc.

If we move on from Vespucci, it is possible to fill out the witch image even more with the addition of devil worship (cf. ill. 3), but that would take us beyond the scope of the present paper.[11] Instead, we now proceed to contrast Vespucci's image of excessive sexual incontinence with an image of excessive continence: the Amazons.[12]

III

Already before Columbus set foot on American soil he had preconceptions of the Amazons he expected to find there. In fact, in Spain there had been

---

[10]   The old hag in the Vespucci woodcut is exceptional in this respect, as Wendt has pointed out (1989: 15 n.5).

[11]   The process of 'demonization' is by no means confined to European perceptions of America. We find it at work, for instance, in the first European accounts of the Hindu gods. Ludovico di Varthema's description of the idol known as Deumo, who was worshipped by the king of Calicut, dating from between 1503 and 1508, owed far more to European demonological conceptions than to perception of Indian gods (Mitter 1977: 16ff.). In fact, it bears a striking resemblance to the idol reproduced in ill. 3.

[12]   Besides a contrast, there is also a connection between witches and Amazons: it is interesting to note that one of the names given to witches was 'broom Amazons' (Duerr 1985: 174 n.2).

interest in Amazons at least since the thirteenth century (Irizarry 1983). [13]
The many readers of Mandeville's *Travels* could find the following account
of them:

> Next to Chaldea is the land of Amazoun, which we call the
> Maiden Land or the Land of Women; no man lives there, only
> women. This is not because, as some say, no man can live there,
> but because the women will not allow men to rule the kingdom.
> There was once a king in that land called Colopheus, and there
> were once men living there as they do elsewhere. It so happened
> that this king went to war with the King of Scythia, and was slain
> with all his great men in battle with his enemy. And when the
> Queen and the other ladies of that land heard the news that the
> King and the lords were slain, they marshalled themselves with
> one accord and slaughtered all the men left among them. And
> since that time they will never let a man live with them more
> than seven days, nor will they allow a boy child to be brought up
> among them. But when they want to have the company of man,
> they go to that side of their country where their lovers live, stay
> with them eight or nine days and then go home again. If any of
> them bears a child and it is a son, they keep it until it can speak
> and walk and eat by itself and then they send it to the father —
> or they kill it. If they have a girl child, they cut off one of her
> breasts and cauterize it; in the case of a woman of great estate,
> the left one, so that she can carry her shield better, and, in one of
> low degree, they cut off the right, so that it will not hinder them
> shooting — for they know very well the skill of archery. There
> is always a queen to rule that land, and they all obey her. This
> queen is always chosen by election, for they choose the woman
> who is the best fighter. These women are noble and wise
> warriors; and therefore kings of neighbouring realms hire them to
> help them in their wars. This land of the Amazons is an island,
> surrounded by water, except at two points where there are two
> ways in. Beyond the water live their lovers to whom they go
> when it pleases them to have bodily pleasure with them. (Man-
> deville 1983: 116-117).

Columbus' informants told him that the anthropophagous inhabitants of the

---

[13]   For a brief survey of the Amazon tradition see Gerritsen 1985. The
archaic Greek, nineteenth- and twentieth-century traditions are extensively treated
in J. Blok 1991.

island of Carib have intercourse once a year with the women of the island of Matininó, though the explorer himself was more interested in the reports of precious minerals to be found there (Colón 1984: 115, 119). Columbus' willingness to accept the existence of Amazons on the island of Matininó was in line with the European tradition in which the Amazons were particularly aggressive and militaristic. However, they disappear from Columbus' later account. In fact, when Columbus finally did land on the island of Matininó in June 1503, he made no reference at all to the mythical component of the island.

It is worth noting that there is also considerable evidence for the existence of native Indian beliefs concerning a tribe of women without men, first recorded by Fray Ramón Pané in 1494 (Sued-Badillo 1986). Some accounts add references to the vast mineral wealth of the territory of the Amazons, a theme which may have been used, like the myth of El Dorado, as a ploy by the Amerindians to lure the gold-hungry Europeans away. For example, when the German expedition in which Ulrich Schmidel participated was looking for gold, the 'king' of an Indian tribe told the foreigners to set out on a two-month trek over land to a kingdom near the island of the Amazons, where they would find the gold and silver they were looking for (Schmidel 1597: ch. XX).

In his *Singularités de la France antarctique*, which was first published in 1557, the cosmographer André Thevet seized upon the military aggressiveness of the Amazons and presented the following horrific account:

> Elles font la guerre ordinairement contre quelques autres nations, et traitent fort inhumainement ceux qu'elles peuvent prendre en guerre. Pour les faire mourir, elles les pendent par une jambe à quelque haute branche d'un arbre; et après l'avoir laissé quelque espace de temps, quand elles y retournent, si par cas extraordinaire il n'est pas trépassé, elles tireront dix mille coups de flèches; et elles ne le mangent pas comme les autres sauvages, mais le passent par le feu jusqu'à ce qu'il soit réduit en cendres. Davantage, quand ces femmes approchent pour combattre, elles poussent des cris horribles et merveilleux pour épouvanter leurs ennemis. (Thevet 1983: 167).

The Amazons are here presented as embodying the inversion of normal relations. For instance, they invert the position of their male victims by hanging them by the leg instead of by the neck (ill. 6). [14] There is a curious parallel to this upside-down punishment in an account preserved in the 17th century *Crónica mexicáyotl* of Don Fernando Alvarado Tezozomoc:

> Au sortir d'Aztlan, les Mexicas étaient passés par Chicomoztoc; expulsés du paradis, ils étaient issues des Sept Cavernes du corps de Tlecltecuhli. Avant d'atteindre Mexico, il leur faut donc repasser par Chicomoztoc. Tezozomoc raconte qu'après la défaite que leur infligèrent les Colhuas indignés, les Mexicas parvinrent à Acatzintitlan. Là, ils capturèrent Acatzin, 'Derrière d'Acatl'; ils le culbutèrent la tête en bas et lui tirèrent des flèches dans les fesses. Le lieu fut appelé ensuite Mexicatzinco, 'Derrière des Mexicas'. (Graulich 1987: 242).

ill. 6

---

[14]   This was also a form of judicial punishment on the European continent, documented everywhere from Germany to Spain. It was reserved especially for suicides, Jews and homicidal animals, particularly pigs. It was a particularly protracted form of execution, since the victim might remain alive for several days before death occurred. See E. Cohen 1989, 1990.

If Michel Graulich is correct in seeing this incident as the reflection of a rite of taking possession, it might be possible to apply the same reasoning to the case of the Amazons: instead of women being possessed by men, it is the women who here take possession of the men, thereby reversing the usual distribution of male and female roles in terms of activity and passivity. In fact, as in the Greek tradition (Carlier-Detienne 1980-81), the Amazons are anti-men in two senses: they are both *in opposition to men* (anti-men) and *able to take the place of men* (in a male-free society). Anti- is here the glyph of supplementarity, as the Amazons both replace and supplement the male order.

Their ability to dispense with men can be seen in one of the traditions going back to the Greeks that the Amazons only had intercourse with men once a year (Strabon XI.5.1). This near celibacy is thus only broken to ensure the procreation of future generations, and not for any sexual pleasure. [15] Moreover, in some traditions the conjunction of the sexes in the act of procreative intercourse serves only to widen the disjunction between the sexes when the offspring is born. In the eleventh century *Gesta* of Adam of Bremen, for instance, girls born in the northern *terra feminarum* become beautiful women, while boys who are born there become dog-headed *cynocephali*.

As for their location on an island, this too emphasizes their separation from the continent of the men. Cortés, quoting the lords of the province of Ciguatán as his authority, places this island ten days' journey away (1972: 300). The island, like the desert, featured as a spot beyond the civilized world in medieval literature (Le Goff 1985: 64). Not only is it separated from *terra firma*, but its traditionally circular form is an image of self-sufficiency which also implies that it can get along nicely without the mainland (cf. Marin 1973: 137ff.).

The continence of the Amazons is also reflected in the extreme treatment of the flesh of their male victims, which is excessively cooked by the reduction to ashes. In this they form a counterpart and contrast to the excessive lack of cooking in the consumption of raw meat by the anthropophagi. Theirs is rather a case of continence: they abstain from eating human flesh and reduce it to ashes instead.

---

[15]   Curiously, there is no ancient tradition crediting the Amazons with parthenogenesis (Loraux 1981: 91 n.84).

If we find excess in the portrayal of the Amazons, it is thus an
excessive continence, a culture of deprivation — the deprivation of one
breast, the deprivation of a diet of human flesh, the deprivation of social
or sexual contact. Instead of engaging in the maternal pursuits connected
with life with men, they engage in warfare, the antithesis of marriage. [16]

IV

If we were structuralists, the right and proper thing to do at this stage
would presumably be to turn from images of women to images of men, to
explore them in terms of continence/incontinence, keeping a close watch
for mirror inversions and the like, and then to fill in the four corners of a
rectangular structure with + and - signs.

One obstacle to such an interpretative framework is the presence of
'impure' forms, which a structuralist approach can only dub as 'intermediate', 'anomalous', or the like. Take the following account of Brazilian
Amazons from Pero de Magalhães de Gandavo's *Historia de provincia
Sancta Cruz* (1576):

> There are some Indian women who determine to remain chaste:
> these have no commerce with men in any manner, nor would they
> consent to it even if refusal meant death. They give up all the
> duties of women and imitate men, and follow men's pursuits as
> if they were not women. They wear the hair cut in the same way
> as the men, and go to war with bows and arrows and pursue
> game, *always in company with men*; each has a woman to serve
> her, to whom she says she is married, and they treat each other
> and speak with each other as man and wife. (Magalhães de
> Gandavo 1922: 89-90; my italics).

There certainly is a mechanism of inversion at work here. In particular, the
detail that the women wear their hair cut in the same way as men has its

---

[16]   For ancient Greece, Vernant notes, marriage is to the girl what war is to
the boy. Hence, he adds, the Amazons of myth correspond structurally to the
virgin goddesses of the Greek cults such as Athena: their warrior status is likened
to their virgin condition, both of which oppose them to the role of married women
(Vernant 1974: 38).

mirror inversion in Columbus' report that the anthropophagous male inhabitants of the island of Carib, with whom the women of the island of Matininó have intercourse, wear their hair long like women (Colón 1984: 145). However, though the women in the above account are Amazon-like in many respects, they fight in the company of men — an awkward detail for any scheme of binary oppositions.

For those who do not see the inevitability of a binary opposition of the sexes in terms of male/female — these categories are constituted within linguistic praxis, and we may wonder with Shirley Ardener (1975: xviii) whether the category 'women' might not be entirely an intellectual creation which one day may disappear — such an approach is bound to raise more questions than it is likely to solve. But since there is no harm in raising questions, we will start off in that direction. So where are the incontinent males?

One simple answer is: in the dirty minds of the Europeans. To take a modern example, Brazilian soldiers asked the Trumai Indians (Upper Xingú) if they could marry any woman at all, i.e. all the categories of possible wives. The Trumai response was 'Yes, we can marry any woman at all', i.e. all the categories of *permitted* wives. In the discrepancy between the two statements arose the misunderstanding that Indian men were promiscuous. Tellingly, the Indians' comment was: 'Mince! C'est dégoutant! Et eux, alors? C'est plutôt eux qui font ça!' (Becquelin Monod 1988: 298-299).

But there is another form of incontinence which is attributed to Amerindian males: sodomy. In September 1513 Balboa attacked the Indians of Quaraco province (Panama), ancestors of the contemporary Cuna, and threw twenty of them alive to his dogs on a charge of sodomy. The event is recorded by Petrus Martyr, and illustrated by De Bry in Part Four of the *Great Voyages* (1594) (ill. 7).

Traditionally, unnatural vices had been imported into Europe from the Orient during the Crusades (Chiffoleau 1990: 298), but it was not difficult for America to assume the same function once it had been added to the repertoire of Europe's others. Hence some form or other of sexual deviance soon became a commonplace in the European sources dealing with the people of America. Hernán Cortés reported in his first letter from Mexico that all the men were sodomites (1972: 37). Cieza de León was surprised that the men went in for sodomy even when they had access to beautiful women, and Gonzalo Fernández de Oviedo commented on the

ill. 7

vice of anal intercourse practised between Arawak men and women as an unnatural act. The line on sodomy and other practices had been made clear by Aquinas. Sodomy was viewed as unnatural because it occurred between inappropriate sexual partners; masturbation was viewed as unnatural because it involved the sexual act 'in a vessel not ordained for it'. On a par with these acts was cannibalism, because it involved the consumption of unnatural foodstuffs (cf. Pagden 1982: 176).

Jean de Léry was more cautious in suggesting what he had not been able to confirm:

> [...] quelquefois en se dépitant l'un contre l'autre, ils s'appellent Tyvire, c'est-à-dire bougre; on peut donc conjecturer de là (car je n'en affirme rien) que cet abominable péché se commet entre eux. (Léry 1980: 200).

There was another ground for conjecturing the existence of such practices in the Americas: the alleged presence of monstrous human figures there, the so-called Plinian races, which feature in accounts of the New World from Columbus and Vespucci on. It was commonly assumed that the birth of deformed babies was due to sexual deviation on the part of the parents or mother. The *Secreta Mulierum*, for instance, a text attributed to Albertus

Magnus, assumes that monstrous births may be caused by the adoption of an 'unnatural' sexual position during intercourse, copulation during menstruation, or an act of bestiality (whether it took place in fact or only in the mother's imagination) (Céard 1977: 36). Thus the presence of monstrous humans in the New World could be seen as 'evidence' of the prevalence of sexually deviant practices on the part of the New World inhabitants. The opposite argument was put forward by the apologist for the Indians, Bartolomé de las Casas. He argued that the longevity of the Indians (Vespucci's mention of life spans of 150 years is no exception) was the result of their sexual continence, for otherwise the enervating effects of sex would have prevented them from reaching such an advanced age (Rech 1985).

Soon after the failure of the French expedition to Brazil in which de Léry had participated, France diverted its gaze to North America, sending an expedition to Florida in 1562. Two years later a second group of colonists arrived there, led by René de Laudonnière. We have valuable information about the Timucua Indians of Florida from de Laudonnière himself and from the paintings of them by Le Moyne, which found their way into De Bry's compilation (cf. Hulton 1978). The French were fascinated by large numbers of what they referred to as Hermaphrodites, who were assumed to have a social status equivalent to that of the women, but at the same time to be stronger than the other male members of the tribe. They are thus not hermaphrodites in the sense of the Plinian race bearing that name, which was credited with the possession of both male and female sexual organs. In the case of the Timucua, the term refers to their social position, but also to their physical appearance. They have long curly hair (perhaps recalling the traditional medieval image of the sodomite, like Chaucer's Pardoner), and they wear skirts (ills. 8 & 9).

Other travellers to North America recorded the presence of a group of men who dressed as women and performed female labour. Dumont de Montigny spent twenty-two years among the Natchez of Louisiana, devoting a chapter of his account of them to the 'Hermaphrodites'. Charlevoix and La Hontan noted similar practices among the Illinois, and Bossu did the same for the Choctaw (Duviols 1982: 37).

So throughout the eighteenth century it was commonly assumed that homosexual practices were prevalent in the Americas, North and South. Voltaire discussed them under the heading of 'Amour nommé socratique' (1967: 18-21), and Diderot and Buffon also assumed it to be the case,

ill. 8

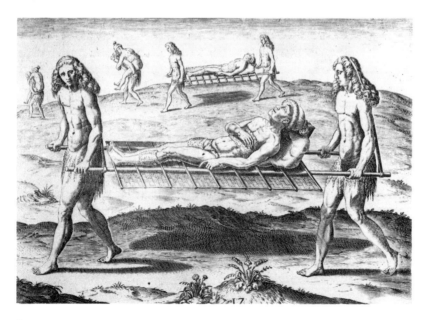

ill. 9

though each of them offered a different explanation for it (references in Duchet 1971: 264f., 304, 446). But as this brief survey shows, the existence of sexual practices that deviated from the European norms was deduced from the flimsiest evidence: linguistic arguments, style of dress, or a female role in the division of labour.

Moreover, the terminology is bewildering and confused. Are we to assume that the Indians were sodomites, homosexuals, transvestites, hermaphrodites, bisexuals, or nothing of the kind? In a sense, there is little point in trying to attain analytical precision, for the European observers were simply not interested in precision of this kind. The reason is equally simple: the act of sodomy was conceived as the *summum* of a life of deviancy which might include celibacy, masturbation or even failure to comply with the sexual obligations of marriage.[17] Because of the diffuseness of these phenomena, any sign which could be read as pointing in this direction was sufficient to label its bearer as deviant, and thereby fully capable of indulging in all the other forms of deviancy too.[18] There was no need to go further into the specific forms which this deviancy might take.

The details of the practices of the males are not so important, compared with the general and generalized image of their sexual incontinence as such. What is important, however, is its articulation with the forms of female continence/incontinence discussed earlier. To get some idea of this relation, it is instructive to compare a report of sodomy which, though drawn from a different geographical provenance, goes some way toward indicating the inner logic of the relation in question:

> Every man and man-child among them, hath a nayle of Tynne thrust quite through the head of his privie part, being split in the lower ende, and rivetted, and on the head of the nayle is as it were a Crowne: which is driven through their privities when they be yong, and the place growth up againe, without any great paine to the child: and they take this nayle out and in as occasion serveth; and for the truth thereof, we our selves have taken one of these nayles from a Sonne of one of the Kings, which was of

---

[17]   For the eighteenth century see Th. van der Meer 1984: 27.

[18]   This could extend beyond forms of sexual deviancy, of course. Thus from the tenth century on there was a tendency to assimilate sodomy and heresy on the European continent (Chiffoleau 1990).

the age of tenne yeeres, who did weare the same in his privy member. This custome was granted at the request of the women of the Countrey, who finding their men to be given to the fowle sinne of Sodomie, desired some remedie against that mischiefe, and obtained this before named of the Magistrates. [...] Moreover, all the males are circumcised, having the foreskinne of their flesh cut away. These people wholly worshippe the Devill, and oftentimes have conference with him, which appeareth unto them in most ugly and monstrous shape. (Samuel Purchas, *Hakluytus Posthumus; or Purchas His Pilgrimes*, 20 vols., 1625, cited in J. Boon 1982: 165).

This text relates to the southern Philippines, not directly to the Americas, although there is in fact a tenuous historical link in that Purchas attributed the malpractices of circumcision, sodomy and devil worship to the nefarious influence of the Spaniards in the area. Its usefulness here, though, is morphological: it indicates a pattern in which the incontinence of the males in checked by the females. [19] It is the women who impose a sexual order on their menfolk. They do so by means of a nail, capped by a crown: as the (metonymic) instrument by which the women impose their sexual order, the nail thus shows who is wielding sexual power now: the women have a monarchical power. As for the male, he is penetrated in 'the head of his privie part' — the symbolism associating the head with male rule here suffers an infraction of that rule, split by the instrument wielded by the women. [20]

The argument for seeing the Philippine case as an inversion of the norm can be strengthened by looking at a case in which the norm is forcefully presented using similar imagery. This time we turn to Tahiti and the description of sexual barter recorded by the master of Captain Wallis' ship, the *Dolphin*, which landed in Tahiti in 1767. [21] Tahitian girls granted the sailors of the *Dolphin* their favours in exchange for nails. The

---

[19]   The term 'morphological' is used in the sense given it by Carlo Ginzburg (1989). It should be apparent that the morphological approach adumbrated in the present article is very heavily indebted to Ginzburg's recent work.

[20]   At least some of Purchas' readers must have been sensitive to the biblical overtones too: Sisera had killed Jael with a nail in the head (*Judges* 4).

[21]   I am here drawing on the witty presentation of the Pacific material by Roy Porter (1989).

price was soon hit by inflation as the girls demanded increasingly longer
nails. What better symbol of European incontinence can one imagine than
the disintegration of the *Dolphin* because so many nails were prised loose
from its timbers? Behind the amusing sexual innuendos of this language
in which a nail is the price of a screw one can detect an implicit statement
of the norm: it is men who are supposed to be in charge of the supplies of
nails by which they secure the submission of women. And since power is
differential, the nails are involved in a symbolism which can also express
differences: the master of the ship, who is dressed differently from the
other members of the crew, is therefore supposed to be in possession of
longer nails by the Tahitian girls. Nail symbolism and the vestimentary
code reinforce one another and the vesting of power in the hands of their
owner.

                                        V

The texts discussed above carry both political and sexual-political
overtones. In the Philippine case, the patriarchal model of phallocentric
monarchy has been disrupted and the power of the males has been usurped
by the women as a result of the sexual incontinence of the men. The same
internal logic structures the earliest accounts, as well as the pictorial
images, of the relations between Amerindian men and women. The
continence of the Amazons enabled them to dispense to a large extent with
men for their sexual pleasure. The sodomy of the Amerindian males is an
attempt to dispense with women. But the Amazon/sodomite dichotomy
implies an asymmetrical power relation, for while the Amazons are a
womanlike, aggressive people, the effeminate sodomites are subser-
vient. [22] This pattern of articulation in male/female relationships contains
both a relative separation between the sexes *and* a subordination of males
to females. It is here that the issue becomes more complex, because this
is also the point at which European/American relations are articulated.

    We can now introduce the Europeans to the scene. And see how
they come!

_____

[22]   Within this perspective, the Timucua hermaphrodites cannot be seen as
occupying an intermediate status between the Timucua warriors and the women,
pace Bucher (1981: 153). Their position is not intermediate, but subordinate.

Victorie of them may be gained in many waies: by force, by
surprize, by famine in burning their Corne, by destroying and
burning their Boats, Canoes, and Houses, by breaking their
fishing Weares, by assailing them in their huntings [...] by
pursuing and chasing them with our hourses, and blood-Hounds
to draw after them, and Mastives to tear them, which take this
naked, tanned, deformed Savages for no other than wild beasts.
(E. Waterhouse, *A declaration of the state of the colony and
affaires in Virginia*, London, 1622: 24; cited in L. Pennington,
1978: 193)

Waterhouse can be seen as a representative of the new line in British
policy after the massacre of the Virginian colonists in 1622. The anti-
Spanish thrust of earlier propaganda is now watered down as Waterhouse
espouses the same methods as those followed by Balboa and his dogs a
little over a century earlier. [23]

Unwittingly, then, the various European colonial powers become
interchangeable in their use of the brute instruments of domination. There
is a further step in this process, for not only do the Europeans come to
resemble one another; the Europeans themselves come to resemble their
picture of the 'savage' Amerindians whom they have come to civilise.
Take for instance Columbus' scepticism about the early reports of
cannibals. He assumes that *canibales* must mean 'soldiers of the Can' (i.e.
the Great Khan), and to refer to a people that is well-armed and therefore
endowed with reason. However, the sub-text suggests that these canibales
are in fact just like the Spaniards — well-armed, intelligent, cultured,
inspiring fear — an identification which 'hints that the real "canibales" of
the Journal are in effect the Spaniards themselves' (P. Hulme 1989: 35).

In its quest for self-legitimation, the European presence was
justified, deliberately or not, by a number of techniques. For instance, the
sixteenth century debate on whether the Indians were natural slaves or not
was at the same time a debate on the legitimacy of their enslavement. As
early as 1512 the Junta de Burgos met to discuss the rights and wrongs of

---

[23]   According to Robert Schomburgk, the Spaniards first used mastiffs against
the Indians on Haiti. One of these dogs, Bezzerillo, was trained to pursue Indians
and drag them back to camp by the arm; if they showed any signs of resistance
they were torn to pieces. He concludes 'the race of Bezzerillo was propagated
from the island to the continent for the destruction of the unfortunate Indians on
the main' (Schomburgk, in Ralegh 1970: 138 n.1).

the subjection of the Amerindians to the *encomienda* system, following the first protest against the treatment of the Amerindians which Antonio de Montesinos had made in a sermon at the end of 1511. The debate continued for decennia, culminating in the exchanges between Sepúlveda and Las Casas in Valladolid in 1550-51 (see Pagden 1982).

To take a second example, persuasive definitions of the lack of Amerindian agriculture were put forward to justify the appropriation of 'uncultivated' land by those who claimed to know how to work it better. Given their alleged lack of civil society, and thus of property relations, the Amerindians could make no claims to ownership when confronted by invaders out to seize their lands. For their lands were not *theirs*, but were viewed as open spaces which they fortuitously happened to inhabit (Pagden 1990: 15).

The present discussion yields a third example, revealing how the issue of incontinence on the part of the American continent might be seen to necessitate external intervention to redress the balance and put matters right.

The following hypothesis might be advanced: the images presented to the Europeans by the Amerindians became particularly charged (whether positively or negatively) at the point at which they came to occupy what Freud called the *innere Ausland*. Ethnological and psychoanalytical categories seem to converge at the point where the strangeness of the foreign, or exotic, culture evokes an unsettling strangeness within the psyche. Symptomatic in this respect is a print from the end of the sixteenth century by Adriaen Collaert in which a number of these themes are combined (ill. 10). In the background to the right is a 'Black Legend' scene of an armed clash between Europeans and Amerindians; in the background to the left is the stock image of a human limb being roasted on a spit; [24] the unfamiliar fauna include a parrot — a symbol of the exotic *par excellence*; and the monstrous armadillo in the foreground, whose evil

---

[24]   This image can lay claim to being one of the earliest, if not the earliest, stereotypes of America. In a catalogue of 'extant illustrations prior to de Bry and having some claim to ethnographic accuracy' compiled by William Sturtevant in 1976, the first entry is a Portuguese manuscript map (Kunstmann II) of the coasts of the South Atlantic dated to 1502. The Brazilian coast bears a scene of a white man skewered on a spit being turned over a fire by a kneeling, naked, curly-haired, bearded, brown-skinned man (Sturtevant 1976: 420).

Illa quidem nos tris dudum non cognita terris,
Faᶜta brevi auriferis latè celeberrima venis,

Visceribus scelerata suis humana recondens
Viscera feralem pretendit AMERICA clavam,

ill. 10

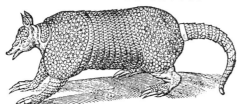

ARMADILLO CLVSII.

ARMADILLO GENVS ALTERVM CLVSII.

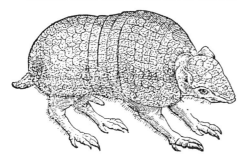

ill. 11

aspect is enhanced by the addition of a pair of devil-like horns,[25] bears
the unsettling figure of an almost nude but heavily armed female warrior.

To borrow a Freudian morphology for the time being, the European
contact with alleged Amerindian *mores* may be a case of this kind. The
Amerindians as a whole are characterized by *lack*: lack of discrimination
in sexual and culinary matters, lack of religion, lack of agriculture, lack of
clothing...[26] And within the Freudian scheme, lack has the double connotation of i) the female lack of the phallus, and ii) the threatened lack of
the phallus in the case of the castrated male. The Amerindian men and
women pose a threat of precisely this kind: emasculated men, aggressive
women who sometimes take the Freudian role of castrator literally (cf. the
use of venomous insects cited above).

Only two implications will be mentioned here. Firstly, the anchoring
of the alleged social lack of the Amerindians within such a psychological
framework might help to explain the determination of the Europeans to
exorcise the spectre of the castrating female and the castrated male by
putting matters to rights. It would then be yet another example of the rule
formulated by Stallybrass and White (1986: 193) as follows: '[...] the
exclusion necessary to the formation of social identity [...] is simultaneously a *production* at the level of the imaginary'.[27] The theme of inversion
is a common one in the sources on America, so the Europeans could see
it as their burden to reverse this inversion and thereby put America on a
European footing.

Not that the Europeans always know how to handle the mechanism
of re-inversion. De Léry was perplexed by the refusal of the Tupinamba
women to wear clothes. In fact, if his men had not forced them to dress by
whipping them, they would have preferred the scorching and heat of the

---

[25]   Of course, this would only be a significant detail if one could indicate that
European representations of armadillos do not usually feature horns. This is
demonstrably the case: the armadillos depicted in Juan Eusebio Nieremberg's
Historia naturae (1635), for example, have pointed ears but no horns (ill. 11).

[26]   Lack is in fact one of the recurring *topoi* in descriptions of the New
World, for it was precisely this absence which made it possible to 'turn over a
new leaf' and to reinscribe history on an unwritten page. For the later development of this theme in North American literature see T. Martin 1985.

[27]   How a negative factor like exclusion can play a positive role is discussed
in Karskens' important contribution to the present volume.

sun to enduring any clothing on their bodies.

So the women are whipped to put on clothes. But they are also whipped to take them off. A member of Columbus's second voyage, M. de Cuneo, relates how he captured a beautiful Carib woman. When she resisted his attempts to rape her, he whipped her until they came to an 'agreement', after which she behaved like a well-trained whore (Todorov 1982: 53-54).

Is this contradictory attitude not that of the voyeur — often a synonym for the anthropologist — who derives his/her pleasure from gazing at what is denied? We also encounter resistance to this voyeurism, but — as happened on the European continent too — those who failed to conform to the European norms of continence (whether in dietary, sexual or other terms) were qualified as monstrous: the casting of the Amerindians as Plinian monsters, the casting of certain individuals in Europe as witches, the casting of the inhabitants of both continents as cannibals... Anthropological nomenclature itself bears the scars of this vision in terms of resistance or acceptance: in the Caribbean area, 'Arawaks' are those who are prepared to accept the Spaniards, while 'Caribs' are those who defend their territory and way of life (Hulme 1986: 72), paying the price in the deformation of their name to 'Caliban' and 'cannibal'.

Secondly, the use to which this Freudian scheme is put raises inevitable questions about that scheme itself. As Raymond Corbey has argued, (1989: Ch. VI; and his contribution to the present volume), Freud's very reference to female sexuality as a *dark continent* is symptomatic of the dependence of his metaphors (and more besides?) on European discourse on Africa, and involves, he claims, a subordination of Freudian theory to the same constraints as the European anthropologist-explorers. In fact, as a symptomatic instance of psychoanalysis' own desire to know, this can be seen as just one of the many instances where 'the exposition of Freud's theory of the psyche acts out its own theorization', where 'the structure of Freud's thought, as it develops, becomes immanent as theme' (J. Fineman 1981: 46-47).

Attitudes toward the seriousness and the implications of this theoretical self-reflection will vary. While some may see in it a coincidence of Freud's hermeneutics with the object of their inquiry, others will see them as examples of the ways in which Freud at times reproduces late-nineteenth-century theories without subjecting them to a full critique (and what critique could ever be full?). [28] At any rate, one criticism that cannot be neglected here is the obvious phallocentrism of the Freudian scheme: if we were to adopt it as an explanatory model, we would fall prey to the very same motivations which led the Spaniards and other encroachers on American soil to perpetrate such excesses (ill. 12). This does not necessarily mean a rejection of Freud; it can rather be seen as a strategy of *Freud contre Freud*, the movement summed up by Beckett as IMAGINATION DEAD IMAGINE, which we might paraphrase here as ANALYSIS DEAD ANALYSE. As we shall see in looking at the case of Foucault, it is the

ill. 12

---

[28]   Here I can do no more than refer to Derrida's remarks on what is to be done: 'nécessité d'un immense travail de déconstruction de ces concepts et des phrases métaphysiques qui s'y condensent et s'y sédiment. Des complicités métaphysiques de la psychanalyse et des sciences dites humaines [...]' (1967a: 294).

question of how one might provide an account of what is beyond the boundaries of *logos* without lapsing into an irrationalism which is itself no more than the inversion of *logos* — a form of 'anti-ism' against which Derrida has issued so many warnings. [29]

VI

1990: 250 years on from the birth of the Marquis de Sade. 1992: 500 years after the 'discovery' of America by Columbus (though how many millennia after the discovery of America by *homo sapiens*?). Columbus and De Sade, two pioneers in the expansion of the limits of the European imagination, meet in the Marquis' cell in the Bastille, where De Sade projected a philosophical essay (*'savante dissertation'*) on America to complete the first volume of the *Portefeuille d'un homme de lettres* (Sade 1986: 527-529).

We know that De Sade possessed at this time a copy of C. de Pauw's controversial *Recherches philosophiques sur les Américains* (Berlin 1768), which presented a very pessimistic view of the inhabitants of America related to climatological theories (cf. Gerbi 1973: 81 and *passim*), going much further than Buffon had done. De Pauw did not see the New World as a fresh, new territory, but as a degenerate land of Indians who were little better than animals or children. It is a strikingly negative portrayal of the radical alterity of America, which was denied a place in world history and condemned to remain perpetually in a state which was completely outside the 'stages of humanity'.

Voltaire's reaction to De Pauw was generally enthusiastic, and it seems likely that De Sade also intended to take up a position in this debate. While imprisoned in Vincennes, he was also making notes and extracts from what he read, this time including a note from 1780 on man's animal ancestry:

> En sorte que, comme certaines couleurs claires ne sont que des dégradations des plus sombres, nous ne sérions à le bien prendre qu'une très belle espèce de bête. (Sade 1986: 471).

---

[29] See, for example, Derrida 1967b: vi-vii; 1972: 39; 1978: 64-65.

It is not difficult to see how a reading of De Pauw some years later might have been in a similar vein, the Americans lending themselves for addition to the Hottentots and other exotic peoples listed by De Sade.

But besides De Sade the philosopher, there is De Sade the sensationalist. One of the few fragments (fragments of a lost work? or fragments of a work that only existed in De Sade's imagination?) of the *Portefeuille* is a brief and pathetic account of the massacres of Protestants at Mérindol and Cabrières in Provence in 1545. [30] This picture of mass rape and killing is presented as an image of Hell, and all in the name of a God of peace. This is how the women are treated:

> Plusieurs sont attachées à des arbres et déchirées à coups de four-
> che, quelques-unes poignardées, au même instant qu'elles
> assouvissent malgré elles les effroyables désirs de ces monstres.
> (Sade 1986: 530).

Inevitably, such scenes recall the Spanish treatment of the Indians as denounced in Bartolomé de Las Casas' *Brevissima relación de la destruyción de las Indias occidentales* (1552). Ill. 13 is just one of the many gruesome scenes which can be found in the later volumes of De Bry's *Great Voyages*. [31] They also recall judicial proceedings, at a time when official acts of torture and official acts of the desecration of the corpses of certain criminals can be seen to anticipate some of the acts performed by rioting crowds (Davis 1975: 162). But such scenes from the

---

[30]   Voltaire mentioned these massacres a number of times too, but de Sade's references are more insistent. For instance, in borrowing from Voltaire's *Questions de Zapata* (question 53) for a passage in *La Nouvelle Justine*, de Sade illustrates Voltaire's reference to the massacre of innocents with the examples of Saint-Barthélémy, Mérindol and Cabrières. Given their setting in the Provence, it is not surprising that Mérindol and Cabrières recur at the end of *Les Harangeurs Provençaux* and in *Le Président Mystifié*. No doubt some of the resentment of these passages is connected with the condemnation of De Sade himself in Aix in 1772. De Sade returned to them in another litany of the crimes committed in the name of Christianity in *Aline et Valcour* (Sade 1990: 629). For de Sade's practice of borrowing and rewriting, with particular reference to Voltaire and d'Holbach, see J. Deprun (1970).

[31]   Incidentally, Dutch translations of Las Casas were used to support a Nornhern equivalent of the Spanish *leyenda negra* (Schama 1987: 84).

ill. 13

conquest of the Americas also recall scenes from the *120 Journées* — what does this tell us about history and fiction? [32]

---

[32]   For another case of this kind it may be noted that Pigafetta and Snelgrave had absurd tales of the butchery of human flesh by the Jagas, which resonate in the *Encyclopédie* article 'Jagas' attributed to Holbach. The legend persists in Sade's *Aline et Valcour* (Sade, 1990: 551; cf. Duchet, 1971: 81 n.102). For other examples of Sade's reworking of American ethnographic material in the same fictional travel narrative, *Aline et Valcour*, see J.-Cl. Sanglier (forthcoming).

To turn from De Sade to an opposite vision — Thomas More's *Utopia* — the same question of the blending of history and fiction arises. Vasco de Quiroga, a Spanish humanist who became bishop of Michoacán, set up two Indian settlements, both called Santa Fé, in which the communities were organised along lines which recall More's *Utopia*. Even though the link with More has been exaggerated by some scholars,[33] this might still be seen as an example of fiction preceding action. On the other hand, More's *Utopia* itself is 'rhetorically indistinguishable from the description of an actual foreign nation', claims Mary Campbell (1988: 217). Here the American continent seems to function as a testing ground for various combinations of 'fiction' and 'reality'.[34]

The twin aspects which were available to De Sade (the philosophical issue of the alleged degeneracy of the peoples of America and the sensational theme of European excesses under the banner of Christianity) provided incontinence on both continents: the childlike incontinence of the Amerindians and the incontinence of the *conquistadores* in the combination of sexual and physical abuse. (It would obviously be begging the question to label the Europeans as sadists *avant la lettre*.) At the same time, and in an inverse movement, the behaviour of his fellow Europeans raises questions about whether it makes any sense to refer to the marquis as a sadist. But such questions will be left aside here.

The case of De Sade is especially relevant for our present purposes, however, because it raises a question of an apparently different kind: what are we to make of the incontinence of the writer, or the incontinence of the text? In other words, the ensemble of articulations we have considered so far — male/female relationships in the Americas, European/American relations — needs extending further to cover the articulation of these

---

[33]   Compare the remarks on the limits of Quiroga's humanitarianism and on his debt to More in Pagden 1990: 25.

[34]   One attempt to come to terms with the fictive nature of American reality can be found in Taussig's recent work (1987). And if the suggestion that we might read De Sade as an ethnographer in some sense of the word seems strange to some, it is worth noting Susan Stewart's remarks (1989: 68 n.5) on what she calls 'the later "ethnology" of the Marquis de Sade. The closed world of the chateau at Silling, for example, with its costumes, manners, ceremonies, customs, and social ranks, presents us with a spectacle of narrative testimonies which refuse to realize themselves as events.'

themes with the text which describes, or inscribes, them. It is this aspect which is the subject of the following section.

VII

> Mais il faudrait interroger justement ce thème si fréquent que le sexe est hors discours et que seule la levée d'un obstacle, la rupture d'un secret peut ouvrir le chemin qui mène jusqu' à lui. [...] Il ne faut pas oublier que la pastorale chrétienne, en faisant du sexe ce qui, par excellence, devait être avoué, l'a toujours présenté obstinément, mais ce qui se cache partout, l'insideuse présence à laquelle on risque de rester sourd tant elle parle d'une voix basse et souvent déguisée. Le secret du sexe n'est sans doute pas la réalité fondamentale par rapport à laquelle se situent toutes les incitations à en parler — soit qu'elles essaient de le briser, soit que de façon obscure elles le reconduisent par la manière même dont elles parlent. [...] Ce qui est propre aux sociétés modernes, ce n'est pas qu'elles aient voué le sexe à rester dans l'ombre, c'est qu'elles se soient vouées à en parler toujours, en le faisant valoir comme *le* secret! (M. Foucault 1976: 48-49).

Foucault has a place in the present discussion for at least three reasons. First, he accorded a significant place to discussion of the work of De Sade in his *Les Mots et les Choses* (1966). Secondly, the three volumes of his history of sexuality which appeared before his death are highly relevant to the question of the *effects* of writing about sexuality. Thirdly, it was Foucault who formulated the problem of how to write an account of madness that was on the side of madness, that did not collude in the acts of violence which were themselves constitutive of 'madness' as such. By analogy, in the present case, how are we to suppose that it might be possible to write about continental incontinence while remaining aloof from that incontinence itself? After all, was not the text on the Orient a pre-text for the presentation of salacious details by Burton and others (Kabbani 1986: 37-66)? And — to take the argument a step further — how would the content of such a discussion itself remain divorced from the container in which the discussion was being put? Is America once again no more than a foil, dragged in as the form to contain the content of the present (European) text? Frame/form/content; inside/outside — the metaphysics implied by such oppositions no longer seem to make much sense.

Inadvertently, we seem to have moved a long way away from the structural oppositions with which we began — proof of the *efficacy* of the text.

I would like to single out three aspects of Foucault's text at this point. First, we should briefly indicate where the complicity between Foucault's text and its subject lies. Look at the language he uses — it involves a slippage from 'le sexe' as 'sex' to 'le sexe' as the *female* genitals. 'Le sexe' is something that is hidden (*caché*). It speaks with a low, seductive voice like the female Sirens of antiquity. Speech about sex, on the other hand, is aroused (*incité*). It tries to break (*briser*) the secret. It is importunate (*obstiné*). In short, this is the language of sexual penetration. Like Freud, Foucault is continuing a discourse which relates the images of male discovery to the images of the female as object of discovery. A few pages further on, Foucault remarks on children's sexuality that it is surrounded by 'des lignes de *pénétration* indéfinie' (1976: 58; my emphasis). And if 'le sexe' has not ceased to provoke a sort of 'éréthisme discursif généralisé' since the eighteenth century (*ibid.*: 45), it is hard to avoid seeing in this a state of generalized sexual excitement provoked by the hidden female sexual organs.

Secondly, as a result of the slippage from a neutral to a decidedly masculine text, Foucault tends to minimize the effect of sexual misconduct with young girls for the individuals concerned (cf. 'ce quotidien de la sexualité villageoise', referring to an account of the sexual abuse of minors by a simpleton, *ibid.*: 43-45), a bias which can only be labelled sexist.

Thirdly, the generalized erethism to which he refers becomes a hallmark of his own text.

Some might just see a use of metaphor here, but the important point is the choice of *the particular metaphors* to which Foucault resorts and their *effects*. For one of these effects is to align Foucault's discourse with the prying tendency he is actually describing. In this respect, Foucault is simply following in the footsteps of Diderot and his other Enlightenment predecessors. Suzanne Rodin Pucci (1989) has recently offered a valuable analysis of the imbrication of exoticism in the Enlightenment. There is a remarkable congruence between the metaphor of the harem, where the impenetrability of women's difference is a function of their existence as discrete entities with their own (sexual) truths, and the impossibility of resolving the truths with which the experimental scientist is confronted into a systematic philosophy. In both cases — the sexual and the scientific — the (male) observer is still the point of reference for the process that he

initiates: as writer, as philosopher, and as 'sultan'. Even more striking is
the suggestion that this congruence may not just be a question of metaphor,
but that there may actually be a metonymic relationship at stake. The same
paradigm structures both the process of knowledge and the structure of
(sexual) desire. [35] Though she does not make the connection herself, there
is a resemblance between her analysis of the masculine thrust of metaphysical desire in the work of Diderot and Jacques Derrida's suggestive
remarks on the play of masculinity and femininity in Nietzsche (Derrida
1978).

The case of Foucault has been chosen to suggest some of the ways
in which the texts we have been discussing relating to incontinence are
themselves articulated with the continence/incontinence of the discussion
itself. At one level, this is simply confirmation of De Sade's proud boast
that no reader would be the same again after reading *120 Journées de
Sodome*. Every word I write is a case of incontinence, a determination to
vent the pent. Or to put it another way: every text is excessive. Or, as
Musil described it in *The Man Without Qualities*, it is

> the well-known incoherency of ideas, with their way of spreading
> out without a central point, an incoherency *that is characteristic
> of the present era* [my emphasis] and constitutes its peculiar arith-
> metic, rambling about in a multitude of things, from a hundred
> possibilities to yet a thousand others, and always without a basic
> unity.

There is a precise term that can be evoked to refer to this state of affairs:
decadence. To quote:

> Il n'y a donc rien de paradoxal à ce que la conscience struc-
> turaliste soit conscience catastrophique, détruite à la fois et
> destructrice, *destructurante*, comme l'est toute conscience ou au
> moins le moment décadent, période propre à tout mouvement de
> la conscience. (Derrida 1967a: 13).

---

[35]   Compare the discussion of the parallel between the Franco-Persian
philosophe's desire to understand, to 'know' the exotic Other, and the overriding
(and likewise never satisfied) desire in *Lettres persanes* to know what women are
all about, in Leerssen 1987.

Derrida's text marks the relation of the present remarks to the 'struc-turalist' suggestions made earlier. They are situated in and as a moment of decadence, the moment when the vacant edifices of a ghost town still reveal the traces of their previous glory and have not yet given way to a return to nature.

This is where the argument can be given another twist to send it in yet a different direction. To recall the rhetoric of emptiness which called for suppletion by the colonial presence, we saw how tempting it was to place this within a morphology owing something to Freud and to see this move as the male compensation for the female lack. But the critique of phallocentrism involves the critique of phal-*logo*-centrism. This is why, 'malgré les apparences, la déconstruction du logocentrisme n'est pas une psychanalyse de la philosophie' (Derrida 1967a: 293). In a certain way, the text — any text — whatever we mean by 'text' — seems to share in this movement of suppletion. It fills in what has been lost through the lapse of historical time; it fills in as a present what is otherwise absent, elsewhere; and in some cases — and this is particularly true of 'structuralist' inspired texts — it claims to penetrate below the surface to get at hidden, under-lying, 'deep' structures.

It seems that, in writing about either continence or incontinence, the writing itself will be marked by incontinence, a fluctuating movement within the closure and fissure of the text, which leaves as its trace in the text — difference. A deferral of *the* text on (in)continence to a point in the future which will never be reached. And a difference which inscribes the text sexually in a reverse movement to the textual inscription of sex to which Foucault has drawn so much attention. A text *on* continence, a text *about* continence, a text *of* continence: this is where 'the' problem lies — in the on, in the about, in the of. And in the (in).

Sources

S. ARDENER, 1975. 'Introduction', in *Perceiving Women*, ed. S. Ardener (London).
A. BECQUELIN MONOD, 1988. '"La parole des Blancs nous fait rire": ethnographie de la citation', *L'Homme* 106-107, avril-septembre: 296-317.
J.B. BLOK, 1991. 'Amazones Antianeirai. Interpretaties van de Amazonenmythe in het mythologisch onderzoek van de 19de en 20ste eeuw en in archaïsche Griekenland' (Dissertation, Leiden).
W. BOER, 1973. *Epistola Alexandri ad Aristotelem*. Beiträge zur klassischen

Philologie, 50 (Meisenheim/Glan: Anton Hain).

J.A. BOON, 1982. *Other Tribes, Other Scribes* (Cambridge University Press).

B. BUCHER, 1981. *Icon and Conquest. A structural analysis of the illustrations of de Bry's Great Voyages*, tr. Basia Miller Gulati (University of Chicago Press [Fr. ed. 1977]).

B. BUCHER, 1982. 'Zur graphischen Repräsentation des Kannibalismus in de Bry's America', in *Mythen der neuen Welt*, ed. K.-H. Kohl (Berlin: Frölich & Kaufmann): 75-91.

M.A. CAMPBELL, 1988. *The Witness and the Other World. Exotic European Travel Writing 400-1600* (Cornell University Press).

J. CARLIER-DETIENNE, 1980-81. 'Les Amazones font la guerre et l'amour', *L'Ethnographie* CXXIIe année, tome LXXVI, nos. 81-82: 11-33.

J. CÉARD, 1977. *La nature et les prodiges. L'insolite au XVIe siècle, en France* (Genève: Droz).

J. CHIFFOLEAU, 1990. 'Dire l'indicible. Remarques sur la catégorie du *nefandum* du XIIe au XVe siècle', *Annales E.S.C.* 45 (2): 289-324.

E. COHEN, 1989. 'Symbols of culpability and the universal language of justice: The ritual of public executions in late medieval Europe', *History of European Ideas*, 11: 407-416.

E. COHEN, 1990. '"To Die a Criminal for the Public Good": the Execution Ritual in Late Medieval Paris' in *Law, Custom and the Social Fabric in Medieval Europe. Essays in Honor of Bryce Lyon*, ed. B.S. Bachrach & D. Nicholas (Studies in Medieval Culture XXVIII, Medieval Institute Publications; Western Michigan University, Kalamazoo): 285-304.

C. COLÓN, 1984. *Textos y documentos completos*. Prólogo y notas de Consuelo Varela (2nd ed. Madrid: Alianza Editorial).

R. CORBEY, 1989. *Wildheid en beschaving* (Baarn: Ambo).

H. CORTÉS, 1972. *Letters from Mexico*, tr. & ed. by A.R. Pagden (Oxford University Press).

N.Z. DAVIS, 1975. *Society and Culture in Early Modern France* (Stanford University Press).

J. DEPRUN, 1970. 'Quand Sade récrit Fréret, Voltaire et d'Holbach', *Roman et Lumières au 18e siècle*, (Centre d'Etudes et de Recherches Marxistes; Paris: Editions Sociales): 331-340.

J. DERRIDA, 1967a. *L'écriture et la différence* (Paris: Seuil).

J. DERRIDA, 1967b. *Marges* (Paris: Minuit).

J. DERRIDA, 1972. *La Dissémination* (Paris: Minuit).

J. DERRIDA, 1978. *Eperons. Les styles de Nietzsche* (Paris: Flammarion).

M. DUCHET, 1971. *Anthropologie et Histoire au siècle des Lumières* (Paris: Maspero).

H.P. DUERR, 1985. *Dreamtime. Concerning the Boundary between Wilderness and Civilization*, tr. F. Goodman (Oxford: Basil Blackwell [1978]).

J.-P. DUVIOLS, 1982. 'La colonie de Florida (1562-1565) et la découverte de nouveaux "sauvages"', in *Etudes sur L'Impact Culturel du Nouveau Monde* II

(Paris: Harmattan): 31-43.

J. FINEMAN, 1981. 'The Structure of Allegorical Desire', in *Allegory and Representation*, ed. S.J. Greenblatt (John Hopkins University Press): 26-60.

M. FOUCAULT, 1966. *Les Mots et les Choses* (Paris: Gallimard).

M. FOUCAULT, 1976. *L'histoire de la sexualité* I (Paris: Gallimard).

CL. GAIGNEBET & J.-D. LAJOUX, 1985. *Art profane et religion populaire au Moyen Age* (Presses Universitaires de France).

A. GERBI, 1973. *The Dispute of the New World. The History of a Polemic, 1750-1900*, rev. and enlarged ed., tr. Jeremy Moyle (University of Pittsburgh Press).

W.P. GERRITSEN, 1985. 'De omgekeerde wereld van de Amazonen', in *Middeleeuwers over vrouwen*, ed. R.E.V. Stuip & C. Vellekoop, I: 157-176.

C. GINZBURG, 1989. *Storia notturna. Una decifrazione del sabba* (Turin: Einaudi).

M. GRAULICH, 1987. *Mythes et Rites du Mexique ancien préhispanique*, Academie Royale de Belgique, Mémoires de la Classe des Lettres.

L.L. GUNDERSON, 1980. *Alexander's Letter to Aristotle about India*, Beiträge zur klassischen Philologie, 110 (Meisenheim/Glan: Anton Hain).

P. HULME, 1985. 'Polytropic Man: Tropes of Sexuality and Mobility in Early Colonial Discourse', in *Europe and its others*, ed. F. Barker *et al.* (University of Essex Press), II: 17-32.

P. HULME, 1986. *Colonial Encounters. Europe and the Native Caribbean 1492-1979* (London: Methuen).

P. HULME, 1989. 'The Log of Christopher Columbus', *Culture & History* 6: 25-36.

P. HULTON, 1978. 'Images of the New World: Jacques Le Moyne de Morgues and John White', in *The Westward Enterprise. English activities in Ireland, the Atlantic, and America 1480-1650*, ed. K.R. Andrews, N.P. Canny & P.E.H. Hair (Liverpool University Press): 195-214.

E. IRIZARRY, 1983. 'Echoes of the Amazon myth in medieval Spanish literature', in *Women in Hispanic Literature. Icons and Fallen Idols*, ed. B. Miller (University of California Press): 53-66.

H. JORIS DE ZAVALA, 1983. 'L'allégorie de l'Amérique dans l'art européen', *Jahrbuch für Geschichte von Staat, Wirtschaft und Gesellschaft Lateinamerikas* 20: 563-574.

R. KABBANI, 1986. *Europe's Myths of Orient. Devise and Rule* (London: Macmillan).

L. KEYMIS, 1596. *A Relation of the Second Voyage to Guiana* (London).

K.-H. KOHL, 1987. *Abwehr und Verlangen* (Frankfurt: Qumran).

J. LE GOFF, 1985. *L'imaginaire médiéval* (Paris: Gallimard).

CL. LECOUTEUX, 1982. *Les Monstres dans la littérature allemande du Moyen Age* (3 vols. Göppingen: Kümmerle).

J. LEERSSEN, 1987. 'Montesquieu's Corresponding Images: Cultural and Sexual Alterity in Pseudo-Oriental Letters', *Comparative Criticism* 9: 135-154.

J. DE LÉRY, 1980. *Histoire d'un voyage faict en la terre du Brésil* (Paris: Plasma).

N. LORAUX, 1981. *Les enfants d'Athéna. Idées athéniennes sur la citoyenneté et la division des sexes* (Paris: Maspero).

P. DE MAGALHÃES DE GANDAVO, 1922. *The Histories of Brazil*, translated & annotated by John B. Stetson, Jr., with a facsimile of the Portuguese original of 1576 (New York: Cortes Society).

J. MANDEVILLE, 1983. *The Travels of Sir John Mandeville*, translated with an introduction by C.W.R.D. Moseley (Harmondsworth: Penguin).

L. MARIN, 1973. *Utopiques: jeux d'espace* (Paris: Minuit).

T. MARTIN, 1985. 'The Negative Structures of American Literature', *American Literature*, 57 (1): 1-22.

TH. VAN DER MEER, 1984. *De wesentlyke sonde van sodomie en andere vuyligheden: sodomietenvervolgingen in Amsterdam 1730-1811* (Amsterdam: Tabula).

P. MITTER, 1977. *Much Maligned Monsters. History of European Reactions to Indian Art* (Clarendon Press).

A. PAGDEN, 1982. *The fall of natural man. The American Indian and the origins of comparative ethnology*. Cambridge Iberian and Latin American Studies (Cambridge University Press).

A. PAGDEN, 1990. *Spanish Imperialism and the Political Imagination* (Yale University Press).

L.E. PENNINGTON, 1978. 'The Amerindian in English promotional literature 1575-1625', in *The Westward Enterprise. English activities in Ireland, the Atlantic, and America 1480-1650*, ed. K.R. Andrews, N.P. Canny & P.E.H. Hair (Liverpool University Press): 175-194.

R. PORTER, 1989. 'The exotic as erotic: Captain Cook at Tahiti', in *Exoticism and the Enlightenment*, ed. G.S. Rousseau & R. Porter (Manchester University Press): 117-144.

S.R. PUCCI, 1989. 'The discrete charms of the exotic: fictions of the harem in eighteenth-century France', in *Exoticism and the Enlightenment*, ed. G.S. Rousseau & R. Porter (Manchester University Press): 145-174.

W. RALEGH, 1970. *The Discovery of the Large, Rich and Beautiful Empire of Guiana*. Introduction and notes by R.H. Schomburgk (New York: Lennox Hill [reprint of 1848 edition by The Hakluyt Society, London]).

B. RECH, 1985. 'Bartolomé de las Casas und Aristoteles', *Jahrbuch für Geschichte von Staat, Wirtschaft und Gesellschaft Lateinamerikas*, 22: 39-68.

D.A.F. DE SADE, 1986. *Oeuvres I* (Paris: Pauvert).

D.A.F. DE SADE, 1990. *Oeuvres I* (Paris: Gallimard).

J.-CL. SANGLIER, 'Een achttiende-eeuwse etnograaf van Amerika: de markies de Sade', *José Martí Journaal* (forthcoming).

S. SCHAMA, 1987. *The Embarrassment of Riches. An Interpretation of Dutch Culture in the Golden Age* (London: Collins).

U. SCHMIEDEL, 1597. *Warhafftige unnd liebliche Beschreibung etlicher fuernemmen Indiani...*

P. STALLYBRASS & A. WHITE, 1986. *The Politics and Poetics of Transgression* (Cornell University Press).

S. STEWART, 1989. 'Antipodal Expectations. Notes on the Formosan "Ethnography" of George Psalmanazar', in *Romantic Motives. Essays on Anthropological Sensibility*, ed. G.W. Stocking, Jr. (History of Anthropology Vol. 6; University of Wisconsin Press): 44-73.

W.C. STURTEVANT, 1976. 'First Visual Images of Native America', in *First Images of America. The Impact of the New World on the Old*, ed. F. Chiapelli (University of California Press) I: 417-454.

J. SUED-BADILLO, 1986. 'El mito indoantillano de las mujeres sin hombres', *Boletín de Estudios Latinoamericanos y del Caribe* 40: 15-22.

M. TAUSSIG, 1987. *Shamanism, Colonialism and the Wild Man. A Study in Terror and Healing* (University of Chicago Press).

A. THEVET, 1983. *Les singularités de la France antarctique*. Choix de textes, introduction et notes de Frank Lestringant (Paris: La Découverte/ Maspero [1577-78]).

T. TODOROV, 1982. *La conquête de l'Amérique. La question de l'autre* (Paris: Seuil).

J.-P. VERNANT, 1974. *Mythe et société en grèce ancienne* (Paris: Maspero).

A. VESPUCCI, 1984. *Il Mondo Nuovo di Amerigo Vespucci. Vespucci autentico e apocrifo*, a cura di M. Pozzi (Milan: Serra e Riva).

F.-M. VOLTAIRE, 1967. *Dictionnaire philosophique*, ed. R. Naves & J. Benda (Paris: Garnier).

A. WENDT, 1989. *Kannibalismus in Brasilien. Eine Analyse europäischer Reiseberichte und Amerika-Darstellungen für die Zeit zwischen 1500 und 1654* (Frankfurt/Main etc.: Peter Lang).

IMAGE AND POWER [1]

Jan Nederveen Pieterse

Western hegemony also means the hegemony of western culture. In the course of centuries this cultural hegemony has taken shape in science and fiction and mixtures thereof. Initially, nautical and geographic knowledge were particularly strategic but in the course of time nonwestern societies and cultures were mapped as well. Knowledge and power grew in tandem. In the colonial era ethnology served the administrative interests of colonial administrations. Western hegemony also manifested itself in works of art and literature concerning the nonwestern world. New impressions mingled with medieval fables and notions inherited from the bible and the classics. Visual arts, poetry, theatre, opera, popular prints, illustrated magazines, novels, youth and children's literature — in a broad stream of imagination the non-European world was represented as part of European scenarios. Science and fiction interacted, as in Orientalism, which took shape in paintings and novels as well as in scholarly studies of Asia and the Middle East. In the course of the nineteenth century, along with the advance of

---

[1]   This article, presented in an earlier version at the conference *Alterity, Identity, Image,* is an adjusted version of chapter 15 in Nederveen Pieterse 1990. The English edition of this book, *White on Black: Images of Africa and Blacks in western popular culture,* is due to be published by Yale University Press in 1992.

western imperialism, repertories of image production expanded to include photography and later film. Cheaper print techniques enabled a wider distribution and popularization of images, also by means of advertising and packaging.

Many of these images — the accumulated harvest of five hundred years of western expansion and hegemony — still circulate. Meanwhile, a process of decolonization has taken place, at least in a political sense. A process of intellectual decolonization is also in motion, in the sense that perspectives critical of western colonialism are gaining ground also in the western world. Cultural decolonization, however, still has to take place.

This is an inquiry into the politics of intercultural representation. It is an unfinished exploration of relations between representations of 'otherness' and dynamics of power. This straddles two terrains, each of which are complex in their own terms. The focal area of this reflection is the depiction of Africa and blacks in western popular culture. Since the assessment of what representation means in terms of power and hierarchy depends on how representation is analysed in the first place, a few remarks on method preface this reflection.

Imagologic

Inquiries into the representation of 'otherness' first took shape in analyses of western literature about the nonwestern world. As a consequence the leading approaches in literary analysis — structuralism, semiotics and deconstruction — have become dominant approaches in interrogating the representation of otherness. These approaches in their turn have been shaped by structural linguistics.

Among the social sciences, anthropology, sociology and social psychology made contributions to this field. In anthropology, Lévi-Strauss adapted structural linguistics to the analysis of societies in the form of structuralism. Later critical anthropology introduced critical reflections upon anthropological theory and practice. In sociology studies of deviance produced relevant perspectives. Social psychology contributed key concepts such as prejudice, ethnocentrism, attitude, stereotype or schema, prototype and script. Social psychology focuses primarily on minorities within the western world; in the 1950s antisemitism in Europe and 'racial' tensions in the United States were its first subject matter. Political psychology examines propaganda and the formation of enemy images (Keen 1986).

There is a growing body of media studies and research into representation in photography, film, comic books, illustrated magazines, advertising, and communications media generally. At times this line of research is more preoccupied with the logic of the medium itself than with the thematic of representation and othering as such.

Does it make a difference that the inquiry into representation of otherness generally has been patterned by the analysis of representation in texts? Every picture tells a story — also visual imagery has a narrative character and structure. To Roland Barthes (1957) it made no difference whether popular ideologies took shape in word or image. Even so, it is worth noting that the pile of literature on representation in texts and documents far exceeds the pile of literature on visual imagery, and that critical inquiries into visual representation tend to follow the model of the study of texts and documents.

At the basis of research into visual imagery stands art history with iconography and iconology (Panofsky 1962). One of the approaches to the study of representation is referred to, presumably in analogy with iconology, as *imagology*; this too is a school of literary research (Steins 1972).

It is obvious that the analysis of representation and otherness itself is historically and culturally determined. There is no Archimedean point, no objective position beyond history from which historical processes of imagining and othering can be monitored and interpreted. Analyses of representation themselves carry and imply certain representations — which, hopefully, reflect a more inclusive collective awareness. In the meantime it is not uncommon for analyses of stereotypes to produce new stereotypes — for instance, simplifications and clichés with regard to 'western culture'.

Frequently in the literature more attention has been bestowed on analysing *conquest* than on analysing *domination*. A case in point are studies of the Spanish conquest of America and the subjugation of the Indians, which abound (e.g. Todorov 1976; Bucher 1977/1981), whereas there appears to be far less interest in the actual institutionalized and routinized exercise of power which *followed* upon the conquest. While the conquest took place over a relatively brief time span, domination went on for centuries and extends into the present.

Does this bias stem from the general fascination with the sixteenth century, the encounter with the *New World*, treading in the footsteps of Columbus? Is it that the act of *conquest* with its violence and penetration is more dramatic and thus more interesting than the routines of institution-alized domination? Does the interest concern *newness* rather than *otherness*? Is the new, unknown other more interesting, because full of possibilities, than the subjugated and known other? Is the onset of occidental hegemony, and the threshold of modernity, a more rewarding problematic than the actual, and ongoing, exercise of occidental hegemony?

In structuralist approaches representation is regarded as being structured in terms of binary oppositions, such as male/female, young/old, light/darkness, civilization/nature, clothed/naked, and so forth, possibly in combination with a third mediating term. Thus, images of Africa may be dissembled into cognitive coordinates and accounted for, ultimately, as a matter of thinking in terms of oppositions.[2]

There are several disadvantages to this kind of approach. First, it tends to be ahistorical — in 1600 it would be as attractive to think in terms of opposites as in 1900; in other words, it is difficult to monitor and account for *change* with this approach. The *process character* of represen-tation, the shifts in imagery and or meaning over time, tends to be underplayed in structuralist approaches because of the inclination to resolve every difference into a binary opposition. Second, it is idealistic, in the sense that ideas and representations are explained in terms of ideas and not in terms of social relations and interests. Third, it may be tautological to the extent that cognitive patterns are explained in terms of cognitive patterns.

Structures (presumably of a mental character) make up the centre of this approach and *history* is marginalized. Roland Barthes once defined the basic principle of myth as the conversion of history into nature (myth as 'depoliticized speech'). In structuralism, the tendency is towards the conversion of history into structure. This is of course the classical argument against structuralism. Accordingly structuralist discourse may produce a view of 'western culture' which is more homogeneous and static, also in its representations of others, than is valid.

Other leading approaches in the analysis of intercultural represen-

---

[2]   Instances of a structuralist approach (although these studies are also richer than this particular methodology) are Mudimbe 1988 and Corbey 1989, as well as Todorov 1976 and Bucher 1977.

tation are discourse analysis and deconstruction. Originally, in the work of Michel Foucault and Jacques Derrida, these were mainly modes of *intra*cultural analysis; but they have been turned into methods of *inter*cultural analysis as well in the work of Edward Said (1978/85), who applied Foucault's methods of discourse analysis to orientalism, and among others Gayatri Spivak (1987), who applied deconstruction to representations of women and the third world. Both typically are scholars of nonwestern origin who living in the west have turned western discourses and discourse analyses into instruments critical of western hegemony. Discourse analysis is also a wider field examining the production and reproduction of social relations in discourse, in everyday discourse and the media (e.g., Smitherman-Donaldson and Van Dijk 1988).

Deconstructionist analyses, in the footsteps of Jacques Derrida (1981), are concerned with 'a complete overturning of cultural domination'. While structuralism searches for the structure behind the representation, deconstruction pursues the ambiguity behind the structure. Deconstruction has in common with structuralism that everything is converted into text — as if the narrative structures of reality were more important than reality itself. Besides, deconstruction proceeds *ad infinitum* — there is no end of the line, only transfers are possible. The endpoint of deconstruction is that there is no endpoint. There are 'no facts, just interpretations' according to Paul de Man. Deconstruction is an application of the art of paradox. As Merquior (1986: 234) observes with respect to Derrida, 'it is always the same trick: what is denied is at once affirmed, what is denounced survives in the very gesture of denunciation'. Is this indeterminacy not in conflict with the aims of the *Kulturkritik* of western hegemony?

As poststructuralism, deconstruction carries some of the luggage of structuralism and thus a potential for overrating the homogeneity of western culture. Indeed, *Kulturkritik* does not just take place in texts, it is not the domain of radical literati alone: there is also the *Kulturkritik* of social movements and mentality changes which are operative as ferments within western cultures. Countercurrents also form part of 'western culture'. To arrive at a more complete picture, a combination of culture critique and historical analysis is required.

Otherness is historical

The approach to images of Africa and blacks in western popular culture
followed here builds on the above-mentioned approaches and combines
them within a larger context of comparative historical analysis. Historical
because a significant feature of representations of others is their *historicity*,
the fact that images of others shift and change over time. Comparative
because of the *diversity* of stereotypes according to cultural contexts. And
analysis in terms of the perspective that these variations correlate with
varying modes of domination, varying over time and across different
regions.

     Thus with respect to images of Africa and blacks there are
significant variations among western countries, in particular between
America and Europe (that is, North America and Western Europe). A
review of some of the findings of our research reveals patterns of
stereotyping and patterns of domination both divergent and similar.

     In the United States (roughly between 1800 and 1950), key images
of black males are the Brute Nigger, Sambo and Uncle, and of black
females the Mammy. The brute nigger is the black male as beast, who, by
means of *lynching* (emasculation), either physically or symbolically, is
'tamed' and transformed into Sambo, the clownish figure of the harmless
entertainer or fool, or into the easygoing Uncle. The Mammy is the type
of the desexualized black female who is amply represented in figures such
as Aunt Jemima, Dinah the cook and so forth. Images of the sexually
attractive black female are (or until fairly recently, were) absent in
American popular culture — not because her charms are not noticed, but
because their cultural acknowledgment would go against the grain of
American ethnic stratification.

     In the United States, the decisive, formative episode in white-black
relations is slavery; for Europe it is colonialism and relations with Africa.
The decisive arena for white-black relations in the United States used to
be the South; the 'south of Europe' is Africa. The equivalent of the
American image of the brute nigger is the European image of the African
savage. If in America the brute nigger is transformed into Sambo, in
Europe the savage is transformed into the *Moor*. In America this occurred
by means of actual lynching, in Europe it takes place by means of
symbolic methods of domestication and castration, in particular the
diminution and *marginalization* of blacks in representation, following

traditions which long predate colonialism. Popular black types in European cultures such as *Zwarte Piet* in the Netherlands, *Sarotti-Mohr* in Germany, the *Golliwog* in England, *Père Fouettard* in Belgium, are typically tiny childlike servant types.

The quasi-oriental costume worn by many of Europe's Moors (striped trousers, pointed shoes, turban) suggests that the image of the black Moor was adopted from Arabic culture (i.e., Moorish culture in the Iberian peninsula and Sicily). Thus the black Moor represents a form of European orientalism. It reflects the fact that relations between Europe and sub-Saharan Africa have been mediated by 'oriental' traditions and examples. The prominence of the *eunuch* in occidental depictions of black males is another instance of this.

The black Uncle and Mammy do not figure in European popular culture, simply because the proximity and quasi-family relationship with black people as developed in the context of American slavery did not exist in Europe. Images of the *black Venus*, however, the sexualized black female, do occur in Europe, unlike in the United States, for precisely the same reason. In at least one European culture, France, the *Vénus noire* is amply represented in a literary and iconographic tradition. It is telling that Josephine Baker, an embodiment of the black Venus, became famous in Europe and not in the United States. In European cultures the appeal of African and black females could be acknowledged because they were scarce and could not pose a risk to the social structure. The sexual gains of colonialism could find cultural expression in metropolitan culture, but the sexual gain of *domestic* ethnic stratification in the United States had to remain hidden.

American and European images of black *males* are fundamentally similar. Generally, images of black males in western popular culture are eunuch types — males stripped of their virility. With regard to images of black *females*, on the other hand, there are significant differences. The divergence in the representations of black males and females in different contexts signals the importance of gender as a dimension of hierarchy.

'We have met the enemy and he is us'

Thus the approach followed here stresses the *historicity* and *diversity* of images of others while arguing that these variations correlate with specific patterns of hegemony. The main principles and arguments of this approach are the following.

1. All the attributes assigned to non-European peoples have also and first been attributed to European peoples, in a gradually expanding circle from neighbouring to further removed peoples. This applies to the entire complex of savagery, bestiality, promiscuity, incest, heathenism, cannibalism, and so forth. Accordingly these qualifications are in no way specific for non-European peoples.

Already in ancient times mention was made of man-eating — did not Herodotus discuss the *androphagi?* But where were they located? On a world map made on the basis of Herodotus' descriptions the *androphagi* are indicated in the area where they typically occur — namely in northern Europe, in an area centered on contemporary Poland (Arens 1979: 10).

Were we to take into account only the period of European colonialism and render a structural analysis of then current images, we would as it were immortalize what was but a temporary configuration and search for cognitive patterns behind what are in reality historical relations.

2. Assigning attributes of otherness serves multiple functions for the labelling group. It may be an expression of critical social distance, of a claim to status on the part of the labelling group. It may serve to negotiate internal group relations by reference to an out group.

3. Often we may find similar negative imagery vice versa among the labeling as well as among the labeled group. It is however the view of the dominant group which prevails and survives. Power also means cultural power. Thus, colonized Africans also suspected Europeans of cannibalism. Besides, how were they to know that the Vatican was not located in Transsylvania? Also in this sense, images of otherness are not specific to a particular group. (Cf. Forbes 1979)

4. Generalizations are inevitable and nuances imperative. A basic precaution is to avoid the singular for the plural. The singular suggests uniformity and is static. Thus, here we are concerned not with *the image of the black,* but with *images of blacks.* This also applies to *western culture* — a concept which is necessary and sufficient for a certain mode and level of analysis, but if we are to further the analysis, the plural may be required here also — *western cultures.*

5. Different circles and levels of analysis, then, include a global plane and the global hegemony of western culture, the various national cultures and their particular projects of 'othering', and finally, the

differentiation within each national culture.

Mainstream culture is not of one cloth — there are distinctions between elite culture and popular culture, and among urban, suburban and rural culture, subcultures and countercultures. 'Popular culture' itself is a mosaic, an arena in which different tendencies press for prominence. Images of otherness, of minorities and foreign peoples may be among the issues of conflict. They are not always important but episodes such as the American Civil War, the French Dreyfuss Affair and the Nazi epoch (not to mention international conflicts), suffice to remind us of what may be at stake in images of otherness.

6. Subcultures may be regionally based, related to differences of class or age, or to specific occupational or interest groups. Instances of the latter are colonial interests and the mission. While the missions were influential producers of propaganda about the nonwestern world in word and image, they were not identical with hegemonic western culture. In fact, missionary representations of otherness, of deeply-sunk heathen in far-off places, were also a means of polemicizing with secularizing tendencies *within* European culture. By means of missionary activities the European churches rejuvenated themselves.

In addition to subcultures, there are counterpoints or counter-tendencies to hegemonic culture, either 'new beginnings' or institu-tionalized countercurrents (Nederveen Pieterse 1988). Thus political satire mocks the pretensions, or some of them, which predominate in hegemonic culture. Abolitionism, on the other hand, was a counterpoint which became a countercurrent and, ultimately, the hegemonic pattern.

Accordingly, specific representations of otherness may reflect global hegemonic culture, national mainstream culture, subcultures, or counter-points.

7. When hegemonic culture shifts and the countercurrent becomes the mainstream, other effects may enter into operation. Subgroups may be mobilized into action to assert their views. Thus, the nineteenth century for the major part was a period of clashing and contending images of blacks in western popular culture — images based on prevalent prejudices, counterposed abolitionist propaganda, and again counterpropaganda from Southern planters (in the United States) and West Indian interests (in Europe). These contending images of otherness correlated with divergent views and forces in relation to political economy and labour relations (industrialization or plantation economy, free labour or slavery) and

society. Representations of otherness formed part of the negotiation of the future.

8. Not only images themselves change but also their meaning or function, sometimes radically. Some of the images of abolitionist liberation (such as 'Uncle Tom') later became vehicles of segregationist oppression.

9. An ideology of *alter* involves an ideology of *ego* (cf. Therborn 1980). Representations of otherness therefore are also indirectly representations of self.

Accordingly, images of Africa and blacks in western cultures must be interpreted primarily in terms of what they say about western cultures, not in terms of what they say about Africa or blacks. It is not that they do not convey any information regarding Africa or blacks but this information is onesided and perverse.

Images of 'others' do not circulate on account of their truthfulness but because they reflect the concerns of the image producers and consumers. Some images owe their currency precisely to their distortion of realities, as if magic formulae, or talismans of difference. Sambo, Jim Crow and Rastus were antidotes to the spectre of the rebellious slave, antidotes to Nat Turner and Denmark Vesey, and to *Santo Domingo*, which engendered hysterical fears in the planters community.

10. Others are plural. Many analyses by focusing on 'the other' in the process of generalizing objectify and reify otherness. But the point is precisely that there is no 'the other', there are *others* — they are many and their identities vary according to time, place, relationship, gender, and so forth. Pontificating on 'the other' means losing sight of this multiplicity and complexity and introducing an essentialism of otherness.

11. Otherness is historical. In structuralist perspectives the process character of images of otherness tends to be marginalized; but this is essential as indication of shifting relations and patterns of domination.

Changes in representations of otherness according to time and place tend to reflect, not changes in the characteristics of the labeled group, but rather changes in the circumstances of the labeling group, or changes in the relationship between the labeling and the labeled group.

Thus, the *savage* has undergone many changes correlating with different positions and shifts in European culture and stages in European colonialism: the *noble* savage (with aristocratic connotations) and the *good* savage (a bourgeois notion), the savage cannibal (a counter-utopia), the *ferocious* savage and the warrior (enemy images of incipient or early colonialism), the *childlike* savage (the savage turned subject, an image of mature colonialism), the *westernized* savage (late colonialism or neocolonialism).

The image of the childlike savage corresponds to the *child/ savage* image of blacks in the United States. This suggests a certain symmetry of patterns of domination between mature European colonialism in Africa and white hegemony in the United States. Corresponding representations of otherness may suggest similar modes of domination or control.

12. Images of others relate not merely to the control over others but also to the control over self. Thus, representations of others relate to power not merely in the sense of imperial power but also in the sense of the *disciplinary power* exercised by the bourgeoisie within metropolitan societies, or power as it permeates the *society of normalization* (cf. Foucault 1980 and 1975).

Otherness is the boundary of normality. As such images of otherness exercise a disciplinary function, as mirrors of difference, as markers and warning signals. The savage is indispensable in establishing civilization's place in the universe. The cannibal represents a counter image to bourgeois morality — Caliban in the seventeenth century signalled that the New World was *not* paradise; in the second half of the nineteenth century popular cannibal lore in Europe reaffirmed this with respect to Africa and the Pacific; twentieth-century cannibal humour articulates the difference between westernization and civilization in the neo-colonial world.

These boundaries were firmly established in Victorian anthropology. In nineteenth-century criminology, medical sciences, psychology and psychiatry, the profiles of the primitive and the savage correlated with those of the abnormal and the criminal, the insane and the prostitute. In Social Darwinism historical evolution was assimilated and equated with natural evolution, as if both were the outcome of 'natural selection'. 'Race' played a key part in this equation, the cement between worlds and discourses, the masterkey of difference. Concepts and images derived from 'race' negotiated hierarchies large and small, global and domestic — as if the classical Great Chain of Being was transmuted into the Great Chain of Empire. In other words, imperial hierarchy interacted with domestic hierarchy.

13. Representations of otherness participate in the production and reproduction of social inequality. The culture of difference is a hierarchical

culture.

In the second half of the twentieth century 'race' is no longer the masterkey of difference. It has been succeeded by the discourse of ethnicity, a system of differences founded not upon biology but upon *culture*. In the United States, however, ethnic stratification still retains many 'racist' characteristics. Since the days of slavery, stratification on the basis of class has been substituted in the United States for stratification on the basis of pigmentation. Even so, the hierarchy of culture is not profoundly different from the hierarchy of race — the rhetoric of 'race' was embedded in a wider culture of hierarchy and many of these features live on in contemporary representations of otherness.

Image and power are interdependent in many ways. Impression management and image management are as much a part of politics as propaganda is. Image manipulation has been institutionalized through the participation of advertising agencies in political campaigns. Image management can also play a significant part in psychological warfare and covert operations.

Five hundred years of occidental hegemony leave deep imprints. The culture of difference instituted as part of colonialism is being reproduced and reworked in the framework of neocolonialism, in conjunction with discourses of 'development' and 'aid'. While the logic of othering has a history as long as the history of representation itself, these dynamics are being multiplied and intensified in the media age.

References

W. ARENS, 1979. *The Man-Eating Myth. Anthropology and Anthropophagy* (New York).
R. BARTHES, 1957. *Mythologies* (Paris).
B. BUCHER, 1977. *La sauvage aux seins pendants* (Paris).
R. CORBEY, 1989. *Wildheid en beschaving. De europese verbeelding van Afrika* (Bilthoven).
J. DERRIDA, 1981. *Positions* (Chicago).
J.D. FORBES, 1979. *A world Ruled by Cannibals. The Wétiko Disease of Aggression, Violence and Imperialism* (Davis, CA).
M. FOUCAULT, 1975. *Surveiller et punir. Naissance de la prison* (Paris).
M. FOUCAULT, 1980. *Power/Knowledge*, ed. C. Gordon (New York).
S. KEEN, 1986. *Faces of the Enemy. Reflections of the Hostile Imagination* (San Francisco).

J.G. MERQUIOR, 1986. *From Prague to Paris. A Critique of Structuralist and Post-structuralist Thought* (London).

V.Y. MUDIMBE, 1988. *The Invention of Africa* (Durham, NC).

J.P. NEDERVEEN PIETERSE, 1988. 'Counterpoint and Emancipation', *Development and Change*, 19 #2 (April).

J.P. NEDERVEEN PIETERSE, 1990. *Wit over zwart. Beelden van Afrika en zwarten in de Westerse populaire cultuur* (Amsterdam/Den Haag).

E. PANOFSKY, 1962. *Studies in Iconology* (New York).

E.W. SAID, 1978/1985. *Orientalism* (Harmondsworth).

G. SMITHERMAN-DONALDSON & T. VAN DIJK (eds), 1988. *Discourse and Discrimination* (Detroit).

G.C. SPIVAK, 1987. *In Other Worlds* (New York/London).

M. STEINS, 1972. *Das Bild des Schwarzen in der europäischen Kolonialliteratur 1870-1918. Ein Beitrag zur literarischen Imagologie* (Frankfurt/Main).

G. THERBORN, 1980. *The Ideology of Power and the Power of Ideology* (London).

T. TODOROV, 1976. *La conquête de l'Amérique. La question de l'autre* (Paris).

ALTÉRITÉ DANS *VENDREDI*
OU LES LIMBES DU PACIFIQUE DE MICHEL TOURNIER:
UNE ANALYSE DÉCONSTRUCTIVE

Els Schrover

Identité/altérité

Depuis Freud, la quête de l'identité, du sujet aussi bien que de la culture, s'est montrée une des problématiques les plus fascinantes, sinon la plus fascinante de toutes, de la pensée occidentale du XXe siècle.

De l'écriture automatique des Surréalistes au récit fragmentarisé du Nouveau Roman, toute la tradition littéraire du XXe siècle fait preuve d'une recherche inlassable des limites du 'moi', de ce qui divise ce 'moi' de l'autre que l'entoure.

La psychanalyse de Freud, et après, celle de Lacan ont beaucoup attribué à rendre plus précaire encore la différence, censée si sûre avant eux, entre le même et l'autre. 'Quel est donc cet autre à qui je suis plus attaché qu'à moi, puisque au sein le plus assenti de mon identité à moi-même, c'est lui qui m'agite?', se demande Lacan.[1] Question fort rhétorique d'ailleurs, car voici la réponse de Freud: 'c'est l'inconscient, le ça, noyau de votre personnalité, qui vous sera toujours étrange.'

Si la différence entre la propre identité du sujet et l'autre, ce qui lui est étrange, se trouve aussi radicalement mise en question, non seulement dans la psychologie, dans la littérature, mais encore dans la philosophie, celle de Derrida par exemple, il faut constater que la problématique qui lie

---

[1]   Lacan 1966: 524.

l'identité à l'altérité est une des caractéristiques de la culture occidentale contemporaine.

Dans un cadre plus large, ce même problème s'est manifesté jusqu'ici dans une tradition littéraire (et philosophique d'ailleurs) qui oppose la propre culture à celle des barbares, des sauvages, bref, qui raconte de la rencontre de la culture (occidentale) avec *l'autre*. La théorie freudienne a montré qu'il n'était pas nécessaire d'aller si loin pour rencontrer l'autre, puisqu'il se trouvait au sein même du sujet, mais cela n'est qu'une différence qu'on pourrait qualifier de 'topique': les problèmes que nous pose l'opposition identité/altérité restent bien les mêmes.

La tradition littéraire: Confrontation de la culture européenne avec son 'autre' — les sauvages.

The Tempest, de Shakespeare, nous présente un des exemples les plus illustratifs de la confrontation de la civilisation européenne avec l'état sauvage. Caliban, le sauvage qui habitait l'île avant la venue de Prospero et de sa fille, est devenu leur esclave, avec toute la rancune et la mauvaise foi envers son maître qui en est l'inévitable conséquence. Inaccessible à la culture qui le domine, il n'a appris la langue (Miranda la lui a apprise) que pour jurer, il est peint comme un presqu'animal, méchant, grossier, et surtout, menace sexuel: il a manqué violer Miranda.

La servilité qui le fait changer de maître aussitôt qu'il aperçoit des nouveaux-venus à l'île, et qui d'ailleurs sera répété plus tard par Vendredi dans le roman de Tournier, est présenté comme signe de son infidélité envers ceux qui pourtant se sont efforcés (le père et la fille le répètent) de le faire profiter de leur propre culture plus élevée. Comme Vendredi, il ne choisit pas bien ses nouveaux maîtres: dans les deux cas, il s'agit de marins sans culture, bien inférieurs à Prospero et Robinson. On pourrait l'interpréter comme signe de naïveté, qui ne voit pas l'essentiel dans l'autre culture: Caliban est impressionné par l'alcool, comme Vendredi le sera par la voilure du bateau, des détails insignifiants d'une culture qui aurait pu leur apporter de meilleures connaissances.

Notons d'ailleurs, que Shakespeare a quand-même donné à Caliban quelques traits humains qui lui assurent sinon la sympathie, du moins la pitié du lecteur: il a été le roi de l'île; dominé par les étrangers il est devenu leur esclave. Il a donc raison de leur en vouloir! Et encore, outre la basse vulgarité de la sexualité avec laquelle il menace Miranda et Prospero ('thou didst prevent me: I had peopled else the isle with Calibans', I.ii), il fait signe d'une admiration sincère pout Miranda. Ce n'est pas la seule manifestation de son esprit poétique: en parlant des merveilles de son île aussi, il fait preuve d'un émerveillement qui dans le contexte culturel de l'époque est réservé toujours aux êtres d'une noblesse naturelle.

Il est curieux que tous les traits attestés dans la figure de Caliban, traits animaux aussi bien que poétiques, vont revenir dans les autres manifestations du même genre. L'autre sera toujours cela: plus bas, plus instinctif, voir plus animal que 'nous', mais aussi plus naturel, dans un entendement plus direct avec la nature et ses merveilles, et qui par là peut servir parfois à châtier les imperfections de la civilisation. Outre par le 'bon sauvage' de Rousseau, ce dernier rôle est joué aussi par le Vendredi de Tournier: dans les deux textes, la description de l'état sauvage a la tendance d'avertir contre les maux d'une civilisation que l'auteur et son lecteur partagent. [2]

Diverses appréciations de l'autre: le sauvage dans la tradition littéraire

La littérature anglaise abonde en exemples du sauvage civilisé par une culture (celle de l'Europe) supérieure. Dans *Robinson Crusoe* de Daniel Defoe, la 'domestication' de Vendredi en est un exemple. L'idéologie implicite est celle de l'expansion du Commonwealth, qui ne concevait pas une valeur propre aux cultures étranges des territoires occupés: seule l'adaptation à la civilisation anglaise pouvait élever le sauvage au niveau humain (cf. *VP*, p. 227).

Au XXe siècle, une réaction contre cette idéologie éducative commence à se dessiner: dans *Heart of Darkness* de Conrad, par exemple, mais aussi dans *Lord of the Flies* de Golding, il est montré comment, au lieu de civiliser le sauvage, les protagonistes, représentants du monde civilisé, y tournent sauvages eux-mêmes. Dans ces romans, c'est la nature qui l'emporte sur la culture. En effet, ce qui se montre aussi, c'est que 'l'autre'

---

[2]   Dans son commentaire sur *Vendredi*, Tournier lui-même n'est pas de cet avis. cf. *Le vent Paraclet*, p. 228. Nous y reviendrons.

n'est pas si loin que ça, puisque 'la nature', c'est bien ce qui se trouve de façon latente dans chacun des voyageurs. Dominé en Angleterre par tout un système de règles de conduite, 'l'autre' se libère lorsque les circonstances se montrent favorables. Ainsi, dans *Lord of the Flies*, quelques dizaines de garçons bien élevés tournent en cannibales dans les quelques semaines après un accident d'avion qu'ils habitent seuls une île déserte.

Ce qui importe pour notre étude, c'est que malgré l'opinion favorable ou défavorable de 'l'autre' qui peut se présenter dans ces romans, le réseau sous-jacent qui oppose le même (la propre identité) à l'autre, ne change pas. Peu d'importance alors, si c'est la nature ou la culture qui l'emporte, puisque l'opposition irréductible se maintient.

'Vendredi' de Tournier: la synthèse du même et de l'autre?

Le roman de Michel Tournier peut se lire comme réponse au *Robinson Crusoe*, de Defoe. Defoe a fait entreprendre à son Robinson la tâche de civiliser Vendredi, l'idée implicite étant que ce dernier se trouve sur un niveau de culture bien inférieur à celui de Robinson (cf. *VP*, p. 227). L'opposition entre culture et nature est nette, et double celle de la propre identité de Robinson et l'altérité radicale de Vendredi. L'abîme qui sépare les deux hommes ne sera traversé (en apparence, seulement) que lorsque Vendredi aura accepté les valeurs de la culture de Robinson.

Dans le roman de Tournier c'est l'inverse qui se produit: au début du roman c'est bien la structure de Defoe qui semble se répéter, parce que le Robinson de Tournier aussi entreprend de domestiquer Vendredi, mais le lecteur, déjà averti par le titre où ne figure que le nom de Vendredi, voit vite échouer ce projet. C'est alors, dans la deuxième partie, que va se déployer la matière principale du roman, qui est une inversion complète des idées de Defoe. Il faudrait s'imaginer Prospero devenu disciple de Caliban[3] pour concevoir l'étendu de la nouveauté que Tournier présente

---

[3]   Vendredi est présenté comme génie aérien. Il semble donc unir les traits de Caliban avec ceux d'Ariel. En effet, Tournier, qui parmi ses prédécesseurs ne nomme pas Shakespeare, fait pourtant allusion à Ariel dans une description de Vendredi qui rappelle *The Tempest*: 'Le principe de Vendredi est aérien, éolien, *ariellien*' (*VP*, p. 234). Les traits de Caliban dans Vendredi, pour ne pas être attestés par Tournier, sont pourtant évidents aussi; cf. notre commentaire *supra*.

au lecteur: c'est Vendredi comme l'indique le titre, qui dans cette deuxième partie est devenu le maître, l'exemple, l'appui de Robinson. Les caractéristiques de l'ordre représenté par Vendredi ont alors la valeur d'exemple, pour Robinson, mais aussi pour le lecteur qui partage en effet la même culture occidentale avec lui.

Nous retrouvons en quelque sorte la pensée romantique Rousseauiste dans ce que représente Vendredi: l'ordre de la nature opposé à celui de la civilisation de Robinson et du lecteur, est une critique implicite de tout ce qui caractérise la culture occidentale du XXe siècle.[4] Ainsi Vendredi ne connaît ni l'obsession du temps qui coule, ni l'idée d'un ordre hiérarchique comprenant maître et esclave. Plus important encore, Vendredi ne connaît pas le souci de l'avenir, ni le remords du passé: il vit dans le présent, d'une manière infiniment plus riche, dans un entendement plus fin avec la nature et les animaux, qui pourrait rappeler l'ingénuité de Caliban. Vendredi ne réfléchit pas sur sa propre existence, il ne connaît pas le doute de soi qui fait de Robinson le maître tourmenté de l'île administrée:

> quoi que fît Robinson, il y avait toujours quelqu'un en lui qui attendait un événement décisif, bouleversant, un commencement radicalement nouveau qui frapperait de nullité toute entreprise passée ou future. (*Vendredi*, p. 150)

A la fin du livre, Robinson a beaucoup appris de la sagesse sauvage de Vendredi. Il s'est même approprié beaucoup des qualités de Vendredi. Comme il le constate lui-même,

> il existait désormais — par un phénomène de mimétisme bien explicable — une ressemblance évidente entre son visage et celui de son compagnon. Des années durant, il avait été à la fois le maître et le père de Vendredi. En quelques jours il était devenu son frère — et il n'était pas sûr que ce fût son frère aîné. (p. 191)

---

[4]   Tournier, bienque niant cette ressemblance avec l'oeuvre de Rousseau, voue un quart de son explication du roman *Vendredi* dans *Le vent Paraclet* à une critique intransigeante de la société occidentale: cf. *VP*, pp. 221-7, 236-7. Originairement, le roman aurait dû être dédié même à 'la masse énorme et silencieuse des travailleurs immigrés de France, tous ces Vendredi dépêchés vers nous par le tiers monde' (*VP*, p. 236): le lien avec une critique de la société occidentale a en vérité toujours été évident.

Quelques pages après, Robinson compare leur union avec celle des Dioscoures: les jumeaux à la jeunesse éternelle. Le Robinson de Tournier est devenu le frère jumeau de Vendredi, leur union est telle que Robinson se hasarde même à répondre de la sexualité de Vendredi. Si l'on regarde l'attitude vis à vis de la sexualité comme ce qu'il y a de plus caractéristique de l'individu, il faut constater avec ces mots de Robinson que Vendredi et lui font vraiment un: 'En vérité, au suprême degré où nous avons accédé, Vendredi et moi, la différence de sexe est dépassée' (p. 230).

Est-ce que le roman de Tournier signifie le point tournant de la tradition littéraire qui a codifié dans une opposition bien nette jusqu'ici l'identité et l'altérité? Est-ce que l'opposition se trouve transcendée dans cette nouvelle union de Robinson et de Vendredi?

Il semble pourtant y avoir quelques indices qui font douter à l'harmonie parfaite. Curieusement, ce sont les expressions de Robinson qui aspire justement à plus de ressemblance à Vendredi qui vont donner l'idée d'une différence ineffaçable entre lui et Vendredi: 'Soleil, rends-moi plus semblable à Vendredi' (p. 217); 'Saurai-je jamais marcher avec une aussi naturelle majesté?' (p. 221).

A l'intérieur, l'unité manifeste une différence qui provient paradoxalement du désir de l'un des frères jumeaux de plus ressembler à l'autre. Ainsi, pour avoir voulu mieux mettre en évidence la grande différence qui sépare son Robinson de celui de Defoe, Tournier a, sans le vouloir, simultanément montré en quoi la différence est insurmontable: Robinson est le seul à aspirer à cette union; pas Vendredi.

La déconstruction du récit philosophique et romanesque

Jacques Derrida est le contemporain de Tournier: *De la grammatologie* a paru en 1967, *Vendredi* en 1969. Il serait intéressant de tracer les nombreux points de concordance des deux projets. C'est surtout la mise en question de la position supérieure du monde occidental et de ses relations avec d'autres cultures, qui leur est commune. On pourrait argumenter aussi que c'est un examen rigoureux des frontières qui séparent l'esprit occidental de son 'autre' qui est commun à Derrida et Tournier: une méfiance à l'égard de la stabilité du sujet, et du pouvoir de la langue de transmettre un sens indubitable. G. Deleuze a travaillé dans ce sens en examinant 'la structure d'autrui' dans *Vendredi*. Le projet de Derrida, comme celui de Tournier, pourrait être caractérisé comme la déconstruction de ces frontières qui organisent le savoir en des couples d'oppositions rigides qui ont codifié la pensée occidentale. Nous avons vu comment Tournier a fait sauter l'opposition maître/esclave héritée de Defoe, regardons maintenant de plus près la théorie de Derrida.

La théorie de la déconstruction

La déconstruction a pour objet des *textes*, aussi bien philosophiques que littéraires. Chaque texte présente une unité: une quantité délimitée de mots et d'idées. Par conséquent, l'auteur du texte a dû asssigner une limite à son texte, en décidant ce qui en ferait partie, et ce qui serait exclu. La stratégie de la déconstruction est de se concentrer sur ce genre de démarcations d'un texte: des décisions de l'auteur restées implicites, mais qui se font tracer dans son texte. C'est ici que se manifeste ce qui a été appelé plus haut 'l'examen des frontières': dans *L'écriture et la différence* Derrida a posé pour la première fois le problème de délimitation dans la langue. Il oppose au texte *fini*, ou au *livre*, le système de la langue, qui, malgré les implications du mot 'système', ne connaît pas de limites. Dans *De la grammatologie*, qui a paru en 1967 comme *L'écriture et la différence*, le prochain fragment présente en résumé ces idées:

> L'idée du livre, qui renvoie toujours à une totalité naturelle, est profondément étrangère au sens de l'écriture. Elle est la protection encyclopédique de la théologie et du logocentrisme contre la disruption de l'écriture, contre son énergie aphoristique et, nous le préciserons plus loin, contre la différence en général. (Derrida 1967b: 30-31)

'La disruption de l'écriture', son 'énergie aphoristique': selon Derrida l'idée de significations fixes et de délimitations nettes est incompatible avec le procès signifiant de la langue. La production de sens ne s'arrête pas:

> Et si le sens du sens, c'est l'implication infinie? Le renvoi indéfini de signifiant à signifiant? Si sa force est une certaine équivocité pure et infinie ne laissant aucun répit, aucun repos au sens signifié, l'engageant, en sa propre *économie*, à faire signe encore

et à *différer*? (Derrida 1967a: 42)

Ce principe de renvoi indéfini, Derrida lui a donné le nom de 'différance', nom dont le *-ance* signifie un mouvement constant. C'est entre autres dans *La dissémination* que Derrida a élaboré les conséquences d'un tel concept de langue pour l'analyse littéraire:

> Le mot *pharmakon* y [dans le texte de Platon] est pris dans une chaîne de significations. Le jeu de cette chaîne semble systématique. Mais le système n'est pas ici simplement celui des intentions de l'auteur connu sous le nom de Platon. Ce système n'est pas d'abord celui d'un vouloir-dire. Des communications réglées s'établissent, grâce au jeu de la langue, entre diverses fonctions du mot, et, en lui, entre divers sédiments ou diverses régions de la culture. [...] ces liaisons s'opèrent d'elles-mêmes. Malgré lui [Platon]? grâce à lui? dans *son* texte? *hors* de son texte? mais alors où? entre son texte et la langue? (Derrida 1972: 108)

La langue une fois définie comme ce mouvement d'échos perpétuels, elle tend à faire sauter les limites. C'est pourquoi l'unité du texte (du roman) est devenu problématique dans l'optique déconstructiviste. Avec elle tout le système métaphysique qui soustend la production de textes est étudié de nouveau: basée sur des oppositions fixes de termes qui s'excluent mutuellement, la métaphysique depuis Platon implique le respect des limites que la déconstruction a mis en question. Tout comme Vendredi qui dans les mots de Tournier 'sème le doute dans un système qui ne tenait que par la force d'une conviction aveugle' (*VP*, p. 234).

Ainsi la stratégie de la déconstruction, selon Derrida, est de travailler dans les marges de textes pour mettre en question la logique sousjacente: ce ne sont pas les oppositions qui importent, mais le principe qui a pu les générer:

> [...] il faut chercher de nouveaux concepts et de nouveaux modèles, une *économie* échappant à ce système d'oppositions métaphysiques. [...] Notre discours appartient irréductiblement au système des oppositions métaphysiques. On ne peut annoncer la rupture de cette appartenance que par une *certaine* organisation, un certain aménagement *stratégique* qui, à l'intérieur du champ et de ses pouvoirs propres, retournant contre lui ses propres *stratagèmes*, produise une *force de dislocation* se propageant à travers tout le système, le fissurant dans tous les sens et le *dé-*

limitant de part en part. (Derrida 1967a: 34)

On pourrait lire ceci comme un exposé théorique de ce que fait Vendredi de l'île administrée par Robinson. Le travail dans les marges sert à montrer des liens entre les termes d'une opposition qui souvent restent inaperçus: la déconstruction aide à mettre en valeur les implications d'un concept opposé. Souvent le texte tend à *miner* l'opposition qu'il semble supporter:

> The deconstruction of a text does not proceed by random doubt or generalized skepticism, but by the careful teasing out of warring forces of signification *within the text itself*. (Johnson 1981: xiv)

Il s'agit maintenant d'analyser si le texte de Tournier présente de tels 'warring forces' qui mineraient l'unité idyllique de Vendredi et Robinson, et par là peut-être même le message philosophique du roman.

Tournier et l'autre: Robinson et Vendredi

Il est évident que Tournier a des aspirations philosophiques avec son roman: 'Bien de tous les hommes, Robinson est l'un des éléments constitutifs de l'âme de l'homme occidental' (*VP*, p. 221). Le commentaire de Tournier sur le Robinson de Defoe montre assez la direction nouvelle qu'il voudrait signaler à la culture occidentale:

> Or qu'était Vendredi pour Daniel Defoe? Rien, une bête, un être en tout cas qui attend de recevoir son humanité de Robinson, l'homme occidental, seul détenteur de tout savoir, de toute sagesse. Et quand il aura été dûment morigéné par Robinson, il deviendra tout au plus un bon serviteur. (*VP*, p. 227)

L'erreur de Robinson, selon Tournier, c'est de se croire supérieur à Vendredi, et de ne lui donner qu'un rôle bien humble comme serviteur, sans percevoir que lui-même aurait pu apprendre des qualités humaines de la personnalité 'autre' de Vendredi. Le Robinson de Tournier échappera à cette erreur: il verra en Vendredi son maître. Dans *Le vent Paraclet* (= *VP*) Tournier explique curieusement pourquoi:

> Là [au musée de l'homme] j'avais appris qu'il n'y a pas de
> 'sauvages', mais seulement des hommes relevant d'une civilisa-
> tion différente de la nôtre et que nous avons grand intérêt à
> étudier. L'attitude de Robinson à l'égard de Vendredi manifestait
> le racisme le plus ingénu et une méconnaissance de son propre
> intérêt. Car pour vivre sur l'île du Pacifique ne vaut-il pas mieux
> se mettre à l'école d'un indigène rompu à toutes les techniques
> adaptées à ce milieu particulier que de s'acharner à plaquer sur
> elle un mode de vie purement anglais? (*VP*, pp. 227-8)

Dans ce fragment Tournier fait preuve d'une modestie vis à vis des autres
cultures qu'on chercherait en vain dans les écrits de Defoe. Pourtant il s'y
manifeste aussi une ressemblance inquiétante avec l'idéologie utilitaire de
ce dernier, qui si longtemps a dominé l'esprit occidental. Tournier a
reproché à Defoe de regarder Vendredi 'tout au plus [comme] un bon
serviteur': c'est-à-dire de négliger les qualités humaines de l'autre en vue
d'un bas principe d'utilité qui mène à l'esclavage. Personne ne doutera de
l'horreur de Tournier à l'égard de cet esprit utilitaire, qui d'ailleurs est
dénoncé à la fin du même article, où Vendredi est comparé aus voyageurs
immigrés en France.

Pourtant, quand Tournier conseille à l'Occident de 'se mettre à
l'école' des autres, la suite de l'argument étonne: ce n'est pas pour
apprendre des vérités humaines qu'il faut écouter les autres, non, c'est
parce que les indigènes sont 'rompus à toutes les techniques adaptées à ce
milieu particulier'. Ceci implique: les indigènes peuvent vous être plus
utiles que vous ne croyez. Après l'exploitation des ressources de l'île,
condamnée comme caractéristique de l'attitude coloniale de l'Occident,
c'est l'exploitation des ressources de Vendredi qui est conseillée ici.

Ainsi la teneur du roman: ne donnez pas de leçons aux indigènes,
soyons modestes et allons apprendre d'eux au contraire, pourrait se lire
finalement comme un conseil à mieux tirer profit des autres: Robinson qui
a exploité les ressources de l'île Speranza a trouvé un nouvel objet.
Désormais il profitera de celles de Vendredi. Evidemment ceci n'a jamais
été l'intention de Tournier, ni la teneur de son roman. Rappelons que
Tournier avait voulu le dédier auz travailleurs immigrés en France, 'Cette
population baillonnée mais vitale, tolérée mais indispensable [...] Tous ces
Vendredi dépêchés vers nous par le tiers monde' (*VP*, pp. 237, 236).

Le mot-clé ici, c'est 'indispensable': les travailleurs immigrés le
sont à l'Occident, tout coame Vendredi l'est à Robinson. Le roman de

Tournier, c'est la relation de l'évolution de Robinson qui a dû l'apprendre. L'intention consciente de Tournier est évidente. Une analyse déconstructiviste pourtant semble tourner les implications de cette évolution contre l'intention de l'auteur. Quand, dans *Le vent Paraclet*, Tournier décrit les phases de l'évolution de Robinson en schéma, ce sera le suivant:

Terre + Air = Soleil
Robinson terrien + Vendredi [5] = Robinson solaire (*VP*, p. 235)

En regardant de plus près la dernière formule, on constate une erreur mathématique:

Robinson + Vendredi = Robinson!

Dans sa simplicité élémentaire, la formule découvre ce que Tournier aurait voulu contester: la nécessité absolue de Vendredi, proclamée par le titre du roman, où ne figure que son nom, est minée par l'intérêt porté exclusivement au développement de Robinson. Ici, comme en France, Vendredi n'est pas indispensable du tout. Cette structure a placé Vendredi exactement dans la position des travailleurs immigrés de France: tout comme leur place pourra être occupée par d'*autres* travailleurs immigrés, pourvu que la *structure* se maintienne, c'est-à-dire que le travail soit fait, de la même façon Vendredi peut être remplacé par un autre étranger qui (détail ironique) obtiendra le nom de *Jeudi*. Le titre du roman ne couvre pas le contenu: non seulement le récit commence avant la venue de Vendredi, mais, plus significatif, tout continuera, après qu'un autre aura pris sa place.

Une explication possible du paradoxe que nous venons de constater me semble la suivante: Tournier avec son roman *Vendredi* a voulu réagir contre l'idéologie occidentale, qui ne vise qu'à élargir l'horizon de son influence, tout en asservissant l'autre. Au contraire, Tournier, avec l'exagération caractéristique d'une réaction critique, propose que Robinson aille apprendre de Vendredi. L'influence de l'autre doit s'aggrandir. Ainsi Robinson apprend beaucoup de Vendredi, mais Vendredi n'apprend rien de lui: victime d'une trop grande modestie, cette dernière phase de la domination occidentale, Vendredi dans le roman n'acquiert pas le statut de l'humanité: il ne change pas, il ne connaîtra ni les doutes, ni les remords.

---

[5]   Vendredi a été dépeint comme génie aérien (cf. note 3).

Le lecteur ne connaîtra ni ses sentiments, ni ses pensées. On ne lira pas la motivation de son choix de quitter Robinson, seules les conjectures de ce dernier, qui d'ailleurs ne sont pas trop flattantes. Tournier les répète dans *Le vent Paraclet*:

> Le principe de Vendredi est aérien [...] C'est d'ailleurs ce qui le perdra, car il ne saura pas résister à la séduction du fin voilier anglais [...] (*VP*, p. 234)

Les qualités humaines dont témoigne Robinson à la fin du roman: pitié de Jaan, le souci de Vendredi (danger de l'esclavage), le remords d'avoir pris à lui seul la décision de rester avec Vendredi sur l'île, sa confiance en Vendredi, Tournier ne les attribue pas à Vendredi. Vendredi 'ne saura pas résister à la séduction' — c'est comme Caliban qui n'a pas su résister à celle de l'alcool et celle de Miranda [6]. Même, à la fin, il perd son nom, il n'est indiqué qu'avec celui de sa race après la découverte de son départ:

> Allait-il falloir tout recommencer [...] en attendant la survenue d'un nouvel Araucan [...] (p. 251)

> '[...] j'ai vu un homme aborder en pirogue. C'etait votre serviteur métis. Il a repoussé du pied la pirogue, et il est entré chez le second qui paraissait l'attendre. J'ai compris qu'il resterait à bord [...]' (p. 252)

Voici la dernière action de Vendredi, relatée par Jaan. Le 'second qui paraissait l'attendre' prouve que Vendredi a quitté son ami délibéremment, sans une motivation qui pourrait réconcilier le lecteur au désespoir de Robinson:

> [...] il courut, trébuchant et criant, désespérément convaincu au fond de lui-même que ses recherches étaient vaines. Il ne comprenait pas comment Vendredi avait pu le trahir, mais il ne pouvait plus reculer devant l'évidence qu'il était seul dans l'île, seul comme aux premiers jours. Cette quête hagarde acheva de le

---

[6]   En effet, Tournier a encore écrit un conte où il raconte la suite des aventures de Robinson et de Vendredi (ceux de Defoe), retournés parmi les hommes. Vendredi y est présenté succombé aux deux tentations de Caliban: à l'alcool et aux femmes.

briser [...] (p. 250)

Tout ce qui rend humain Robinson: le doute, un développement spirituel, le désir de s'améliorer ('Soleil, rends-moi plus semblable à Vendredi'), est absent dans Vendredi. Il y a même un leger soupçon de culpabilité dans la description de son départ furtif par Jaan. Même l'auteur du roman n'échappe pas à la manifestation d'une certaine irritation, quand dans *Le vent Paraclet*, il constate sèchement que la qualité aérienne perdra Vendredi. Pourquoi se perdra-t-il en abordant le navire anglais? Pourquoi les autres Anglais n'arriveront-ils pas à percevoir les qualités de Vendredi que Robinson avait découvertes? Questions pénibles qui amènent le lecteur à une triste constatation: en le présentant comme exemple pour la civilisation occidentale, Tournier a omis de donner à Vendredi des traits humains: en lui niant la possibilité d'un développement, il a exclu Vendredi de l'humanité. A la fin du roman, ce manque d'humanité finit par replacer Vendredi dans la structure que Tournier avait voulu détruire: celle de l'altérité radicale, représentée avant lui par Caliban et tant d'autres: la place des êtres douteux, dangereux et infidèles, incompréhensibles et incapables de relations humaines. La place de l'altérité inaltérable.

Littérature

C. DAVIS, 1988. *Michel Tournier, Philosophy and Fiction* (Clarendon Press).

G. DELEUZE, 1967. 'Michel Tournier et le monde sans autrui', postface in M. Tournier, *Vendredi et les limbes du Pacifique*.

J. DERRIDA, 1967a. *L'écriture et la différence* (Paris: Seuil).

J. DERRIDA, 1967b. *De la grammatologie* (Paris: Minuit).

J. DERRIDA, 1972. *La dissémination* (Paris: Seuil).

L.A. FIEDLER, 1973. *The Stranger in Shakespeare* (London: Croom Helm).

B. JOHNSON, 1981. 'Translator's Introduction' in *Jacques Derrida: Dissémination* (University of Chicago Press).

J. LACAN, 1966. *Écrits* (Paris: Seuil).

M. TOURNIER, *Vendredi ou les limbes du Pacifique* (Paris: Gallimard, 1972).

M. TOURNIER, *Le vent Paraclet* (Paris: Gallimard, 1977).

ALTERITY/IDENTITY: A DEFICIENT IMAGE OF CULTURE

Paul Voestermans

> There are no intrinsic reasons why cultural
> processes should not be incorporated in the hard
> center of the social sciences, modifying the
> concept of the rational agent by setting him in a
> well-analyzed social context and allowing for his
> internalization of its moral and political attitudes.
> Mary Douglas, *Natural Symbols* (1982).

> When thou didst not, savage,
> Know thine own meaning, but wouldst gabble like
> A thing most brutish, I endow'd thy purposes
> With words that would make them known.
> *The Tempest*, I.ii

Setting the stage

'Alterity' can broadly be defined as discourse on the otherness of people,
particularly people outside one's domestic ken. 'Identity' is the affirmation
of who we are by contrasting nearly every element of our way of life with
that of others. This self-other dialectic is the core of the debate on alterity
and identity: they invest each other with meaning, one does not go without
the other. Usually the opposition is between cultures. The way distinct
groups of mankind comprehend each other and the records of their success
or failure to do so: all this undoubtedly constitutes, in a way, an area of

culture; in what way precisely, is what I aim to assess in the following pages.

The Alterity/Identity theme has an epistemological dimension. The impression is created that alterity/identity formations are mental constructs, susceptible to our critical analysis. The documentary record offers us the following picture: The life of aliens in distant lands is set off against familiar life at home; the resulting impressions tend to be recorded in a biased fashion, so that it becomes impossible to get any idea of what was actually experienced. The initial experience is from the outset soaked up, as it were, by the discursive activity, central to which is the practice of classification, representation and mis-representation. However, it is rarely this psychological process which is studied in the alterity/identity debate; rather, current practice takes its point of departure in finished mental products - texts. A simple example shows what happens. Explorers of a still undiscovered shore, who often came from prosperous cities in Europe, were, of course, struck by the fact that there were no cities, at least not in the way they were familiar with. The most important hallmark of civilization was absent. What were they to conclude? In an effort to understand they fell back on the discursive activity of classifying what they saw, in terms like 'uncivilized'. It is this type of phraseology, which tends to serve as a starting point for subsequent critical study.

Moreover, the Alterity/Identity debate seems to be primarily a debate about beliefs. The linguistic protocols in which meetings with the other were recorded document a large set of beliefs, opinions, attitudes or similar, propositionally organized realms of thought.

So we have 'culture', 'mind' and 'belief'. These three taken together form the dominant triangular locus in which discussions about alterity and identity take place. This triangle is also the main locus and source of the main theme in the Alterity/Identity debate: the cultural idiom of 'wildness' and 'civilization'.

I want to consider the triangle culture-mind-belief as a (somewhat problematic) particularization of another, more basic one. That is the one formed by connecting culture with body and sentiment. The use of 'image' in the title of this paper — not so much the image of 'other' and 'self' but of culture — alludes to my strong conviction that the common view of culture is wrongly situated within the confines of that triangle culture-mind-belief. Such an image of culture is defective and impaired and wrongly constrictive. Placing the concept of culture in connection with the more basic principles of body and sentiment will provide a more fruitful approach to cultural phenomena. Let me say in advance that the contrast between the two 'triangular loci' of culture, which I devised for the purpose of what I want argue in this paper, is not simply a matter of idealist versus materialist notions of culture. Idealism and materialism in the present context amount to two sides of the same coin. Both have their shortcomings, and their opposition needs to be circumvented.

The limitations of an ideological approach

The critical analysis of the twin concepts of alterity and identity (and the articles in the present collection may count as a representative sample) betrays a preoccupation with epistemology and ideology — not in the sense of basic questions such as 'what makes knowledge possible' or 'how valid and reliable is our perception of the world', but rather in the sense of some sort of sociology of knowledge. The central question is whether the image of the Other can exist outside the social realities of the self. It is, of course, a legitimate approach to past and present western thinking about Others; but the epistemological approach and the ideology business suffer severely from occidental logocentrism and preoccupation with literacy. Let me address, by way of a preliminary, this particular bias.

The term 'ideology' is often used to designate a belief system. Consequently ideological conflicts are conflicts of beliefs. Yet, beliefs are only partly responsible for the monitoring of behaviour. Social groupings differ widely with respect to the degree in which belief systems regulate behaviour, and even within a given society not every behavioural domain is equally and ubiquitously organized by beliefs. On the other hand, the concept is far from useless and should not be abandoned. There is great value, for example, in anthropologists' critical self-reflection on its ideological biases. Ton Lemaire (1986) justly raises the question whether it is possible to know the Other without getting trapped in the dilemma of objective vs. subjective knowledge. In the context of trying to get to know the 'otherness' or difference of another group of humanity, subjective knowledge necessarily remains confined to the historical attitudes which gave the impetus to the inquiry into 'others' — aliens, savages — in the first place. Two attitudes which immediately come to mind are, on the one hand,the experience of dissatisfaction with our own 'civilization', and on the other, of ethnocentrism. Globally speaking, one led to starry-eyed exoticism, the other to wholesale denigration and inferiorization.

Lemaire concludes that we never can really know the Other and its otherness, since the science and philosophy we need in order to describe what we see can never be free from ideological influences. A possible way out is that we acknowledge the existence of our biases and learn from them by continual reflection upon our own presuppositions whenever we presume to speak of others. Knowledge of others is inextricably bound up with self-knowledge. These dialectics may help an evolution towards some form of tolerance and modesty. The past has shown that this is possible at times.

My point is that reflection on 'ourselves' whenever we presume to confront ourselves with 'others' is not just a matter of texts and critical analyses of discourses. Self-reflection is not solely an epistemological affair, and I do not believe that the fabric from which our dealings with 'other' people are made will be properly elucidated that way. Of course, literacy and the unraveling of knowledge structures have a high cultural profile. What else are books about? But that does not mean that textuality is all there is. Although identity and alterity are mainly laid down in texts, from Plato and Aristotle onwards, what is written down has its origin in experience rather than words. It is this pre-verbal experience, in all its complexity, that we have to address.

It is hazardous to raise, let alone to query, the issue of words and concepts. The philosopher will, in an understandable gesture, turn his back on you. He will sit there, silently, indicating that nothing will happen anymore unless things will get named again and thoughts and feelings will again find their linguistic expression. The 'semiotic warfare' must go on. Language is paramount, sole vehicle of meaning. However, the empirical scientist is more skeptical of 'meaning'. After all, what exactly is in a word? Let me give an example. Newly coined terms such as 'automobility', which seems to have such a realistic and meaningful appearance (especially given its functions in the heated political debates nowadays), are easily dismissed by the empirically oriented researcher. Why? Simply because such a concept proves to be empty as soon as the issue is raised of what it is that makes even intellectuals hold on to their cars so tenaciously. In that context, a term like 'automobility' ceases to have a precise meaning and seems to be a mere stand-in for something like 'convenience'. However, 'convenience' is not something with a recognized central status in all the heated debates around traffic logistics. 'Convenience', in this context, hardly conceptualizes anything at all. It merely summarizes our day-to-day praxis; what this praxis involves we can't really pinpoint. We don't know why 'convenience' has this strong impact; why it causes people to take out their cars every morning, thoughtlessly, in a habitual pattern which seems unshakeable, except by severe measures such as raising the costs of driving a car to an almost intolerable degree.

The same can be said about what regulates courtship practices. Men and women hardly can meet without getting involved in some form of relationship which tends to obstruct an unburdened exchange. Again, what is written or otherwise explicitly stated about emancipation seems to leave these interactive patterns largely unchanged. And to tie this back to our subject at hand: Why, in intercultural confrontations, did the vast majority of observers get so upset with what they failed to recognize as a regulation — tribal, different, but a regulation all the same — of interaction between the sexes? All they saw was incontinence and lasciviousness. The enigma remains: what makes people react so vehemently, and with such a strange blend of fascination and disgust, to inhabitants of other parts of the world?

These examples show 'culture' at work without much recourse to words or explicit concepts. I am by no means implying that there are no 'ideas' involved. Culture to some extent is a system of ideas. But from a psychological point of view, 'ideas' exist in many forms or types. These range from an articulated, argumentatively and propositionally organized set of concepts, to a vague and loose feeling or an iconic sensation which organizes responses.

Beyond ideology

In the accepted view, a critical analysis of what Western man (men, mostly) projected into the inhabitants of the New World or Africa — the Indian, the Negro — is highly problematic, since that critical analysis will itself betray another, albeit different distortion. When, for example, in a book on the cultural bias of our forebears, a wood-cutting of Amerindian women around a camp fire is reproduced, with a summary of the seventeenth-century description of a masturbatory gesture testifying to their incontinence and wildness,[1] then the twentieth-century critic may in turn be read as tacitly appreciating the unproblematic and relaxed sexual mores of these people. A modern commentator may even go so far as to replace the notion of their 'wildness', by that of their 'naturalness', in sexual matters. That, of course, would be misguided, since there was no such thing as 'sexual matters' at that time. But instead of trying to account for the mere difference, it is commonly assumed that both texts are 'cultural' products and should be treated as such. The view of the twentieth-century critic, then, is a clear product of the modern Western discourse on sex; the views of the seventeenth-century artist and writer a product of then-current inhibiting tendencies. In other words, what we have here is a culture clash.

But what do we mean by 'culture' in this clash? Does visual and written material become 'cultural' simply because a seventeenth-century man represented the values of his period by depicting the Indian woman the way he did? And is our modern interpretation 'cultural' for the same reason, again because it represents some of the values which dominate our present outlook? It is not difficult to see how easily 'cultural' gets equated with 'ideological'. But that is in itself a hidden culture theory. The suggestion is made that in 'picture' and 'text' something ideological is going on and that we all know what that is. But what about the experience of 'wildness' and our present critical appraisal thereof in terms of the structuring of feelings, emotions, bodily awareness, etc.? Does all that belong to the realm of 'ideology' as well? Is there anything to say about this side of 'culture' without pre-emptying its content solely in terms of ideology? Is that all there is to culture, or can a more encompassing theory be formulated?

Let me elaborate on this issue by citing Mieke Bal's analysis on the occasion of an exhibition held in 1989 on the colonial nude on picture-postcards.[2] In connection with this exhibition and the accompanying book by Raymond Corbey (Corbey 1989) she raises the question whether the 'western imagination of "Africa"' is exhibited with sufficient critical distance. What about self-criticism? Why did Corbey call the postcards

---

[1]   Cf. Peter Mason's contribution to the present volume.

[2]   I refer to Bal's unpublished opening speech ('De wetenschapper als wildeman. Naar aanleiding van de expositie "De Koloniale Verbeelding"'), of which I had occasion to peruse the MS.

'erotic', even though the women on the cards often look very defensive and give the onlooker a grumpy look? The fact that the colonial photographers are criticized for their racism and sexism does not preclude an ongoing typification of the depicted women as 'real', 'attractive', and 'erotic', notwithstanding their visible abhorrence at being at the photographer's command. One should have made use of pictorial material in a much more careful way, Bal argues. But how? By pointing the accusing finger at the colonial photographer? That will cause misuse again. By not presenting the material at all? Bal dislikes binary choices and recommends a third route: bring out, wherever possible, the picture's author, the depicter, and analyse the white male subject. One way of doing this is to pay some attention to materials in which the situation is reversed: for example, black women who look at white males; that is, the white image in black literature.

Bal couches her playful rebuttal in narratological jargon. She asks for 'the focalizer', the subjective perspective through which the women then (as now, at this particular exhibition) have been brought into focus. Only the recognition of 'the fascinated brains' behind it all, in this case of the male colonial and exhibitor (!), gives the Self-Other-dialectic a chance, she feels. If one wants to get an answer to the question what this probing into men's brains (for men they were) implies for Bal, and if one wants to know what sort of criticism she thinks it involves, one discerns in her text the vague contours of something in 'culture' which hardly ever is brought to the fore: In order to give flesh and blood to the 'focalizer' she demands an affective vocabulary. She wants preferences, e.g. feelings of repulsion or attraction. These, too, are part of culture. Formulated in somewhat more general terms, she would like to have these men pay attention to the specific function of the visual material. For isn't it true, so Bal surmises ironically, that men get their castration anxiety from visual experience? It is a typically male problem, she adds. 'I would like to hear more about that. But, if possible, directly rather than through racism and sexism, be these scientifically legitimated'. This suggested to me that ideology somehow needs to be bypassed by addressing oneself to a form of culture-bound 'imagery' which as yet is untouched by the polarity of alterity and identity, not yet structured by a set of arguments about otherness or sameness, be it of racist or anti-racist, of sexist or anti-sexist leaning.

In his chapter on 'Wildness and Civilization', Corbey (1989: 81-104) puts his own approach in line with modern comparative literature. He adopts the imagologist's emphasis on affectively charged hetero- and auto-images, which are presented as natural and as given instead of constructed. Corbey analyses the paradigmatic and syntagmatic dimensions of these images. On the paradigmatic dimension all kind of binary oppositions are lined up, 'wild' vs 'civilized' being of course the most prominent one. The syntagmatic dimension is used to reveal the hidden plot and story behind missionary and colonial activities. The semiotic coherence of binary concepts, heroes and villains, but also of unclassifiable, liminal objects should not just explain the rather fortuitous fabric of the stories as recorded in the innumerable books about the inhabitants of other worlds. It should explain particularly why European men told this 'One, Prolonged European Text' about 'the Other', and why they did so predominantly as voyeurs. Corbey invokes Johannes Fabian, who attributes to anthropologists the intention to 'construct ordered Space and Time — a cosmos — for Western society to inhabit, rather than "to understand other cultures", its ostensible vocation' (Fabian 1983: 111-2). What is said of anthropologists can be said of the European imagination in general, Corbey adds (Corbey 1989: 155). He contends that this 'Prolonged Text' has the power of a Kantian a priori. It is a way of world making, even. Corbey labels it 'semiosis', i.e. the practice of categorization of cultures, thereby underscoring that it is a product of a writer behind his desk. It is assumed that a 'living culture' within all these men was at work. Indeed; but how? There is one little allusion to what made this semiosis so powerful. On page 159 Corbey surmises that it was the 'bourgeois mentality or habitus' interwoven with the Christian world view.

I think that in order to understand this aspect of Western culture, we should cease to locate culture exclusively within a process of fabricating constructs. It reduces the notion of culture to some nebulous 'mind stuff'.[3] Let me outline two challenges to a concept of culture which privileges propositional features and ideological tenets over other types of ideas.[4]

---

[3]   The ensuing reduction of culture to 'measurable energy costs' (Harris) stems from the same attitude and is vitiated by the same shortcomings.

[4]   There does not seem to exist a sufficiently refined taxonomy of ideas. The very thought seems far-fetched, but to my mind some sort of classification of ideas must be developed in order to deal with the perplexing phenomenon that human behaviour cannot exist outside the notional domain. I leave aside the

Two challenges to a mind-ridden image of culture

People are, as we all know, generally of the doing type. There have been at least two movements in psychology in which it was doubted whether even very intellectual people do 'think' much in certain important areas of conduct. They do a lot instead. One movement to capitalize on this truism was of course behaviourism; the other the Russian cultural-historical school.

The empty mind of behaviourism

Of course, the behaviouristic claim of an empty mind was initially stated much more rigorously than is the case today. Often arguments are overstretched in order to correct an equally exaggerated view. That pendulum-swing has served, by now, to ridicule earlier claims. We no longer fall for this nonsensical notion that things going on inside us have no explanatory value. In Watson's days and even at the heyday of Skinner it wasn't all that serious. Out of a rebellious dissatisfaction with the smug self-sufficiency of inherited morality, behaviourists voted against the mind and for outer control. The concepts of reward and reinforcement became central to control, which was stated in terms of environmental constraints and facilitations. The former concepts could only be defined empirically, of course. It trapped the behaviourists into a circular argument, because the thing that could be called a reinforcer was something that strengthened behaviour and vice versa. But despite the circularity, it worked and served their send-up of traditional ethics.

Behaviourism is still quite strong, though it has lost its sharp edges. It shows up in the cognitive study of the mind in the guise of the

---

existence of sheer automatic patterns of behaviour which are totally explicable in terms of cognitively completely encapsulated, hard-wired organizing principles. The axis along which ideas can be classified is probably that of involvement. Elements that can be involved in ideas vary from the viscera to cold cognitions. Culture reflects or mirrors elements and grades the way these get triggered. Culture is therefore as articulate or jointed as ideas. Triggers vary from single percepts to rituals.

modularity of mind approach to language (Fodor 1983) and to emotion (e.g. Frijda 1986). Behaviourism survived its youthful excesses because it was firmly rooted in evolutionary thinking, a point often underplayed in the bleak criticism of the so-called 'black box'. Even nowadays we tend to regard consciousness by and large as an automatic central processor of information. In that respect behaviourism is alive and kicking. The top-level processor is assisted in its tasks by various 'top-down' or 'bottom-up' units (some unresolved dispute there) to which behaviouristic insights apply. On the other hand, the 'naturalization of mind programme' initialized by Darwin has left the physicalistic premises to which it was confined in the earlier days, and has moved to 'wet-ware' conceptions of the brain. The brain seems open to the ontogenetical (apart from phylo-genetical) 'wiring in' of behavioural controls. The so-called 'arbitrary codes' of culture have behavioural impact along these lines, it is assumed (Gardner & Gardner 1988). They can be viewed as elaborations of 'obligatory responses'. An important corollary of this assumption is that the body gets transformed from a sack full of fibres and organs into a system which translates something that impinges on it into bodily executable actions.[5] Note that this 'bodily system' is no fact of nature. Since it is open to structuring and restructuring of its components or 'modules' during its lifespan, it is a cultural body we are talking about. I shall return to this point.

Action and practice: the new 'fillers' of mind

The second movement which has been emphasizing 'doing' almost throughout the entire history of the social sciences is that of the Soviet psychologists who belong to the Cultural-Historical School. They start from

---

[5]   Geertz (1973: 44) is wrong in highlighting the programme metaphor when he talks about culture not being complexes of concrete behaviour patterns, but a set of control mechanisms, a 'program', for the governing of behaviour. The point is that people somehow act with their bodies in response to some cultural 'command': 'run', which is addressed to some sort of 'compiler', that translates 'culture-program language' into, let's say, 'body-machine language'. That makes culture tick. All thinking is metaphor, certainly, but one should be a bit more demanding about the choice of one's metaphors.

the astute observation, made also by early phenomenologists, that thinking and consciousness are always action-based. This can easily be observed in children for whom a tree is something to climb into; and when they barely can walk and not yet have mastered the language, they pull and push you near the candy jar in order to get you to take out some sweets. The concept of 'action' is central to the Soviets' attempts to deal with the so called 'social formation of the mind'. Philosophically they bypass Descartes in their search back for a new starting-point, which they find with Spinoza, and particularly around what Il'enkov has termed the 'thinking body'. Spinoza refutes the idea that thought is a 'product' of action. To use his own terminology: it is not a substance, but an attribute. Much as walking is not the product of action, but action itself at the moment of its performance, so too thinking is action. In linguistics there is a comparable trend to view language primarily as action.

What intrigues me personally in this action-based reappraisal of consciousness and language is the 'tool mediated action' (Wertsch 1985), which serves as a fresh start for a theory of meaning. Tool-mediated action implies both the use of objects and of action-delaying considerations of use, e.g. in problem-solving or 'thinking' (by means of words and images) about what can be used best, or differently, or contrary to common usage etc. etc. In the case of the actual use of objects, there is always first the 'inorganic body' which acts through its means of direct access: grips, spatial position, boundaries, openings, ingestions, etc. A hammer, a car, the house which smells or which is clean: these are what they are because of direct bodily access. A hammer can of course be used as a swinging pendulum, or a weight, or whatever in order to solve a particular problem. In problem-solving jargon this is described as breaking through a 'set', in this case departing from the common usage of a hammer as a handy instrument for driving nails into wood. Various heuristics can be used in order to counteract the established way of going about things. Problem-solving research shows that breaking through a 'set' is not merely a perceptual phenomenon or shifting of attention. It is better viewed as a Gestalt-switch, the sudden flip-over of an entire action-configuration.

Thus, bypassing the mind presupposes the integration into an action theory of neo-darwinian views on what enables organisms to detect something. Emotions and feelings are part of these detection mechanisms. Therefore affective structures should be included in the aforementioned 'bodily system'. This implies that emotions and feelings are by no means precultural, natural, or biological alone. They are preeminently cultural. Emotions and feelings are no longer labels for internal states whose essence is presumed to be invariant due to the electro-chemical processes humans share.

The disseminating skill called 'civilization'

These two psychological schools challenge the concept of mind or consciousness as a 'given', and replace it by something which is constituted in practice. As such, consciousness functions as 'practical sense' (Bourdieu 1990). One of the inferences to be made concerns the notion of 'reflection'.

Reflection or discursive activity and reflexivity can probably best be seen as the consequences of disrupted action. Reflection is the counteraction of involvement. It is a subsidiary principle, which can by no means 'undo' the initial reaction. Disruptions sensitize the actor to the means and ends involved, which before the disruption were present in a more 'blurred' way. Reflection turns what was automatic into something 'conscious', but in that case as *opus operatum*, that is as something 'ready made', a finished product, so to speak, not as *modus operandi*, that is as a procedure. We have no access to what actually goes on in the head. [6] Reflection, therefore, presents itself foremost in terms of what enables us to talk about a ready made, 'finished something'. It implies a skill, an ability, which, of course, in turn can become habitually organized. But we should not forget that this skill itself is structured by actual practice. Much of the cultural idiom stems from one important part of this skill and that is skilled literacy. Through skilled literacy the initial responses get moulded. Through literacy one seeks to accommodate the initial awareness of primary sensations (repulsion, attraction, fear or whatever) to existing, communicative vehicles. Language, concepts, stories and conventional judgemental frames enable the appeasement of disruptive experience. Much training has been involved in this practice, but it is practice all the same.

The skill, thus typified, is culturally distributed and mediated. Not

---

[6]   The distinction between *opus operatum* and *modus operandi* is used in Bourdieu (1990) for an elucidation of the 'practical sense'.

everyone possesses this skill in the same degree and certainly not in the same way and in all behavioural domains. The skill varies enormously across distinct groupings of people. It usually gets shaped by the presence of predominant modes of what is considered 'proper action'. Nineteenth- and twentieth-century utilitarianism, in which human activity is charac- terized by application of means to obtain some end, or the view that the a rational human being tends to apply the most useful or 'rational' means to their cause, are examples of such shaping frames. Within such a frame the skill coincides with being civil, or civilized, or polite, or 'cultured'. In sum: Good manners, civility and other signs of civilization are essentially abstractions of ongoing activity. These abstractions are disseminated across the populace. Yet, let us not forget that 'culture', related to practical sense and feeling, is operative in those activities. It is at work also in the distribution and mediatization of skill. I assume that underneath these abstractions culture is always present and has a shaping influence. To the initiated, culture moulds action without conscious effort. In that respect the Europeans who met the 'savages' reacted within the framework of their culturally informed practical sense. But the moment they called what they experienced a different 'culture' they ceased referring to the actual workings of their own frame as confronted with alien stimuli. Instead they referred to arrested content, a finished product, constituted by their verbalizing skill; they accommodated what they saw and felt in ready-made terms. To label such products of skill and accommodating pressures 'a different culture' which heightened the awareness of their own cultural legacy, is only another way of speaking about culture. 'Culture' then becomes a very confusing concept. It signifies a finished product as well as some sort of moulding process.

This process is a highly interesting topic for scientific investigation. This requires that we turn to the forces of the cultural body and to culturally informed feelings and emotions, that is, to sentiments. It is here that the moulding process takes place.

This view is at odds with the mind-ridden notions of 'civilized' and 'uncivilized' people. Suddenly such concepts appear transparent. They merely point to the fact that culture always was (and still is, n think) tacitly presented as a skill, as something substantial, something that has content, something one could poses in certain degrees. Culture as substance and skill marks off 'them' from 'us'.

At this juncture, the question must be raised why Western culture as a moulding force has almost never been analyzed. It seems as if culture as a moulding force receded behind the 'substantial' view outlined above. Let me state it more clearly, and, for the sake of argument, somewhat exaggeratedly: Western culture has removed itself from scientific scrutiny. As a result, alterity and identity, which have been and continue to be constructed by means of the 'substantial' notion of culture have also been placed outside the reach of rigorous scientific scrutiny. Because of a bias towards seeing culture in terms of *opus operatum*, as substance, as content, as 'product', rather than probing into the *modus operandi*, in order to analyze its moulding capacity, culture has remained just another word for nothing else to say. Within such terms, the alterity/identity debate is merely a literary game, and a game, at that, which is played around forces of conduct not yet understood. Corbey's book and many others about Western imagination testify to the fact that all that can be done is to describe again and again how the European imagination went astray. These books are one massive source of data. They contain a wealth of well-documented instances of cultural misapprehension. Yet, an explanation, apart from an attempt to deconstruct the often bizarre representations, is hardly ever offered. Is it sufficient to invoke the notion of 'narrative' and to point out that the boundary between literature and science is blurred? That does not help us to understand the reason why the Western narrative could be so violent. Covetousness has been held responsible for this violence, but to the psychologist such an explanation seems merely to skim the very surface. This poverty of explanation, I suggest, is due to the lack of a scientific analysis of culture as a mould for action.

Despite all anti-scientist criticism, only real scientific scrutiny could formulate a cogent critique of Western identity constructs. This never happened; instead, things went quite the opposite way. We have inflated our own image to a gigantic proportion. Why? In the next section I address this question with reference to cultural forces at a level below the skilled use of the cultural idiom of wildness, civilization, irrationality, brutishness etc. This is also an effort to clear the ground for a more fruitful, *behavioural* approach to culture.

The imperviousness of culture

The cultural idiom in which the confrontation of the old world with the new was couched often had a scientific ring to it. Notions from evolutionary theory have been invoked, for example, which compared the 'primitive' with an early stage in man's ontogeny. Sometimes notions from psychological theories about cognitive functions or intelligent behaviour were used. This well known fact is often explained in terms of the ideological forces in science: the risk that science runs of being manipulated by established interests and of being, consequently, misapplied. That interpretation presupposes that the distortion comes from outside the scientific field. But the history of science abounds with so many examples of false ideas, twisted arguments and stubborn prejudice, particularly in the domain of assessing cultural differences, that there is more to be said.

The point is not that science is misused or applied wrongly, but rather that it isn't applied vigorously enough. In the social domain science's disenchanting forces are often warded off. Science's success in demythologizing nature in order to alleviate the anxieties imposed by ignorance on mankind may have been acclaimed, but only as lo,g as the process posed no threat to the stability of social patterns. Culture, particularly Western culture, has frequently placed a check on the critical probe of scientific thought, safeguarding and indeed maintaining its patterns.

We have no records about what actually moulded the behaviour of those who went forth and conquered, no description of their culture with its bodily and affective structures. What we have instead in Western accounts of culture, particularly of Western culture itself, is 'self-consciousness' and 'reflexivity'. Our culture has always been a fit subject for moral discourse, something that could be pointed out to 'others', particularly by stressing what the others are lacking. Western man always has been quite articulate about his own 'cultural identity' and about the 'alterity' of others.

However, in pointing out what Western man possessed and the others were lacking, something strange happened. Western man has attributed, in scientific discourse, aliens with a biological make-up and 'structures of mind' intended to account for their backwardness, lack of rationality and unfitness for the boons of modern life. This can hardly be called an ideological distortion imposed from outside. Rather, it is a dynamic of science itself, and one which has tended to obfuscate rather than clarify the forces in our own culture.

Receding from science, behind science

What was it that caused the ongoing withdrawal of western culture itself from the analyses that it applied to other cultural systems? Admittedly, judging by philosophical texts, the Western world has been hyperconscious about its own cultural shortcomings. Many intellectuals have pointed out the failures of our civilization. These were skilled reflections. But how come these skilled reflections never called upon the machinery of scientific investigations? Why did the critique of Western society, from the sixteenth century onward, remain only a 'symptom of our own problematic and spoiled identity' (Lemaire 1986: 247)? Lemaire suggests that our reluctance to try to come to terms with our own hidden values makes us hostile towards the values of others. But I would like to offer an additional explanation, which may be gleaned from a tendency in our way of thinking that emerged in the mid-nineteenth century and has been with us since. A tendency which has enabled us (and perhaps still does) to ward off an all-too rigorous assessment of our own cultural frames.

In an earlier section I attributed the vehement reaction of behaviourists against 'mind' and 'consciousness' to moral indignation on their part. Such indignation was endemic in the human sciences in general. From the mid-century onward, discussions about 'progress' or 'change', or about what really could contribute to the improvement of the human condition, took place in a scientific climate that was highly competitive. Witness the effort that went into post-darwinian polemics, notably among biologists and evolutionists of all persuasions, in order to refute the existence of essential 'fixities', particularly fixities of nature and of class. However, the tendency seems to have been to deny such essential fixities in culture and history, not on the defaults of the case at issue, but as part of this competitive, agonistic scientific debate and its quarrel over the shaping influences in human conduct (nature vs. culture, nature vs. nurture). At best, the quarrel was a moral *ad hominem* one: which stance was enlightened, which one reactionary? At worst it was a sheer struggle for power.

A good number of these debates took place in the field of the differential psychology of mental measurement. They constitute a nasty chapter in the annals of the 'mismeasure of man' (Gould 1984). Strikingly, what was at stake was not so much whether real insight could be gained in what determined human behaviour, but whether those sciences which were skeptical toward essential fixities of whatever sort, could pass the test of scientificity. As a result the debate was obscured by an implicit meta-dispute about what type of academic investigation could rightfully call itself a 'science'. No attempt was made to settle the issue by showing the surplus value of the explanatory power of one of the alternatives; instead, a second-degree confusion obscured the scene. Much energy was diverted into demonstrating or refuting the ideological bias of biology and of the social sciences (including cultural anthropology). Scholars appeared to be constantly engaged in mutual accusations and deontological minutiae of scientific methodology. The essential fixity debate was not about issues of understanding, but about second-, or even third-degree derivatives. It was about whether one was rational enough, or materialistic enough, or whether one could be accused of idealism etc. The only effect, as far as I can see, was that science as such got ample opportunity to present itself as the most misleading cultural force of the Western world. Science itself came to appear as the safest device against attacks on our own culture. It enabled culture to recede from science behind science.

Let me elaborate on this. Even today, the debate whether culture as a 'behavioural programme' is motivated, either by a 'referential' or 'symbolic system', or by 'gut affairs' (womb, stomach, muscular or skeletal differentials...) fails to address real issues. The debate, rather, is about the scientific corroboration of the social importance of emancipatory targets: should social emancipation or improvement (issues which the West seems to have a patent on) address, in the first instance, the mind, that is, people's thoughts or discourse, or else the material conditions under which people live? That science should have been called in as an arbiter, even in this issue, has led to a degree of scientific self-righteousness. 'Scientificity' as a mode of self-righteousness has become very deeply ingrained in our culture. What in the ages of the 'Divine Order' formed people's innermost moral guide for political conduct (namely, man's Godlike nature as the source of all good) has been transformed into a secular but no less profound and deeply-held affect: the moral endorsement provided by the standards of scientificity. I think that it hardly can be denied that science and scientific rationality belong to the innermost core of Western cultural values. As such, science has come to serve as the main judgemental frame behind which our 'culture' could withdraw in order to ward off critical analysis. [7]

The question remains how this withdrawal has taken shape. One of the answers lies, I think, in the development of a very specific cultural idiom. The cultural idiom in which non-western people have been described derives from the scientific jargon of various disciplines: evolutionary biology and that human zoology which addresses the hereditary features of human nature and which has formed the foundation of 'differential psychology'. Also, biological theories concerning the defective nature of 'others' drew on that influential discourse which sees the human personality as comprising, at the 'lowest' or 'deepest' level, a miasma of animal passions, instincts and desires. In terms of that discourse, those animal forces were most influential in those who lacked civilization. This begs the question, of course, why only in the Western world (and even there only in certain layers of society) 'civilization' should have succeeded in establishing control over animal passion.

Crowding the human interior

Many scholars have been struck by the fact that during the nineteenth century an elaborate intrapsychic scripting developed as an attempt to link individual desires to social meanings. Foucault has shown that reason and unreason ceased at some moment in history to reside in separate, geographically distinct domains. At some point it became widely accepted that every human being did run the risk of becoming insane. In the nineteenth century this feeling had become all-pervasive and insanity counted as the

---

[7]   The certainty derived from this process can be challenged by asking the simple question: Does science itself belong to the head or to the guts? This question has made some impact in recent post-Popperian decades and in the postmodern climate: reason and evidence show that science does not consist merely of its serene ideals and values, but that scientific practice has developed into a specific culture (mechanical, voracious). Scientists may be seen as forming a tribal culture functioning to a large extent on 'gut' affects; that scientific community can be scrutinized for the way it devises the facts and fables of our time. Exposing the narrative structure of science is the ultimate unmasking of its claims. Yet again, what has turned science into something like a story are its cultural (i.e. behaviourally patterned) underpinnings.

gravest destructive force of culture. Spotting culture threats from within became a fashion.

This development should be seen in the context of nineteenth-century urbanization: a multitude of people who had previously lived the orderly life of the village moved to the anonymous streets and dwellings of the great cities; and this necessitated a social rearticulation of the private world of individual, private wishes and desires. Lionel Trilling (1972) argues that it was the emergence of modern Western urbanized and industrialized society which for growing numbers of people necessitated the focusing and amplification of a 'self'. Therefore, it may well be that 'id-like' functions have followed the appearance of superego-like functions, rather than the other way around.

The intrapsychic emerged, then, as an autonomous domain following the experience of living in a modern city. Desires, things people really want to happen to them or want to get from others, now came to be experienced as distinct from existing cultural scenarios of city life, often felt to be uncongenial. Previously, in a rural or village environment, desires had been conventionalized, ritualized, and justified by the very fact of forming part of traditional life in the community. They were negotiated as such in the public realm. Within the confines of one's familiar locality one acted in accordance with pre-set scenarios to settle the negotiation (success not always guaranteed, of course). Once the conventions and its concomitant behaviour-guiding rituals decayed (as a result of people becoming incapable of stinking to their scripts) a new quality of desire emerged. This new quality was experienced with great uneasiness, embarrassment, anxiety and pain, linked to a general sense of alienation. Much of this distress was experienced (plausibly enough) in sexual terms - sex being one of the more elaborately scripted emotions. What I am contending here is that the 'id' (or man's 'animal nature' as it is sometimes called) is the *product* of the civilizing process and the most modern of psychic functions, not the most archaic one.

Assuming my view of the 'id' (to maintain that terminology) is correct and that my macro-analysis has some plausibility (though it needs elaboration and factual corroboration), we can argue that the human interior of Western man got crowded with desires, emotions and feelings, which have been cut loose from their traditional cultural frame. That very same crowded interior thus became in itself the ultimate frame of reference and was applied to one's assessment of others. What pertained to the people of the West was assumed to pertain to the people of other parts of the world as well, particularly, of course, when those others exhibit deviant behaviour such as cannibalism. The Western cultural frame that was judgementally applied to others was the product of a particular way of dealing with the affective side of human existence: Western cultural values were based on an introjection of emotions and desires that had been dissociated from their original beds of convention, form and ritual.

This brings me to my central contention. Even though this introjection of cultural values was performed under social pressures, the analysis of the resulting value system was not performed by a cultural or social science. Rather, the sciences that were applied to these 'inner' forces were biology, psychiatry and to some extent psychology (particularly psychoanalysis). In dealing with human conduct and human relations, these disciplines classed drives, needs and desires as 'inner' forces under the assumption that they were universal. Psychology performed the trick behind biology's back. Obviously, the concepts of alterity and identity were fabricated from what had thus been misconstrued as 'inner' forces thus misplaced. [8]

We should not be surprised, then, to see that ethnologists did not bother to frame native people's affects in terms of different rituals, forms and conventions. It is merely the consequence of the fact that Western man did not pursue the cultural framing of his own affective life. That pursuit still seems to be in its incipience.

Body and sentiment: a behavioural approach to culture

What, after so much cultural criticism, can be offered by way of an alternative concept of culture?

Since the introjection process outlined above took place at a definite point in time in Western social history and under specific conditions (such as the decay of rituals for the public negotiation of desire), psychoanalytic-ally-oriented approaches to the 'dynamics' of culture are beside the point. Desire has been transformed from something one can get relatively freely

---

[8]   This mislocation resembles the religious habit of locating evil within everyone's heart. Even a very common religious practice became 'natural' as it got secularized.

from others (as 'tribal' societies show) into an elusive intimate sensation that interferes with people's serenity;[9] to articulate this process in psychoanalytic terms, however modified, is itself a cultural phenomenon. Psychoanalysis studies the results of an introjection process which it has itself set in motion. It is impossible to use the product of a cultural change for the explanation of the conditions under which that change took place. In this respect I fully agree with Corbey (1989: 105 ff.; and his contribution to the present collection), who dismisses the psychoanalytic interpretation of 'wildness'-in-others in terms of 'wildness'-within-ourselves: the theoretical tools are couched in the same idiom whose employment it tries to explain. If we are to account for such transformations to which psychoanalysis has been an amplifying asset, we cannot use psychoanalysis as a vantage point, and have to turn to cultural theory instead.

What, then, provides access to the cultural forces? What is at work in fascination and disgust, in the appreciation or denigration of other people's way of life?

The key terms have already been mentioned: the inorganic body, affective structures, practical sense, and the habitual organization and structure of behaviour.

The inorganic body

In modern behaviourism the body was no longer seen as a corpus of organic matter but as a transducer of stimuli and sensations, transforming them into executable acts. Thus even behaviourism pays tribute to some insights in phenomenology. In the phenomenological tradition it is an acknowledged fact that 'sensations' never are 'sense data'. They are 'live-bodily events' (*Leibesvorkomnisse* in Husserl's terminology), which need to be distinguished from mere physical events. They occur in functional correlation with bodily activity. Objects in the external world are, by consequence, always localized in or on my organism. The entire body becomes one sensuous organ. The effort to describe and account for the intentional unification of the various localized fields into one contextually

---

[9]   Anthropologists' fascination with sex in other cultures is puzzling if one does not take into account that in those societies desire did not present itself as a nagging intimate sensation but as something to be negotiated in public.

unified sensuous organ is the primary task of a phenomenology of the body and embodiment (Zaner 1971: 257). Merleau-Ponty contends that there exists a mode of consciousness which is 'non-thetic'. It is called *l'intentionalité opérante* to distinguish it from *l'intentionalité d'acte*. He thus suggests that the body has its own particular brand of intentionality. Since Merleau-Ponty attributes to the body ambiguity, generality and anonymity, this special intentionality is closely related to an already established 'corporeal scheme' outside one's full control. It functions as a very unspecific base, a sedimentation, from which specific and clearly thetic intentional acts emerge.

Merleau-Ponty uses 'scheme' in the singular; I would prefer the plural.[10] Corporeal schemes, which are acquired in all sorts of behavioural domains, constitute a complex of habits, characteristics and usual ways of acting, seeing, touching, assuming postures etc. What goes for corporeal schemes also holds in terms of feelings that have adopted certain cultural forms and are 'lived' as such. They turn the physical body into a social or cultural one. Merleau-Ponty has not addressed this particular issue; as a result his analysis of the body has a kind of naive-optimistic flavour, which, as far as I can see, has done the phenomenological project of the body much harm; even to such a degree that it has come to an halt. According to Merleau-Ponty the body 'knows' things properly, in the sense that one can fall back on it, it is a sense-bestowing device, it expresses existence, it enables lived experience, and endows the world, but also fellow-human beings with meaning. Yet, to return to our subject matter, when body meets body in the context of different life-styles, different forms of dressing, strange eating habits, unusual smells, strange ways of moving around, etc., it can also betray itself as very insensitive organ. The body can take on a harsh posture. It can be appropriated by a group to the effect that the entire person becomes a replica, who gives up his or her individuality and is cordoned off from modes of behaviour other than the condoned standard. As such the body can become a straitjacket or a character-armour, a source of prejudice, impervious to whatever verbal

---

[10]   The emphasis on scheme (singular) is related to Merleau-Ponty's emphasis of 'motility' (i.e., moving around and thereby acquiring a body scheme, which once constituted is always constituted). As such it is a source of awareness for the synergistic system — which the body undoubtedly is. Yet motility is one activity among many other performed by the body as a sensuous organ.

attempt to correct. Such aspects of the body may be elucidated with the help of insights provided by Pierre Bourdieu. [11]

The cultural form of feeling

Pierre Bourdieu is rightfully credited with the insight that social institutions tend to objectify themselves into the human body. The body acquires certain sensibilities and an overlearned, automatic reactiveness, which gear in with the institutional settings in which the individual participates. This complex of acquired sensibilities and dispositions Bourdieu calls *habitus*. Bourdieu undoubtedly got his inspiration from Merleau-Ponty; Zaner has summarized this perspective as follows:

> The de facto regularities in appearances of things in the milieu constituted as 'the same' for each sensuous field (by means of automatic syntheses), these regularities of appearance become constituted as regularities of the self-identical things, happening under circumstances which are essentially connected to this animated organism's actual and potential action 'on' or 'to' these things. Already at the automatic levels, things are experienced by consciousness, not as isolated fragments unrelated to one another, but rather as self-identical unities happening in a regular fashion, undergoing change and alteration, and maintaining regularities with other unities and with the organism itself. (Zaner 1971: 258)

Zaner emphasizes, then, that even at the level of the automatisms of the animated organism, experience presents itself in organized and directional fashion. In this sense the body 'knows' things. Whether or not the body does have its own peculiar brand of intentionality is a question which is fraught with intricacies. One reason for doubt is the fundamental problem of having to postulate an agency which somehow 'reads off' the bodily gathered information. Obviously the word 'to know' is confusing in this regard. It has too strong a connotation of 'ego-relatedness'. The question arises, therefore, whether there exists a mode of relating to the world

---

[11]   After finishing this paper I came across a similar attempt to combine Merleau-Ponty's theory of the body with Bourdieu's theory of habitus: Csordas 1990.

around us in which 'bodily skills' function as monitoring devices, without taking recourse to language (which would make us at the outset into interpreters of the world). Before human beings become semantically inserted in their context (at the onset of explicit intentions), they probably are already involved on the basis of emotions and feelings with a strong bearing on bodily skills. Bourdieu's concept of habitus can be applied here, in conjunction with cultural psychological insight in the affective structuring of behaviour.

The idea that emotions are culturally constituted or — as others prefer to term it — socially constructed or constrained, is by now a truism (Levy 1973; Levy & Rosaldo 1983; Lutz 1988; Harré 1986). However, the conceptualization of cultural constraints is by no means satisfactory. Social constructivism suffers from flawed evidence as regards the constructionist contention that affective labeling can be manipulated within a very wide range (Kemper 1981). The emphasis on so called 'cultural norms' for the interpretation, expression, and eliciting of emotions is an equally flawed corollary. Firstly, the 'wide range' doesn't exist. All kinds of constraints on learning in fact limit flexibility - constraints ranging from obligatory species-specific response patterns ingrained in the organism on the basis of Darwinian principles of biological economy (Gardner & Gardner 1988) to body practices and techniques related to acquired behavioural automatisms.

Second, an overly strong emphasis on norms and values may obscure structural relationships of gender, class, age, and in- and out-group. 'Norm-like' concepts such as 'feeling rules' (Hochschild 1983), 'rules of display' of emotions and feelings (Ekman 1973), and 'emotion work' or 'emotion talk' as part of the 'indigenous psychologies' (Heelas 1986), beg a few questions. Norms are norms, and values are values, because of the emotions involved. This means that these factors (highly important though they are) cannot be invoked as antecedents for an explanation of the cultural construction of feeling and emotion. Emotion work and emotion talk testify to the fact that emotions are already there. They can be hypo- or hypercognized, but no more than that: nuances and (acute or fuzzy) discriminations of feeling are a matter not of feeling, but of the level of reflective activity in the community. This means, as Levy (1973: 324) has also noted, that despite the lack of vocabulary, feelings and emotions are already somehow 'orchestrated' within certain cultural frames. The cultural norm for feelings, which constructionists purport to be the shaping force behind human emotions, thus becomes in fact epiphenomenal. The explanatory core can only be found in response patterns which need to be inferred from the interplay of structural relations in a given society and the nature of affective responses described above.

Much empirical work needs to be done, of course, in order come to come to grips with this feature of human affective life. As Bourdieu has never ceased to emphasize, structural relationships nave a much more direct impact on human functioning through the way these relations become objectified in the bodies of the participants who are subjected to, or else in control of, exerted power. The constraining patterns of response as sketched above play an important role in the establishment of human bonds. The body of knowledge from which proof of this fact can be theoretically derived and submitted to empirical testing is readily available. One can think of the work done by Harris (1977; 1979), which brings out the importance, in the establishment of human organization, of 'measurable energy costs' or ecological pressures or gut-feelings stemming from 'womb and belly and earth and water' (Harris 1979: ix). Yet the persistence of certain behavioural patterns and the way these can be elicited almost effortlessly, cannot really be explained without recourse to something like the concept of 'sentiment'.

The concept of sentiment has had quite a long history. Already in the late twenties Malinowski (1927) based his account of the transition from nature to culture on the analysis of sentiments as undertaken by A.F. Shand (1912).

> Shand was the first to realize that emotions cannot be treated as loose elements, unconnected and unorganized, floating around in our mental medium to make now and then an isolated and accidental appearance. His theory as well as all the newer work on emotions is based on the principle that our emotional life is definitely co-ordinated with the environment; that a number of things and persons claim our emotional responses. (1927: 176)

We all are now quite familiar with the idea that emotions and feelings aren't entities. [12] There are no 'states' or 'traits', lying inside, awaiting expression by means of the mediation of behaviour. Neither have emotions

---

[12]   Much of what follows is my own adaptation from Radley 1988.

and feelings the either/or appearance of verbal symbols which allow us to make propositions in which predicates and negatives are employed. Someone may be angry, but while this word is used to describe the state that person is in, one needs to realize that he or she is also, say, generous. The anger is nothing but the expression of a particular sensitivity toward the one he or she is angry at. In the case of downright, immutable anger not one single state is involved either, as the word unduly suggests. Anger involves, for example, the wish to destruct or to annihilate, which again precludes an either/or, an angry-or-not-angry approach.

Emotions and feelings are analogous communications. These communications posit something, which at best can be described as iconic relationships. The richness of communicative import cannot be exhausted in verbal statements of the actors involved. Since emotions and feelings do involve organized experience, linguistic expression is limited. That is why people often refuse to say that they are angry, or to put in words how they feel or think about somebody. They prefer to act in certain ways, or to express themselves ambiguously. They do, of course, use words, but the intention is to convey a 'picture' of the experience as completely as possible. Emotions, then, are expressive of the relationship of individuals to society; conversely, that relationship takes shape from the various kinds of articulation to which emotions are subjected.

The experience of bodily change is a major source of articulative pressures. Through the involvement of the lived body, emotions and feelings inform us immediately about what is going on. Words like 'love', 'attraction' or 'aggression' are merely verbally coded distinctions of what essentially are patterns in the experience of interchange. On these coded forms culturally prescribed vocabulary indeed has a strong bearing, but despite an (often strong) touch of language and speech, emotions and feelings are realized foremost with or through the body, depending on the experience of being gripped or seized (passive undergoing), or of being placed in the position of enactment (actively expressing or doing something 'with feeling'). Emotions and feelings are as much enacted as they are inflicted upon us.

Enactment implies that some distance is realized with respect to what one is undergoing. The distance is marked by a 'disembodiment of feelings' manifesting itself as 'regulation' or 'control'. Control, therefore, should not be defined in terms of the shaping of an amorphous substance of some sort (arousal, for example). Emotions do not function as an amorphous substratum to cognition. It appears no more appropriate to speak of a cognitive label for emotion than it is to speak of a cognitive identifier of whatever other ideational event (such as memory, intuition, belief, etc). What is remembered, intuited or believed isn't the cognitive identification of a vague substratum of mental going-ons. Emotions and feelings are ideational at the outset, as much as thoughts or beliefs are.

The disembodiment of what, paradoxically, nevertheless remains embodied — for the expression of emotion and feeling is always gestural and postural, however 'controlled' or 'verbally shaped' — is nothing more and nothing less than the effect of the reciprocal relationship between the physical body and the social body. This distinction between two bodies I borrow from Mary Douglas (1973).

Douglas takes issue with the programme of Marcel Mauss (1936), whose main shortcoming is that the denial of the existence of natural behaviour, or of a 'natural body', is derived from a false opposition between nature and culture. According to Mauss the body is cultural in all its appearances and in all the use people make of their body in whatever situation. The notion of 'body techniques' expresses this all-pervasive effect of cultural learning. Douglas considers this an overextension of the nature-culture dichotomy, leading to a complete overruling of nature. She postulates a natural tendency, universal in all cultures, to express situations of a certain kind in an appropriate bodily style. Bodily control is thus an expression of social control. Bodily control will be mandatory in those kinds of situations, or even entire cultures, where formality is paramount. On the other hand, 'the less highly structured, the more value on informality, the more the tendency to abandon reason and to follow panic or crazes, and the more the permitted scope for bodily expressions of abandonment'.

That bodily styles are natural does not mean that they are biological. In all cultures, bodily styles involve obedience to the natural tendency to co-ordinate meaning between two patterns of communication. Thus, Douglas's line of argument hypothesizes that there are pressures to create consonance between the perception of the social and the physiological levels of experience. Such a position sees a close interplay between the physical body and the social body. [13] There is not merely the one single cultural body, as Mauss wanted to have it.

It is a matter of nuance, of course, but I feel positively disposed to the notion of a close interplay between what Douglas calls 'vertical references to physical and social experience'. Where the valuing of 'cultured' forms of behaviour over nature is most emphasized, bodily control will be in evidence. Bodily abandon and unkemptness, or their opposites, are culturally controlled. The inarticulateness of social organization will be mirrored in bodily dissociation. What Douglas tries to demonstrate for trance-like states, which according to her theory must exists in weakly structured societies, can probably be demonstrated for all kinds of separate domains within a given social order.

We now can be more precise about how sentiments need to be theoretically conceptualized. Sentiments are co-extensive with form and are revealed through its mode of production. In this connection it is wrong to state that sentiments are feelings regulated by a social order: for this would presuppose a reduction of feeling to formlessness and inarticulation, whereas in fact feelings are produced through their articulation and thus become sentiments. They manifest themselves as part of an affective system of human bonds. What is particularly important is that this affective system circumvents or even cuts across linguistic or analytical distinctions of mind and body, or of individual and society, or of social structure and agencies operating on or within it. Consequently, sentiments are capable of generating as much order and as much rational procedure as beliefs or arguments do. Their ideational power, however, is derived from the close interplay of the two bodies involved. That is the reason why sentiments can be so strongly felt. One is equipped with fully automatic behavioural patterns with regard to modes of dress, decency, or hierarchical superiors. There also is an easy flow of patterned conduct with respect to how men and women need to relate to each other, or what children may or may not do, or how people who differ from us need to be dealt with, etc. These aspects of human comportment are primarily monitored affectively and bodily. In this monitoring process, culture triggers certain patterns of sentiments, and provides (through rituals rather than through explicitly

---

[13]   The words *physical* and *social* do not indicate different bodies as entities. They express standpoints on a single dimension covering a range of pressure and classification, coordinating the physical and social body together.

stated enjoinders) a possibility for the stylization of its expression and the amplification or inhibition of one's awareness of its presence.

Alterity/Identity and culture revisited

Once the point of view is adopted that for a better understanding of the effects of culture, culture needs to be located in the nexus of body and sentiment, its conventional treatment as an ideational system, which solely emphasizes the mind, or reason, or thinking, is open to doubt. But what does culture boil down to once it is firmly fixed in a triangular relation with body and sentiment?

The observation that culture engraves itself on the bodies of the participants and entails a prolonged and in-depth education of the senses, is one side of the coin. The other side is that there exists something like an 'orchestration' of behavioural patterns by extra-personal templates or moulds. What I mean by that can best be exemplified by the way grown-ups proceed in correcting ungrammatical sentences of the young. One normally isn't aware of what rule exactly is violated; yet, correction is still possible and occurs as if no rule exists. The rule only comes to mind as the result of reflection on what has already been performed by way of an automatic corrective procedure. The correcting response is triggered by the way the utterance didn't 'feel' good. Such feelings probably are the result of some subliminal matching against the proper form of a sentence. In other words, proper forms somehow possess a 'gestalt', whose rule-governed syntactical and semantical composition remains hidden behind the immediate impression the utterance makes. In the case of a mismatch, we often laugh first, particularly if we appreciate the effort of the child. But soon thereafter, we proceed to correct.

The same holds for behavioural patterns, which mismatch cultural forms. But what holds for mismatch, holds for comportment that conforms to existing cultural forms. Again, behaviour is not 'produced' by rules.

It seems relevant to emphasize such matching processes or orchestrations, rather than rules, because 'norms', 'values', 'emotion talk', 'feeling rules' etc. are all behavioural abstractions in the language of psychology or sociology. We should not make the mistake of placing those abstractions back inside people's heads. Culture as a scientific concept, therefore, needs to be seen in terms of a theory of behavioural monitoring.

Use of the term 'culture' in order to designate the 'way of life', or an entire civilization, or the local system of historically derived regularities in people's behaviour, is a loose, everyday 'manner of speaking'. Of course there is an accepted validity in using the term in the colloquial sense of, for example, 'Dutch culture', or 'the culture of the Middle-East', or 'the culture of a firm or of a political party'. However, it becomes objectionable to use the term in a sliding way, sometimes for coherent, shared, or interrelated cognitive systems, simplifying the behavioural life of a community, and sometimes for that part of peoples' conduct which is left unexplained once economic, social and personal determinants are accounted for. It often happens that culture is merely a word for the unexplained and baffling residue that escapes otherwise sophisticated analyses.

The analysis of alterity and identity, I said in the opening lines of this paper, often betrays a preoccupation with epistemology and ideology. In the wake of the imagological approach of contacts between 'cultures', culture is reduced to a system of knowledge or ideology. What fascinates me in the alterity/identity debate is that in an attempt to apprehend the construction of an image, one generally has overlooked what actually governed the exchange. Basil Davidson once remarked in a television interview how in the earliest contacts with Africans, the government officials who were welcomed at the African Courts were greatly impressed with the courtly life of the local emperors and kings. The orchestration of sentiments at the African coast probably was not all that different from the way behavioural patterns were triggered at home. Racist sentiments came in to play later on; Davidson corroborated this contention by showing early Renaissance paintings on which the Black Man was pictured with dignity and pride. How the reactions to the common crowd were, he didn't tell. Records of the first meetings between Europeans and the Japanese mention strong feelings of disgust from the side of the Japanese toward men whose filth and stench was unbearable. Such feelings precluded further feelings of respect. There are also examples of men who were impressed by the beauty of blacks or Asians. Apparently the fit between their sexual or erotic taste and the institutional order in the colonies was much better there than at home. This made them more sensitive to existing cultural patterns.

What all these examples show is the importance of body and sentiment. It is not enough to understand our confrontation with others by bringing our self-image into the picture and juxtaposing the knowledge-structure of our own culture and of the culture of the strangers. The imagological instruments need to be supplemented by the study of the cultural triggers of sentiments, bodily styles and other self-regulating devices. The hermeneutics of the meaning of symbols or rituals should at least be accompanied by a testable theoretical account of what made the sources and texts look the way they look.

I am not implying that this procedure has never been followed yet. Thus, Ton Lemaire (1986: 28 ff.) has noticed an interesting divergence in the way Columbus' description of nature was evaluated: Humboldt praises Columbus for his open-mindedness and candour, whereas Olschky relates how much Columbus couched his account in the literary genre of the time. Psychological studies abounds with experimental evidence for assimilative pressures on all kinds of behavioural domains. The perception of nature's beauty can be counted among them, but also, of course, 'person perception' as it is technically called, and the perception of habit and custom. It is quite interesting to see what kind of frame Montaigne employed (in his essay On Cannibals) for the judgement of warfare among the Brazilian Indians. He called their martial style 'noble and magnanimous'. It had a definite beauty and rivalry for courage seemed to be the sole underlying force. The cannibalism of these Indians was far less barbarous than the Portuguese habit of burning people alive. It is very important, of course, to discern in such judgmental frames as Montaigne's the first traces of cultural relativism. But it is still more important to understand the various ways of dealing with the menacing or dangerous other in terms of the underlying affective principles.[14] Merely to point out that the Western cultural myth of the Noble Savage begins with Montaigne, or to argue, as Lemaire does, that Montaigne's cultural critique foundered in his skepticism (p. 102) betrays, again, a deficient concept of culture.

References

P. BOURDIEU, 1990. *The Logic of Practice* (Cambridge: Polity Press).
R. CORBEY, 1989. *Wildheid en beschaving. De Europese verbeelding van Afrika* (Baarn: Ambo).
TH.J. CSORDAS, 1990. 'Embodiment as a Paradigm for Anthropology', *Ethos*, 18, #1: 5-47.

---

[14]   For a first step in that direction, cf. Rosaldo 1984.

250   PAUL VOESTERMANS

M. DOUGLAS, 1982. 'The Two Bodies', in Id., *Natural Symbols. Explorations in Cosmology* (2nd ed. New York: Pantheon), pp. 65-81.

P. EKMAN, 1973. 'Cross-cultural Study of Facial Expression', in *Darwin and Facial Expression*, ed. P. Ekman (New York: Academic Press).

J. FODOR, 1983. *The Modularity of Mind* (MIT Press).

N. FRIJDA, 1986. *The Emotions* (Cambridge University Press).

R.A. GARDNER & B. GARDNER, 1988. 'Feedforward versus Feedbackward: An Ethological Alternative to the Law of Effect', *Behavioral and Brain Sciences*, 11: 429-493.

S.J. GOULD, 1984. *The Mismeasure of Man* (Harmondsworth: Penguin).

R. HARRÉ, ed., 1986. *The Social Construction of Emotions* (Oxford: Basil Blackwell).

M. HARRIS, 1977. *Cannibals and Kings* (New York: Vintage).

M. HARRIS, 1979. *Cultural Materialism. The Struggle for a Science of Culture* (New York: Vintage).

P. HEELAS, 1986. 'Emotion Talk across Cultures', in Harré 1986, pp. 234-266.

A. HOCHSCHILD, 1983. *The Managed Heart: Commercialization of Human Feeling* (University of California Press).

TH.D. KEMPER, 1981. 'Social Constructionist and Positivist Approaches to the Sociology of Emotions', *American Journal of Sociology*, 87, #2: 336-362.

T. LEMAIRE, 1986. *De Indiaan in ons bewustzijn. De ontmoeting van de oude met de nieuwe wereld* (Baarn: Ambo.)

R. LEVY, 1973. *Tahitians: Mind and Experience in the Society Islands* (University of Chicago Press).

R. LEVY & M.Z. ROSALDO, eds., 1983. *Ethos*, 11 (Special issue on self and emotion).

C. LUTZ, 1988. *Unnatural Emotions. Everyday Sentiments on a Micronesian Atoll and their Challenge to Western Theory* (University of Chicago Press).

B. MALINOWSI, 1927. *Sex and Repression in Savage Society* (London: Routledge & Kegan Paul).

M. MAUSS, 1936. 'Les techniques du corps', *Journal de la psychologie*, 32: 23-29.

A. RADLEY, 1988. 'The Social Form of Feeling', *British Journal of Social Psychology*, 27: 5-18.

A.F. SHAND, 1912. 'Character and the Emotions', *Mind*, 1: 23-57.

M. ROSALDO, 1984. 'Grief and a Headhunter's Rage: On the Cultural Force of Emotions', in *Play, Text and Story. Proceedings of the 1983 Meeting of the American Ethnological Society, Washington D.C.*, ed. E. Bruner.

L. TRILLING, 1971. *Sincerity and Authenticity* (Harvard University Press).

P. WERTSCH, 1985. *The Social Construction of Mind* (Harvard University Press).

R.M. ZANER, 1971. *The Problem of Embodiment* (The Hague: Nijhoff).

NOTES ON CONTRIBUTORS

ERNST VAN ALPHEN (1958) is lecturer in Literary Theory at the Department of Comparative Literature, University of Nijmegen. He is the author of *Bang voor Schennis? Inleiding in de ideologiekritiek* (1987) and of *Bij wijze van lezen. Verleiding en verzet van Willem Brakmans lezer* (1988). A book on the painter Francis Bacon is forthcoming.

IRENE CIERAAD (1952) is a social anthropologist (affiliated to the Department of Anthropology, University of Amsterdam) and the author of *De elitaire verbeelding van Volk en Massa* (1989); she is editor of *Sociodrome*.

RAYMOND CORBEY (1954) is lecturer in Philosophy at Tilburg University. Most of his research and publications concern changing and conflicting interpretations of tribal cultures, human origins, animals and evolution, c1850-c1930, especially in philosophy and anthropology, but also in such contexts as museums, world fairs or missions.

GERT HEKMA is lecturer in Gay Studies at the Sociological Institute, University of Amsterdam. He has co-edited various collections in the sociology and history of homosexuality, such as *Soete minne en helsche boosheit* (1988), *The Pursuit of Sodomy* (1989), *Goed Verkeerd* (1989) and *Het verlies van de onschuld* (1990).

MACHIEL KARSKENS (1945) is Professor of Social and Political Philosophy at the University of Nijmegen. He researches and publishes on the history of philosophy (Hobbes, Leibniz, Foucault), on the development and political function of the notion of subject, and on the notion of power and domination.

THEA VAN DER KLEY (1946) is a philosopher working in Women's Studies; she is currently preparing a dissertation at the University of Nijmegen on gender, *différence sexuelle* and the sexualization of the subject.

JEAN KOMMERS (1946) is lecturer in Cultural and Social Anthropology at the University of Nijmegen, and specializes in the history of ethnography. He has published on image formations, on travel literature and on the history of the Western Pacific.

JOEP LEERSSEN (1955) is Professor of Modern European Literature at the Department of European Studies, University of Amsterdam. He works on cultural confrontations and national stereotypes, especially in the British Isles, and on the theory and methodology of literary image studies. He is editor of the *Yearbook of European Studies*.

RIA LEMAIRE (1943) is Head of the Department of Portuguese Studies, University of Utrecht. She works on medieval literature in the Romance languages, on orality and literacy, on Brazilian culture and literature and on Portuguese literature.

PETER MASON (1952) is a translator working in Amsterdam and author of *The Deconstruction of America* (1990). Recent articles include 'Half a Cow', 'How Doth the Little Crocodile Improve his Shining Tail' and 'Nietzsche's Umbrella and Kant's Horse' (with J.-Cl. Sanglier), as well as a number of ethno-anthropological contributions to recent volumes of *Aufstieg und Niedergang der Römischen Welt*.

JAN NEDERVEEN PIETERSE is senior lecturer at the Institute of Social Studies, The Hague. His areas of research are power and emancipation, social and political theory, and intercultural studies. He is the author of *Empire and Emancipation* (1989) and *White on Black* (1990), and editor of *Christianity and Hegemony* (1991).

ELS SCHROVER (1954) is a research fellow at the University of Nijmegen; she obtained her Ph.D. on a contrastive analysis of Lacan and Derrida. She publishes on literary theory, deconstruction and psychoanalytic criticism.

PAUL VOESTERMANS (1946) is senior lecturer in Cultural Psychology at the University of Nijmegen. He works on the history of psychology and on the psychological ramifications of culture theory. He is co-author (with Jacques Janssen) of *De vergruisde universiteit* and of *Studenten in beweging*.